International Copyright in Computer Program Technology

LAW AND PRACTICE SERIES

Editors

Robert Merkin, LLB, LLM
Professor of Commercial Law, University of Cardiff

Robert Lee, LLB
Professor of Law, University of Cardiff

Loyita Worley
Head of Library, Richards Butler, London

LAW AND PRACTICE

INTERNATIONAL COPYRIGHT IN COMPUTER PROGRAM TECHNOLOGY

Brian Bandey
BA (HONS), PHD

CLT PROFESSIONAL PUBLISHING
A Division of Central Law Training Ltd

Published by
CLT Professional Publishing
A division of Central Law Training Ltd
Wrens Court
52–54 Victoria Road
Sutton Coldfield
Birmingham B72 1SX

ISBN 1 85811 098 X

Produced by Palladian.
Typeset by The Setting Studio.
Printed in Great Britain by Redwood Books, Trowbridge, Wiltshire

Contents

FOREWORD

International Copyright in Computer Program Technology is the first book in a forthcoming series of major practitioner monographs on aspects of intellectual property law, to be published by Central Law Publishing, under the general heading *Law and Practice*. Other subjects which are planned for inclusion in the series are the Internet and the protection of designs. Central Law Publishing has also commissioned works for other *Law and Practice* titles – most importantly, commercial property law and employment law. The Editorial Board would be delighted to receive further suggestions for topics which perhaps in the past have received only the most general of treatment as part of a wide and established area of law, and which lend themselves to detailed analysis in the format adopted by this book.

While the application of copyright to computer programs has frequently been considered by text book writers and, less frequently, by judges, Brian Bandey's book adopts an entirely novel approach to the issue. Rather than trying to fit computer software into the principles laid down by the Copyright, Designs and Patents Act 1988, the author seeks to explain exactly what computer software is, and then demonstrates how copyright law applies to the variety of works which may collectively be referred to as "computer software". Brian Bandey examines how a computer works, how software is created, and, most importantly, how software interacts with hardware. By taking readers through the processes by which computer software is developed and operates, the author is able to highlight the various stages at which copyright issues might arise and to suggest possible solutions to them. This form of analysis throws up the intriguing possibilities that software may qualify as a film or a sound recording as well as a literary, musical or artistic work, with the complex consequences of any such finding.

The reader is also guided painlessly through the maze of jargon used in the software industry, so that those lawyers who have in the past found difficulty in communicating effectively with their clients for want of understanding of the finer technical points of computers and software no longer have any reasonable excuse. It is also to be hoped that those engaged in the design of software will benefit from an explanation of how copyright applies to each stage in production process.

RMM
May 1996

Preface

There is more to computer programs than a large series of lines of what appear to be unintelligible sequences of abbreviated words, symbols and numbers. Rather, I tend to think of computer programs as being *virtual* machines. Imagine having to design a mechanical watch from scratch. One would, I suppose, begin by sketching out for one-self the ideas one had with respect to it. Would it tell the time, day and date? Would it be some form of perpetual calendar or a chronograph? Would it be hand-wound or automatic? Would it be designed for the man in the street, or would it be a specialist time-piece for the diver or aviator? Once one had decided on these general issues, the design work would begin on the mechanism, face and case. Endless streams of design decisions would flow as technical drawings, specifications and prototypes are drawn up and built. Final production would then begin with the manufacture of the concluding version of the time-piece together with, perhaps, a manual to describe its functions and instruct the user in its set-up and use. The surprising thing is that a computer program is made in very much the same way. In a computer program or computer software product of complexity, a considerable amount of time is spent in its conceptualisation in a very similar fashion to the manner in which the watch was conceptualised. Specifications are produced together with flow-diagrams. Manuals are written describing the products operation and use. All of these being items which seem to me to be no different in essence than the technical or engineering drawings, specifications and manuals which have been produced by all engineers from the industrial revolution onwards in the design of their machines and inventions.

Like a watch, computer programs nowadays almost invariably need a display in which the information generated by the virtual mechanism within is communicated to the user. It would probably not be the time, day, date or elapsed time (as in the case of a chronograph or stop-watch) but the requirement overall is identical – to communicate sometimes complex information quickly in a fashion directly accessible by the user. A mechanical watch mechanism would have a number of discrete parts which perform different functions. For example: the automatic winding mechanism which converts the motion of a rotor moved by the wearer's wrist into mechanical energy; the balance wheel oscillating and producing the ability of the mechanism to keep time; or the drive-train transmitting these oscillations to the hands. These discrete sub-mechanisms are connected to each other in an exacting order and to fine tolerances which, if disturbed, inaccurately fashioned or improperly designed, may result in the watch running slow, running fast or, indeed, not running at all. So it is with the virtual machine – the computer software product will usually be made up of hundreds, if not thousands, of individual and discrete computer programs and computer program routines (mechanisms). One mechanism might handle the input of data from a keyboard, another mechanism might perform a particular calculation on a specific set of data, another mechanism might deal with collecting and sorting data in a certain manner. Exactly like the watch, these discrete sub-mechanisms are connected to each other in an exacting order which, if disturbed, innacurately fashioned or improperly designed, may result in the software running slow, or indeed, not running at all. These mismatches between virtual cogs and escapements which stop the virtual machine, or produce an incorrect effect, are called "bugs".

The nature of this virtual machine is that it is inert when existing in the world of human perception. In our world the properties and the essence of the virtual machine are invisible to and unappreciated by the human eye when looking at a diskette or a listing on a print-out. However, when released into the virtual world of the computer, this virtual machine crunches numbers, communicates with its kind across continents, and produces a myriad of displays, images and sounds. This is the nub of the problem when applying the law. Ignore the technology and the computer program becomes a creature unlike any other. Consequently one cannot conceptualise its place in the law nor find suitable analogies for it and thus apply precedent in the way one is familiar with. It is this manner of thinking, in my opinion, that has produced so many unfavourable results for the computer programmer. Why can he not have moral rights in his work if his endeavour is no different in either quality or quantity to the draughtsman who produces the essential documents and drawings for the production of a watch? Why can he not restrain the user of his property from dissecting it so that they can connect their mechanism to his if he does not wish them to do so? He cannot if computer programs are perceived as a technology like no other and represent a specie of property inferior to those that have gone before. But I think the fact of the matter is that computer programs are no different in essence than any other product of taste, judgement and effort. They simply do not exist in our world in the same way a painting or a play does. They exist in the virtual world of the computer.

It is my contention that when considered in this way; when the technology and processes behind and within computer programming are examined; existing areas of the law of copyright are directly and, most importantly, properly applicable. Thus in this work, I have always sought to identify the technology first and allow the legal analysis to follow; thus hoping to prove the logic behind my contention.

I would also like to voice a small word of warning to those using this text. I have been careful, wherever possible and through the use of footnotes, to indicate the date to which any specific area of text is current. This applies, in particular, to the implementation of EU Directives. Thus the reader will need to take care with respect to any implementation of any regulation or other change in the law that has occurred within the unavoidable interim between writing and publication.

When commencing my doctoral thesis, from which this work is derived, I did not know how much it cost to write a book. Apart from the simple and direct financial cost, there is an immeasurable cost to oneself, family and friends. Accordingly I should like to thank my family and close friends for their support and especially the unstinting and unwavering support of my wife Rachel which made the writing of this book possible. I should also like to thank my supervising professor, Robert Merkin, for his guidance, the publishers for this opportunity, and my research assistant Lucy Jane Elliot for her help in the latter stages of the preparation of this book.

Brian Bandey
June 1996

Acknowledgments

Figures 5.2 and 5.3 are reproduced by kind permission of Lotus.
Lotus 1-2-3 is a registered trademark of Lotus Development Corporation, a wholly owned subsidiary of IBM.

Table of Cases

Table of Statutes

United Kingdom

Australia

Austria

Belgium

Denmark

Finland

France

Germany

Greece

Iceland

Ireland

Italy

Luxembourg

Netherlands

Norway

Portugal

Spain

Sweden

Switzerland

United States of America

Table of Statutory Instruments

Table of EU Legislation

Table of International Conventions

Chapter 1

Introduction to the Computer Program and the Modern Law of Copyright

The nature of this work

Underlying concept

The basic premise and concept lying behind this work is that no detailed application of the law of copyright has been made to the technical aspects of computer programming, computer operation and the use of the many types of computer programs. The style and approach employed, therefore, throughout this work are first of all to explain in detail and in non-technical terms wherever possible, the scientific and technical issues connected with computer programs and then to apply the law in an equally detailed manner. Only then will a clear picture emerge of "Copyright Software Law" which should then answer some of the key and critical questions being asked by the software industry throughout the United Kingdom.

Limitations in scope

This work is not, nor is it intended to be, a comprehensive dissertation on the different legal mechanisms which are generally available under English Law to "protect" an owner's rights in computer software. Further editions of this work may very well expand it to address the areas of patent, trade mark and confidentiality protection; but it is submitted that the truth of the matter is that the vast majority of business conducted with respect to computer software in the United Kingdom is addressed in the context of the law of copyright. When the commercial developers, owners and/or manufacturers of computer software derive their revenue from their software products, they do so principally by making licences for the use of copyright works. When software houses enter into agreements with specialists who are to translate a computer software product from one version to another so that the new version will operate under some other operating system or hardware environment, they do so in the context of translation and adaptation agreements. In other words they conduct such business in the context of the law of copyright and it is submitted that they are right to do so. The law of copyright is the best place and the first place to begin any in-depth and technical examination of computer programming technologies in a legal environment.

Now a respectable argument may be put forward that computer programs ought to be the proper subject of Patent Law[1], but an examination of this argument is beyond the scope of this work which is concerned with the application of the law of copyright to computer programs only.

The rationale for this approach is two-fold. Firstly, and by far most importantly, computer software has always been presented to be patented embodied in some other technology (be it specialised computer-integrated circuits, data-processing machinery or video-image manipulation equipment), but before the embodiment of the computer programs in some complimentary technology, the computer program was developed in a manner identical to every other type of "stand-alone" computer program which might, for example, be loaded up into a computer in a traditional fashion and run. It is this fact which always establishes a computer program as *initially* being a creature of copyright. Computer software technology is first and foremost a subject of copyright since before any registration under the Patents Act 1977 or any provision concerned with trade mark law (whether of the United Kingdom or the European Union) the computer program exists as a species of copyright work and its existence as property arises by virtue of the Copyright, Designs and Patents Act 1988 *only.* If the guiding premise of this work is to allow the technology actually employed to cause the legal analysis to follow, then the approach generally of this work in concentrating exclusively on the law of copyright must be the right one.

1 *e.g.* see the article by Ron McQuaker in (1995) 11(5) *Computer Law and Security Report* p 259. For an examination of the concepts associated with the interchangeability of software, firmware and hardware, see the article by Dr Axel von Hellfeld in *Australian Law Journal* (1993) 9(1) p 18. See also the Patents Act 1977 especially s 1. Interesting applications with respect to the "patentability" of computer software include: **Slee & Harris's Appl** [1966] RPC 194; **International Business Machines Corp's Appl** [1980] FSR 564; **Merrill Lynch's Appl** [1989] RPC 561.

When computer software is developed within the confines of patentable technology, it will be developed in a computer programming development environment. This means that it will be written, tested, de-bugged and rewritten as a computer program in a computer programming language or directly into some form of machine code in exactly the same way as every other computer program existing. Before it is subsumed into the hardware or technology that adds to or produces its susceptibility to being patented, it may be tested in a software testing environment identical, in principle, to the manner in which stand-alone computer software applications would be tested during their development. During this time, the computer software is recorded, copied, translated, transmitted, adapted and owned as a copyright work. Before patenting for example, the software technology might be shared, perhaps for valuable consideration, with a third party. Such an agreement would have to take place principally in the context of the law of copyright. As made out before, computer software is always first and foremost a creature of copyright.

The second reason for confining this work to an evaluation of computer software in a copyright context is much more mundane. The matter is one of logistics. Computer programming technology advances at such a pace that new legal analyses need to be conducted on emergent technologies as they emerge. It is hoped that this work addresses itself in an up-to-date fashion to the newest technologies including object-oriented programming and CASE tools.[2] The speed of technological innovation prohibits the production of a work such as this, which seeks to legally analyse and explain the technologies used in real life to an appropriate and significant level of detail, from covering too many topics. By the time alternative legal methods of protection are evaluated to a comparable depth, technology would have advanced and rendered other aspects of the work out of date. In the same manner, some aspects of the application of the law of confidentiality and trade secret law are technology dependant[3] and will therefore be addressed in a subsequent edition.

---

2 Computer Assisted Software Engineering – species of computer programs that are used to write other computer programs.

3 *e.g.* see **Structural Dynamics Research Corp v Engineering Mechanics Research Corp** 401 F Supp 1102, 1117–18 (ED Mich 1975) where it was held that a combination of known elements produced a unique and valuable computer program and as such susceptible of being a secret. However, in **Jostens Inc v National Computer Systems Incorporated** 318 NW 2d 691 (Minn 1982), the court held that a graphics design and manufacturing system consisting of specialist hardware, operating system and specialised application software was not a trade secret, commenting that: "... simply to assert a trade secret resides in some combination or otherwise of known data is not sufficient, as the combination itself must be delineated with some particularity in establishing its trade secret status". Generally, see: **Saltman Engineering Co v Campbell Engineering Co Ltd** [1963] 3 All ER 413; **Seager**

THE QUESTION OF HOW TO APPLY THE LAW OF COPYRIGHT

Computer software in this last decade of the twentieth century has become all-pervading. Silicon or microchips, as they are often called, can be found in household appliances such as electric kettles, toasters and ovens. Integrated circuits can be viewed, in a sense, as a receptacle for the computer software they contain; but when integrated circuits are referred to as being "intelligent", reference is really being made to the fact that their presence increases the perceived efficacy of the item, since it then appears to be able to make control-oriented "decisions" for itself. The truth of the matter is that an integrated circuit has been introduced into the device, containing computer software that is then able to control the device in a limited fashion. Although this computer software might be very small in length (only thousands of characters long) its producers may very well consider it to be a significant marketing, sales and product development and therefore value it greatly, not taking into account the money that would have been invested in its design, development and testing.

And yet for these small computer programs of limited functionality that are to be found throughout the country, English law seems not to have developed any certain answers as to whether copyright subsists within such short works and therefore questions arise as to whether the costly exercise in developing it has created something not capable of being owned. Very short and discrete pieces of computer program code, often called "Microcode" exist in the personal computer that is to be found on almost every executive's desk and in a very significant number of homes throughout the United Kingdom. When the computer is first turned on and before the operating system or application programs are loaded, a small set of computer programs known as "ROM BIOS" operate to check the presence of memory, monitor, disk drives and the like. ROM BIOS are of extraordinary value to the producers of personal computers and are one of the foundation stones of their interoperability. Manufacturers of ROM BIOS in the United States litigate over their infringement, but this species of computer programming technology *seems* little understood within the concepts of English copyright

3 *(cont.)*

v Copydex Ltd [1967] 1 WLR 923; **Coco v AN Clark (Engineers) Ltd** [1969] RPC 41; **Marshall (Thomas) (Exports) Ltd v Guinle** [1978] 3 WLR 116; **Weir Pumps Ltd v CML Pumps Ltd** [1984] FSR 33; **Stephens v Avery** [1988] Ch 449; **Lac Minerals Ltd v International Corona Resources Ltd** [1990] FSR 441 (Supreme Court of Canada); **Smith Kline & French Laboratories (Australia) Ltd v Secretary to the Dept of Community Services & Health** [1990] FSR 617 (Fed Ct of Australia NSW Div).

law and *seems* to occupy a tenuous position within it because of its size and the reluctance of the English courts of law to recognise that copyright ought to arise in a short work due to the amount of time, effort and financial investment that has gone into its creation.[4]

Computer software towards the beginning of the 1990s has also become established in command and control avionics systems in commercial aviation. Computer software is being used to interpret the instructions given by the pilot of a commercial airliner through the use of traditional throttles and yoke so that the optimum attitude, speed, engine thrust etc is being applied appropriately. It is computer software that can fly large commercial aircraft on "auto-pilot" and land them at appropriate airports in zero visibility without direct human interaction from the flight crew – except to engage the system in the first place. Computer software is pervasive in modern society yet *seems* to be unlike anything seen before. Perhaps this is why the legal community finds such difficulty in applying the established law to it.

Turning to commercial software houses who are responsible for the operating and applications software used through government, commerce and industry, of the 283 software houses (and their in house legal advisers where available) questioned during the research of this work, none had any definite view or reasoned opinion to express on, for example, the following issues:

- How many lines of computer code need to be written before copyright will arise and subsist in them?
- Does the law of copyright protect graphic user interfaces?
- How far is the structure of a computer program protected by the law of copyright, if at all?
- How much development, in the sense of maintenance and enhancements, needs to be done to a pre-existing software product before a new copyright arises?
- How much of the copyright in your premier computer software product does the software house own in law, taking into account the use of third party freelance programmers in this country and others?

Even for the software house whose revenue is derived from the licensing, installation, configuration, maintenance and support of computer software products they originate, the nature of computer programs *seems* too alien to the current legal structure for the law of copyright to be applied to it comprehensively so as to answer the questions posed above, and the many others that there are.

[4] See, *e.g.* **Exxon Corp v Exxon Insurance Consultants International Ltd** [1982] RPB 69.

The Answer

It is the contention of this work that the key word in the preceding statements is "*seems*", since it is submitted that the long history of the law of copyright in England has, in fact, answered the vast majority of the questions that arise with respect to computer software already. It is argued that only a meticulous examination of the character of computer software will allow a proper and empirical process of analogy (a process well known in the legal community when applying existing case law to a new situation) and such a process of analogy will reveal that the inapplicability of the law of copyright to modern computer programming technologies is more apparent than real.

Some history of applying the law of copyright

No consideration was given to the needs of the computer industry, which was then in its infancy, when the Copyright Act 1956 was passed. The Whitford Committee in 1977[5] recommended, *inter alia*, that computer software should be treated as literary and artistic works in the then normal way (under the Copyright Act 1956) with the same incidents of ownership and term. The Whitford Committee also recommended that the storage of any copyright material in a computer memory or storage medium should be a restricted act; that the authors of computer-produced works should be the humans who devised and originated the instructions and data; and that the unauthorised use of computer programs in a computer should be an infringement of copyright.[6] Under the aegis of the Copyright Act 1956 and before the enactment of the Copyright (Computer Software) Amendment Act 1985, it was generally thought in the legal community that a computer program expressed in writing or other form of notation onto paper would constitute a "literary work" within the meaning of section 2 of the Copyright Act 1956, so long as it was produced as a result of substantial independent skill or useful labour so that it would be "original" and therefore qualify for copyright protection.

In actions proceeding under the Copyright Act 1956, it was still sometimes argued that the Copyright Act 1956, at least before the Copyright (Computer Software) Amendment Act 1985, did not protect computer software at

5 Cmnd 6732.
6 1977 Cmnd 6732 at p 124.

all.[7] It was thought at the time that if a computer program or collection of data was first expressed in the form of invisible magnetic patterns on a computer tape, and still more if in the form of what was then referred to as "core storage"[8], it was considered doubtful whether this constituted "writing" within the meaning of the Copyright Act 1956. The expression "writing" was defined in the Copyright Act 1956[9] as including "any form of notation, whether by hand or by printing, typewriting or any similar process", and although it was argued academically that the expression "notation" should be given a broad meaning, there was some difficulty in accepting that the expression "notation" included the magnetisation states of an array of rings on wires, since all concrete instances given in the definition involved visible symbols that were directly appreciable by humans.[10]

The Copyright (Computer Software) Amendment Act 1985[11] on the face of it was expected to adopt the general recommendations of the 1977 Copyright Committee[12] so that all computer programs and other items of computer software which have involved a sufficient degree of skill and/or labour in their creation were to be considered as works in the normal copyright sense, and which had been reduced to writing or some other material form from which they can be reproduced and therefore protected by copyright law. The Copyright (Computer Software) Amendment Act 1985 did not say outright that a computer program *was* a species of literary work but presented the position where the Copyright Act 1956 was to apply in relation to a computer program as it applied in relation to a literary work.[13] The information technology legal community took the view that the difference was an academic one and made no real impact on the protection afforded to computer programs by the Copyright Act 1956[14], but this position was never truly reconciled.

---

7 See **Milltronics Ltd v Hycontrol Ltd** [1990] FSR 273; and in **Computer Edge Pty Ltd v Apple Computer Inc** [1986] FSR 537, the majority of the High Court of Australia at Canberra, ruling on the Australian Copyright Act 1984 (which gave a degree of protection to computer programs) applied the usual UK tests and distinguished between the source code of each program, which did qualify as a literary work, and the object code of each program stored as electrical impulses in an integrated circuit, which they held did not qualify as a literary work.

8 Now electronic memory, but then sometimes in the form of electromagnetically charged rings.

9 Copyright Act 1956, s 48(1).

10 See Laddie, Prescott and Vitoria *The Modern Law of Copyright* (Butterworths, 1980).

11 Repealed by the Copyright, Designs and Patents Act 1988.

12 Cmnd 6732 para 520(i).

13 The Copyright (Computer Software) Amendment Act 1985, s 1(1).

14 The application of the Copyright Act 1956 through the vehicle of the Copyright (Computer Software) Amendment Act 1985 was not a problem in, *e.g.* **John Richardson Computers Ltd v Flanders & Chemtec Ltd** [1993] FSR 497.

The Copyright (Computer Software) Amendment Act 1985 was retrospective and applied to computer programs made before its commencement and also afterwards.[15] It had already been held that a computer program written in assembly code was capable of protection as a literary work under the Copyright Act 1956[16] and that computer programs generally were capable of protection as literary works.[17] Anton Pillar orders were granted in respect of the alleged infringement of copyright in computer programs.[18] In adopting the formulations set out by the 1977 Copyright Committee[19], the Copyright (Computer Software) Amendment Act 1985 ensured that the more obvious forms of computer programming "literary" works fell to be protected; such as the eye-readable print-out of the computer program's listing, punched cards, punched tapes, magnetic tapes, magnetic cores, disks, integrated circuits and the like. The Copyright, Designs and Patents Act 1988 included computer programs as a species of literary work but failed to define it, and the Copyright, Designs and Patents Act 1988 has itself begun to proceed down the road of amendment to attempt to keep pace with the speed of innovation with respect to computer programming technology.

The structure of this work

Describing the law

To give voice to the approach of this work referred to above, some general principles of the law of copyright will first of all be briefly examined which are applicable to computer programs. The purpose of this is to lay down an initial exposition of the law which is generally applicable to this area so as to avoid repetition and to enable the following chapters to address the case law which is particularly applicable or helpful with respect to the subject-matter of each chapter. However, this exercise is not intended to be nor should be read as a comprehensive exposition of the general principles of copyright law, such expositions being generally available in traditional textbooks; but each examination will include a short explanation of the principle's applicability to computer programs.

15 **Milltronics Ltd v Hycontrol Ltd** [1990] FSR 273.
16 **Sega Enterprises Ltd v Richards** [1983] FSR 73.
17 **Thrust Code Ltd v WW Computing Ltd** [1983] FSR 502.
18 See *e.g.* **Gates v Swift** [1982] RPC 339
19 Cmnd 6732 para 520(i).

Development

Following this the different processes which are generally recognised within the software industry, and which bring the computer program into being in machine-readable form are evaluated. The stages of testing and market preparation (including such items as market surveys, direct-mailing campaigns and advertising generally that usually follow thereafter) are not discussed, since these do not impinge directly on the copyright issues associated with computer software. Appropriate legal tests are then developed and applied in order to discover what types of copyright works arise in the development cycle of computer programs. Thus, it will also be necessary briefly to review the newer and alternative methods of computer programming; including structured methods and automated methodologies to ensure that the law is applied to all current development techniques.

Execution

Having examined the methodologies employed in the development of computer programs, the next stage in this work will be to assess the different levels of transformations and translations undergone by the computer program during its execution on computer hardware. In this context, the modes in which computer programs exist subsequent to the development cycle will be examined, together with the manner in which fully realised computer programs qualify as different species of copyright works. In doing so this work will explore the very important component of computing known as the "operating system" which is a species of computer program directed not to the applications being processed by an end-user, but towards the computer hardware system itself. An analysis will be carried out of the files that computer programs generate and use during their operation so as to identify the species of copyright works subsisting within them and consider, in depth, the "products" of different types of computer programs as they execute.

"Look and Feel"

Once an understanding of how computer programs are made from the perspective of the law of copyright and how they work, a scrutiny of the law of copyright's applicability to the "look and feel" of computer programs will be conducted. Computer program manufacturers invest inordinate sums of money in research and development to make them visually appealing to the user and easy and recognisable to use. It is therefore not surprising that they are also profoundly interested in the mechanisms that the law of copyright affords them in the protection of this investment.

Ownership

This work then follows this subject with an examination of the legal notion of the ownership of the copyright in computer programs and further examines how ownership arises. Concomitant on such examination, it will consider who is first author with special reference to the use of consultant programmers by software houses and the commissioners of computer software generally; and the development of computer programs by the employees of limited companies, including an examination of the generation of trusts with respect to the ownership of commissioned bespoke software.

Licensing

Having discussed the legal concepts concerned with the ownership of computer programs, an evaluation follows of the mechanisms in which the copyright itself in a work is transmitted from one party to another and further to this, consideration is given to the mechanisms by which rights subsisting under a copyright are transmitted. The computer software industry generally generates the "lion's share" of its revenue through the licensing of its software products to end-users or setting up distribution channels of authorised licensees. Notwithstanding this, the nature of copyright as property in the manner of a *chose in action* is not well understood by either the industry or their advisers. An expectation that the computer software industry fully understands the legal mechanisms involved in licensing copyright works would, it is submitted, be held erroneously.

Infringement

Attention is then turned to the infringement of copyright that subsists within computer programs. In doing so, study will be directed to both primary and secondary infringement; and how the courts may deal with the infringement of the different species of copyright work which subsist within computer programs. Regard will also be made with respect to how, in practice, the courts actually assess the presence of primary infringement (in the sense of copying) in this type of literary work which is not quite like any other.

European Union

Penultimately, the individual structures and mechanisms with respect to the law of copyright in each of the individual Member States of the European Union will be examined with particular reference to the application of the local law of copyright to computer software. It is unavoidable that, in the context of this work, such an examination can only be a brief one and that it can merely be an attempt to highlight and point to the differing mechanisms of copyright application for computer programs that exist throughout the European Union. However, a short examination will be made of the manner in which the local law applies to other species of copyright works since computer software technology, as made out above, can contain, express and/or create many disparate classes of works.

International copyright

Finally, the position of international copyright is briefly examined so as to complete the study of the application of the law of copyright to computer programming technologies.

Chapter 2

GENERAL PRINCIPLES OF COPYRIGHT LAW APPLICABLE TO COMPUTER PROGRAMS

INTRODUCTION

In this chapter some general principles of the law of copyright will be briefly examined which are applicable to computer programs. The purpose of this is to lay down an initial exposition of some of the general principles of copyright law that are applicable to this area so as to avoid repetition and to enable the following chapters to address the case law which is particularly applicable or helpful with respect to the subject-matter of each chapter. However, this chapter is not intended to be nor should be read as a comprehensive exposition of the general principles of copyright law, such expositions being extensively available in general copyright textbooks. It is designed to be a site within this work to which reference may be made to *core* parts of the Copyright, Designs and Patents Act 1988 and *core* quotations from applicable precedents. Each examination will include a short explanation of the principle's applicability to computer programs and this relevance briefly examined, but the methodology adopted in this work is one where the technology is examined first and the law applied second. Accordingly, this chapter will not explain or discuss any such relevance or legal effect in depth, but will leave that activity to the following text.

STATUTORY SPECIES OF COPYRIGHT WORKS

Computer programs as literary works

As section 1(1)(a) of the Copyright Designs and Patents Act 1988 tells us, subject to certain qualifying conditions and constituent elements being met and present, copyright subsists in original literary, dramatic, musical and artistic works. In this respect there is no material difference between this provision and the equivalent provision in the Copyright Act 1956[1] or of the Copyright Act 1911[2], consequently, decisions on matters that are common among the three Acts are still valid and can be used for the proper interpretation of the Copyright, Designs and Patents Act 1988. Works in which copyright subsists under the Copyright, Designs and Patents Act 1988 are described as "Copyright Works"[3] and this terminology will be adopted throughout this work. The species of copyright works are set out in section 1(1) of the Copyright, Designs and Patents Act 1988 as follows:

(a) original literary, dramatic, musical or artistic works,
(b) sound recordings, films, broadcasts or cable programmes, and
(c) the typographical arrangement of published editions.

It should be borne in mind that different statutory species of copyright works may subsist within a computer program contemporaneously[4] and thus it is important to understand what type of copyright work one is attending to when studying the copyright that subsists in computer programs.

Legally defining the computer program

By section 3(1) of the Copyright, Designs and Patents Act 1988, "literary work" is defined as meaning "any work, other than a dramatic or musical work, which is written, spoken or sung, and" includes "a table or compilation", "a computer program" and "preparatory design material for a computer program".[5] No definition of "computer program" is given in the Copyright, Designs and Patents Act 1988; thus for the purposes of this work, although not directly applicable by virtue of the doctrine of *stare decisis*, it is helpful to look at persuasive authority from abroad where intellectual property law may be more developed. In the United States the following definition of a computer program has been adopted:

> "A 'computer program' is a set of statements or instructions to be used directly or indirectly in a computer in order to bring about a certain result."[6]

1 Copyright Act 1956, ss 2(1), 2(2), 3(2) and 3(3).
2 Copyright Act 1911, s 1(1).
3 Copyright, Designs and Patents Act 1988, s 1(2)
4 See Chaps 3 and 4.
5 The inclusion of "preparatory design material for a computer program" in s 3(1)(c) of the Copyright, Designs and Patents Act 1988 was inserted by the Copyright (Computer Programs) Regulations 1992 which came into force on 1 Jan 1993.
6 The 1976 Copyright Act was amended on 12 Dec 1980 when President Carter signed into law Public Law 96-517. Section 10 of that Act (the Computer Software Copyright Act of 1980) provided specific copyright protection for computer programs. The 1980 amendments added a specific definition of "computer program" to § 101 of the 1976 Copyright Act.

Defining "artistic" and "graphic works"

Section 4(1) of the Copyright, Designs and Patents Act 1988 tells us that the term "artistic work" means:

(a) a graphic work, photograph, sculpture or collage, irrespective of artistic quality;
(b) a work of architecture being a building or a model for a building; or
(c) a work of artistic craftsmanship.

Section 4(2) of the Copyright, Designs and Patents Act 1988 defines the term "graphic work" and tells us that it includes a "painting, drawing, diagram, map, chart or plan". This context is an important one, since computer programs and their preparatory design material often contain materials that look like drawings and diagrams.[7]

Defining "sound recording"

In defining a "sound recording", the Copyright, Designs and Patents Act 1988 in section 5(1) follows the position adopted under the Copyright Act 1956[8] by conferring a separate copyright on sound recordings. "sound recording" is defined as being:

(a) a recording of sounds, from which the sounds may be reproduced, or
(b) a recording of the whole or any part of a literary, dramatic or musical work, from which sounds reproducing the work or part may be produced,

regardless of the medium on which the recording is made or the method by which the sounds are reproduced or produced.

Computer programs are currently capable of recording and producing sounds, and thus the inclusion of this definition is germane.[9]

Defining "film"

The Copyright, Designs and Patents Act 1988 follows the Copyright Act 1956 in conferring a separate copyright on films, but casts its definition in a slightly different way. Section 5(1) defines a film as "a recording on any medium from which a moving image may by any means be produced." The essential difference between this definition and that contained in section

7 See Chaps 3 and 4.
8 Copyright Act 1956, s 12(1) and s 12(2).
9 See Chap 4 especially.

13(10) Copyright Act 1956, besides overall simplification, is that the concept of "recording" has been introduced in a much simpler form.[10] Computer programs are capable of generating moving (animated) images either from data held outside of the computer program itself or as a direct product of running the computer program itself without reference to such external data.[11]

Computer program specific provisions in the Copyright, Designs and Patents Act 1988

The Copyright, Designs and Patents Act 1988 contains various provisions that are specific to computer programs or which treat computer programs as an express example or species in a particular provision.[12] In this way the Copyright, Designs and Patents Act 1988 does not treat computer programs as just another type or sub-species of literary work. On the one hand the Copyright, Designs and Patents Act 1988 tends to increase the ambit of its attention to computer programs by specifically addressing or anticipating the uniqueness of computer programs – for example, see section 178 of the Copyright, Designs and Patents Act 1988 below, which deals with computer-generated works. But on the other hand the Copyright, Designs and Patents Act 1988 reduces the value of the literary and artistic taste, judgement and skill that go into making a complex commercial application program or an imaginative games program by excluding the author from the protection of moral rights in his work[13] and limiting his remedies with respect to adaptations.[14] It may well be that it can be argued that the author may receive his moral rights with respect to the artistic and literary works, the music and the films he records in the medium of his computer program. But it is unfortunate that this type of legal sophistry needs to be applied in a situation where the law, so recently changed, ought to be clear.

10 The Copyright Act 1956 defines a "cinematographic film" at s 13(10) as being: "Any sequence of visual images recorded on material of any description (whether translucent or not) so as to be capable, by the use of that material, either of being shown as a moving picture, or of being recorded on other material (whether translucent or not) by the use of which it can be so shown."

11 See Chap 4.

12 The Copyright (Computer Programs) Regulations 1992 (which came into force on 1 Jan 1993) added approximately 12 major new computer program specific amendments in the Copyright, Designs and Patents Act 1988.

13 Copyright, Designs and Patents Act 1988, s 79(2).

14 *Ibid*, s 21(3)(a).

Computer-generated works

Section 178 of the Copyright, Designs and Patents Act 1988 tells us that in relation to a copyright work, the term "computer-generated" means "that the work is generated by computer in circumstances such that there is no human author of the work".

The Copyright, Designs and Patents Act 1988 makes distinctions between computer-generated works as classes of works which are not computer-generated both as to the issue of authorship and the duration of copyright itself. Section 9(3) provides that:

> "In the case of a literary, dramatic, musical or artistic work which is computer-generated, the author shall be taken to be the person by whom the arrangements necessary for the creation of the work are undertaken."

If a work is computer-generated, the copyright subsisting within it "expires at the end of the period of 50 years from the end of the calendar year in which the work was made."[15]

Changes to acts restricted by copyright wrought by the Copyright (Computer Programs) Regulations 1992

With respect to the acts restricted by copyright, before the implementation of the Copyright (Computer Programs) Regulations 1992, section 18 read as follows:

> "**18.** – (1) The issue to the public of copies of the work is an act restricted by the copyright in every description of copyright work.
> (2) References in this Part to the issue to the public of copies of a work are to the act of putting into circulation copies not previously put into circulation, in the United Kingdom or elsewhere, and not to –
> (a) any subsequent distribution, sale, hiring or loan of those copies, or
> (b) any subsequent importation of those copies into the United Kingdom;
> except that in relation to sound recordings, films and computer programs the restricted act of issuing copies to the public includes any rental of copies to the public."

Subsequent to the implementation of the Copyright (Computer Programs) Regulations 1992, section 18 now reads as follows:

> "**18.** – (1) The issue to the public of copies of the work is an act restricted by the copyright in every description of copyright work.
> (2) References in this Part to the issue to the public of copies of a work are

15 *Ibid*, s 12(3).

except where the work is a computer program to the act of putting into circulation copies not previously put into circulation, in the United Kingdom or elsewhere, and not to –

(a) any subsequent distribution, sale, hiring or loan of those copies, or

(b) any subsequent importation of those copies into the United Kingdom;

except that in relation to sound recordings, films the restricted act of issuing copies to the public includes any rental of copies to the public.

(3) References in this Part to the issue to the public of copies of a work where the work is a computer program are to the act of putting into circulation copies of that program not previously put into circulation in the United Kingdom or any other member State, by or with the consent of the copyright owner, and not to –

(a) any subsequent distribution, sale, hiring or loan of those copies, or

(b) any subsequent importation of those copies into the United Kingdom,

except that the restricted act of issuing copies to the public includes any rental of copies to the public."

Here the amendment to the Copyright, Designs and Patents Act 1988 has expanded its ambit to contemplate specifically the position of computer programs. Thus when considering the provisions of section 18 of the Copyright, Designs and Patents Act 1988 with specific respect to computer programs, one applies the broader test as to whether the computer programs have previously been put into circulation in any Member State of the European Union.

Changes to the making of adaptations wrought by the Copyright (Computer Programs) Regulations 1992

Section 21(4) of the Copyright, Designs and Patents Act 1988, before the implementation of the Copyright (Computer Programs) Regulations 1992 dealt with the making of adaptations in the following manner:

"**21.** – (1) The making of an adaptation of the work is an act restricted by the copyright in a literary, dramatic or musical work.

For this purpose an adaptation is made when it is recorded, in writing, or otherwise.

(2) The doing of any of the acts specified in sections 17 to 20, or subsection (1) above, in relation to an adaptation of the work is also an act restricted by the copyright in a literary, dramatic or musical work.

For this purpose it is immaterial; whether the adaptation has been recorded, in writing or otherwise, at the time the act was done.

(3) In this Part "adaptation" –

(a) in relation to a literary or dramatic work, means –

(i) a translation of the work;

(ii) a version of a dramatic work in which it is converted into a non-dramatic work or, as the case may be, of a non-dramatic work in which it is converted into a dramatic work;

(ii) a version of the work in which the story or action is conveyed wholly or mainly be means of pictures in a form suitable for reproduction in a book, or in a newspaper, magazine or similar periodical;

(b) in relation to a musical work, means an arrangement or transcription of the work.

(4) In relation to a computer program, a "translation" includes a version of the program in which it is converted into or out of a computer language or code or into a different computer language or code, otherwise than incidentally in the course of running the program.

(5) No inference shall be drawn from this section as to what does or does not amount to copying a work."

Subsequent to the implementation of the Copyright (Computer Programs) Regulations 1992, section 21(4) of the Copyright, Designs and Patents Act 1988 now deals with the making of adaptations in the following manner, whereby computer programs are completely excluded from the action of section 21(3) and the transformations occurring during the running of a computer program are now included in section 21(5):

"**21.** – (1) The making of an adaptation of the work is an act restricted by the copyright in a literary, dramatic or musical work.

For this purpose an adaptation is made when it is recorded, in writing, or otherwise.

(2) The doing of any of the acts specified in sections 17 to 20, or subsection (1) above, in relation to an adaptation of the work is also an act restricted by the copyright in a literary, dramatic or musical work.

For this purpose it is immaterial; whether the adaptation has been recorded, in writing or otherwise, at the time the act was done.

(3) In this Part "adaptation" –

(a) in relation to a literary work, other than a computer program, or dramatic work, means –

(i) a translation of the work;

(ii) a version of a dramatic work in which it is converted into a non-dramatic work or, as the case may be, of a non-dramatic work in which it is converted into a dramatic work;

(ii) a version of the work in which the story or action is conveyed wholly or mainly be means of pictures in a form suitable for reproduction in a book, or in a newspaper, magazine or similar periodical;

(ab) in relation to a computer program, means an arrangement or altered version of the program or a translation of it;

(b) in relation to a musical work, means an arrangement or transcription of the work.

(4) In relation to a computer program, a "translation" includes a version of the program in which it is converted into or out of a computer language or code or into a different computer language or code.

(5) No inference shall be drawn from this section as to what does or does not amount to copying a work."

This amendment has done more harm than good. On the one hand it seems to negate the proposition that a plot may subsist within a computer program and negatives the proposition that a computer program cannot convey a story wholly or mainly be means of pictures suitable for reproduction in a book or other species of more standard literary work. This is not so, for games programs routinely display a story by means of static and moving pictures[16] and comic strips are now routinely derived from the characterisations to be found in successful computer games programs. The amendment fuels the unsatisfactory quality of this part of the Copyright, Designs and Patents Act 1988 where non-exhaustive lists of the types of activities possible are given which are types of translation. For the first time the concept of an "arrangement" of a computer program is given which is not defined in the Copyright, Designs and Patents Act 1988. One can readily understand with respect to an arrangement of a musical work[17] that what is averred to is the circumstance where a melody written for one instrument is rewritten so that it can be played on another or other instruments whilst maintaining the integrity and qualities of the original piece. But it is a matter of supreme vagueness and uncertainty in this context as to how a computer program may be "arranged".[18]

Changes to the importation of infringing copies wrought by the Copyright (Computer Programs) Regulations 1992

The Copyright (Computer Programs) Regulations 1992 amended section 27(3) of the Copyright, Designs and Patents Act 1988 by the inclusion of a new section 27(3A)[19] and thereby the provisions concerned with the importation of infringing copies changed to the following:

> "(3) Subject to subsection (3A) an article is also an infringing copy if –
> (a) it has been or is proposed to be imported into the United Kingdom, and
> (b) its making in the United Kingdom would have constituted an infringement of copyright in the work in question, or a breach of an exclusive licence agreement relating to that work.
>
> (3A) A copy of a computer program which has previously been sold in any other Member State, by or with the consent of the copyright owner, is not an infringing copy for the purposes of subsection (3)."

16 See Chap 4.
17 Copyright, Designs and Patents Act 1988, s 21(3)(b).
18 A fuller analysis of this provision may be found in Chap 8.
19 The Copyright (Computer Programs) Regulations 1992, s 6.

An analysis of this section in the context of the primary infringement of the copyright in computer programs is to be found in Chapter 8 below.

Changes in relation to fair dealing wrought by the Copyright (Computer Programs) Regulations 1992

The Copyright (Computer Programs) Regulations 1992 amended section 29 of the Copyright, Designs and Patents Act 1988 by the inclusion of a new section 29(4)[20] and thereby the provisions concerned with the fair dealing in Copyright Works changed as follows:

> "(4) It is not fair dealing –
> (a) to convert a computer program expressed in a low level language into a version expressed in a higher level language, or
> (b) incidentally in the course of so converting the program, to copy it,
> (these acts being permitted if done in accordance with section 50B (decompilation))."

Statutory rights for end-users introduced by the Copyright (Computer Programs) Regulations 1992

The effect legally and the impact for the software manufacturing community of this specific area of the application of the amended Copyright, Designs and Patents Act 1988 is analysed in Chapter 11 since it was generated by the European Community so that European Community law could be rationalised and harmonised with respect to computer programs. The Copyright (Computer Programs) Regulations 1992 introduced new sections 50A, 50B and 50C into the Copyright, Designs and Patents Act 1988[21], introducing statutory rights for the end-users of computer programs to make back-up copies of their licensed software, decompile the computer programs licensed to them and to make adaptations of them. The new provisions are framed in the following manner:

> "**50A.** – (1) It is not an infringement of copyright for a lawful user of a copy of a computer program to make any back up copy of it which it is necessary for him to have for the purposes of his lawful use.
> (2) For the purposes of this section and sections **50B** and **50C** a person is a lawful user of a computer program if (whether under a licence to do any acts restricted by the copyright in the program or otherwise), he has a right to use the program.

20 *Ibid*, s 7.

21 *Ibid*, s 8.

(3) Where an act is permitted under this section, it is irrelevant whether or not there exists any term or condition in an agreement which purports to prohibit or restrict the act (such terms being, by virtue of section 296A, void).

50B. – (1) It is not an infringement of copyright for a lawful user of a copy of a computer program expressed in a low level language –

(a) to convert it into a version expressed in a higher level language, or

(b) incidentally on the course of so converting the program, to copy it,

(that is, to "decompile" it), provided that the conditions in subsection (2) are met.

(2) The conditions are that –

(a) it is necessary to decompile the program to obtain the information necessary to create an independent program which can be operated with the program decompiled or with another program ("the permitted objective"); and

(b) the information so obtained is not used for any purpose other than the permitted objective.

(3) In particular, the conditions in subsection (2) are not met if the lawful user –

(a) has readily available to him the information necessary to achieve the permitted objective;

(b) does not confine the decompiling to such acts as are necessary to achieve the permitted objective;

(c) supplies the information obtained by the decompiling to any person to whom it is not necessary to supply it in order to achieve the permitted objective; or

(d) uses the information to create a program which is substantially similar in its expression to the program decompiled or to do any act restricted by copyright.

(4) Where an act is permitted under this section, it is irrelevant whether or not there exists any term or condition in an agreement which purports to prohibit or restrict the act (such terms being, by virtue of section 296A, void).

50C. – (1) It is not an infringement of copyright for a lawful user of a copy of a computer program to copy or adapt it, provided that the copying or adapting -

(a) is necessary for his lawful use; and

(b) is not prohibited under any term or condition of an agreement regulating the circumstances in which his use is lawful.

(2) It may, in particular, be necessary for the lawful use of a computer program to copy it or adapt it for the purpose of correcting errors in it.

(3) This section does not apply to any copying or adapting permitted under section 50A or 50B."

The expression "electronic" and the Copyright, Designs and Patents Act 1988

Section 56 of the Copyright, Designs and Patents Act 1988 is concerned with the transfer of copies of works which are in electronic form and is highly relevant to computer software technology since computer programs execute electronically and are recorded, more often than not, in some form of electronic or electromagnetically actuated medium. Within the Copyright, Designs and Patents Act 1988, "electronic" means "actuated by electric, magnetic, electro-magnetic, electro-chemical or electro-mechanical energy, and 'in electronic form' means in a form usable only by electronic means".[22]

> "**56.** – (1) This section applies where a copy of a work in electronic form has been purchased on terms which, expressly or impliedly or by virtue of any rule of law, allow the purchaser to copy the work, or to adapt it or make copies of an adaptation, in connection with his use of it.
> (2) If there are no express terms –
> (a) prohibiting the transfer of the copy by the purchaser, imposing obligation which continue after a transfer, prohibiting the assignment of any licence or terminating any licence on a transfer, or
> (b) providing for the terms on which a transferee may do the things which the purchaser was permitted to do,
> anything which the purchaser was allowed to do may also be done without infringement of copyright by a transferee; but any copy, adaptation or copy of an adaptation made by the purchaser which is not also transferred shall be treated as an infringing copy for all purposes after the transfer.
> (3) The same applies where the original purchased copy is no longer usable and what is transferred is a further copy used in its place.
> (4) The above provisions also apply on a subsequent transfer, with the substitution for references in subsection (2) to the purchaser of references to the subsequent transferor."

In the context of the subsistence of computer programs electronically, section 66(5) of the Copyright, Designs and Patents Act 1988 becomes germane where it deals with the infringement of rental copies:

> "(5) Copyright in a computer program is not infringed by the rental of copies to the public after the end of the period of 50 years from the end of the calendar year in which copies of it were first issued to the public in electronic form."

The absence of moral rights under the Copyright, Designs and Patents Act 1988

As averred to above on p 16 the right to be identified as author or director of a Copyright Work under the Copyright, Designs and Patents Act 1988[23] does not apply to computer programs by virtue of section 79(2):

22 *Ibid*, s 178.
23 *Ibid*, s 77.

"**79.** – (1) The right conferred by section 77 (right to be identified as author or director) is subject to the following exceptions.
(2) The right does not apply in relation to the following descriptions of work –
(a) a computer program;
(b) the design of a typeface;
(c) any computer-generated work."

The right of the author of a copyright literary, dramatic, musical or artistic work (and the director of a copyright film) not to have his work subject to derogatory treatment[24] produced by the Copyright, Designs and Patents Act 1988 does not extend to computer programs nor to computer-generated works.[25]

However, the right not to have one's work falsely attributed created by the Copyright, Designs and Patents Act 1988[26] includes computer programs.[27] This seems to be somewhat of an inconsistency; since if it is important to the author of a computer program not to have his work falsely attributed, why is it not important for him to be attributed as the author in the first place? This appears to be yet another example of how the Copyright, Designs and Patents Act 1988 does not have a consistent vision as to how computer programs are to fit within the general structure of copyright law and how they are somehow a less worthy species of copyright work, undeserving of the full panoply of protection provided by the Copyright, Designs and Patents Act 1988. Some would argue that the intellectual and creative input necessary to produce a computer program is no less worthy in this sense than that of a novelist or poet.

The circumvention of copy protection under the Copyright, Designs and Patents Act 1988

The Copyright, Designs and Patents Act 1988 introduced new provisions with respect to devices that are designed to circumvent copy protection and this area is analysed in Chapter 9:

"**296.** – (1) This section applies where copies of a copyright work are issued to the public, by or with the licence of the copyright owner, in an electronic form which is copy-protected.
(2) The person issuing the copies to the public has the same rights against a

24 *Ibid*, s 80(1).
25 *Ibid*, s 81(2).
26 *Ibid*, s 84(1).
27 By virtue of their being an absence of any exclusionary provision on this point in the Copyright, Designs and Patents Act 1988.

person who, knowing or having reason to believe that it will be used to make infringing copies:

(a) makes, imports, sells or lets for hire, offers or exposes for sale or hire, or advertises for sale of hire, any device or means specifically designed or adapted to circumvent the form of copy-protection employed, or

(b) publishes information intended to enable or assist persons to circumvent the form of copy- protection,

as a copyright owner has in respect of an infringement of copyright.

(3) Further, he has the same rights under section 99 or 100 (delivery up or seizure of certain articles) in relation to any such device or means which a person has in his possession, custody or control with the intention that it should be used to make infringing copies of copyright works, as a copyright owner has in relation to an infringing copy.

(4) References in this section to copy-protection includes any device or means intended to prevent or restrict copying of a work or to impair the quality of copies made."

Computer software contracts and the Copyright, Designs and Patents Act 1988

The Copyright (Computer Programs) Regulations 1992 introduced a new section 296A into the Copyright, Designs and Patents Act 1988 which deals with the contractual avoidance of certain provisions of the Copyright, Designs and Patents Act 1988 dealing with computer programs:

"**296A.** – (1) Where a person has the use of a computer program under an agreement, any term or condition in the agreement shall be void in so far as it purports to prohibit or restrict –

(a) the making of any back up copy of the program which is necessary for him to have for the purposes of the agreed use;

(b) where the conditions in section 50B(2) are met, the decompiling of the program; or

(c) the use of any device or means to observe, study or test the functioning of the program in order to understand the ideas and principles which underlie any element of the program.

(2) In this section, decompile, in relation to a computer program, has the same meaning as in section 50B."[28]

This amended area of the Copyright, Designs and Patents Act 1988 is treated in Chapter 11.

28 The Copyright (Computer Programs) Regulations 1992, s 11.

THE CONSTITUENT ELEMENTS OF COPYRIGHT SUBSISTENCE

There are certain constituent elements of copyright that must be borne in mind in any consideration of a copyright work. They are: the absence of protection for ideas *per se*; the need for originality (skill, taste and judgement) and the requirement of certainty. A short exposition of some of the leading cases on this subject here (before a full analysis of the subsistence of copyright in computer programs that is to come in the following chapters) is thought necessary so as to crystallise these pre-eminent concepts so that they can be understood with clarity without tackling the complexities of computer programming technologies which is the context in which these concepts are applied.

Concepts and ideas

It should be constantly borne in mind that copyright protection is given to literary, musical, dramatic and artistic works and not to ideas *per se*. Pritchard J gave an important and exemplary analysis of the issue of the subsistence of copyright in ideas in *Plix Products Ltd v Frank M Winstone (Merchants)*.[29] The learned judge's analyses of the two main arguments put forward with respect to this matter are included here as directly applicable to the conceptualisation of computer programs. In his judgment he says:

> "The learned authors of *Copinger and Skone James* (12th ed, paras 2, 103, 179, 156) state unequivocally that the ideas and original thought of the author are not protected – that copyright is concerned only with the concrete forms in which the ideas are expressed. There is an insistent line of authority to support this view, ranging from *Kenrick & Co v Lawrence & Co* (1890) 25 QBD 99 to *LB Plastics Ltd v Swish Products Ltd* [1979] RPC 551, 619.
>
> The concept that copyright does not protect ideas is found unacceptable by the authors of several recent textbooks – e.g. Laddie, Prescott & Vitoria at pages 31 to 33, and Lahore on 'Intellectual Property in Australia,' paragraphs 1121, 1151.
>
> I think the conflict between these two philosophies is more apparent than real, and that if there is any conflict it can be resolved by an analysis of the concept of 'ideas'.
>
> There are in fact two kinds of 'ideas' involved in the making of any work which is susceptible of being the subject of copyright. In the first place; there is the general idea or basic concept of the work. This idea is formed (or implanted) in the mind of the author. He sets out to write a poem or a novel about unrequited love or to draw a dog listening to a gramophone or to make a kiwi fruit pocket pack – or whatever project he has in mind. While this 'idea' remains as a thought

29 [1986] FSR 63.

in the author's mind it is, of course, not copyright. It is accepted by the proponents of the 'copyright in ideas' theory that the mere act of reducing a general or basic concept of this sort to a tangible form does not result in a monopoly in the concept (Laddie, Prescott & Vitoria, para 3.27).

Then there is a second phase – a second kind of 'idea'. The author of the work will scarcely be able to transform the basic concept into a concrete form – i.e. 'express' the idea – without furnishing it with details of form and shape. The novelist will think of characters, dialogue, details of plot and so forth. The artist will think of a certain tilt to the dog's head, to the effect of perspective, colour, light and shade. The pocket pack maker will likewise design the shapes, forms, patterns whereby he believes he can most effectively express the basic idea of pocket packs. Each author will draw on his skill, his knowledge of the subject, the results of his own researches, his own imagination in forming his idea of how he will express the basic concept. All these modes of expression have their genesis in the author's mind – these too are 'ideas'. When these ideas (which are essentially constrictive in character) are reduced to concrete form, the forms they take are where the copyright resides.

So it is true to say (with Laddie, Prescott & Vitoria et al.) that copyright does extend to the protection of ideas – not to basic concepts, but to the ideas which are applied in the exercise of giving expression to basic concepts. It is equally true to say with Copinger & Skone James (and a formidable line of authority) that copyright subsists only in the form of expression and that infringement occurs only when such forms are copied.

The difficulty, of course, is to determine just where the general concept ends and the exercise of expressing the concept begins. It is, as Professor Cornish observes in his recent work, *Intellectual Property*, an 'ill-defined boundary'. There can be no general formula by which to establish the line between the general idea and the author's expression of the idea. The basic idea (or concept) is not necessarily simple – it may be complex. It may be something innovative; or it may be commonplace, utilitarian or banal. The way the author treats the subject, the forms he uses to express the basic concept, may range from the rude and simplistic to the ornate, complicated – and involving the collation and application of a great number of constructive ideas. It is in this area that the author expends the skill and industry which (even though they may be slight) give the work its originality and entitle him to copyright. Anyone is free to use the basic idea – unless, of course, it is a novel invention which is protected by the grant of a patent. But no one can appropriate the forms or shapes evolved by the author in the process of giving expression to the basic idea.

So he who seeks to make a product of the same description as that in which another owns copyright must tread with care. If he copies the details which properly belong to the expression and not to the basic concept, he will infringe the copyright. That is why, when the basic idea is expressed in a crude, or simplistic form, the potential plagiarist or business competitor can, without offending, come very close to an exact reproduction of the copyright work. But where the expression is ornate, complex or detailed, then he must keep his distance: the only product he can then make without infringing may bear little resemblance to the copyright work."[30]

30 *Ibid* at 92–93.

Although an admittedly lengthy quotation, it is submitted that the learned judge's words speak for themselves and are the correct interpretation of the question concerning the existence of copyright in ideas and concepts. The general basic idea or concept of a computer program to address, say, the needs of the wine-making market or the interest of persons in science fiction would not be susceptible to copyright. While the concept remains in the mind of the author it is not copyright, nor does the mere reducing of that concept to some form of tangible medium constitute a copyright work. Then, as the learned judge expounds, there is a second form of "idea". The author of the computer program begins to transform the basic concept into a concrete form. The developer of commercial software will design the algorithms, logic and processes by which he can most effectively express his basic idea of a wine-maker's application. The developer of a games or entertainment computer program will think of the characters he is to involve, the details of the plot and the interaction of the characters and the technologies he is to invent for them. All of these modes of expression have their genesis in the author's mind and are, as such, "ideas" too. When these ideas are reduced to concrete form, copyright resides in the form in which they are expressed. The learned judge then recognises that the test as to where the end of a general conceptualisation lies or where the expression of the concept begins is a difficult one to construct and no general test can be fashioned.

Originality, Skill, Taste and Judgment

Originality

It is the original skill and labour in the execution of the work to hand which gives rise to copyright and not the originality of thought that is required. A useful dictum can be found in the judgment of Peterson J in *University of London Press Ltd v University Tutorial Press Ltd*[31] where he says that:

> "The word 'original' does not in this connection mean that the work must be the expression of original or inventive thought. Copyright Acts are not concerned with the originality of ideas, but with the expression of thought in print or writing. The originality which is required relates to the expression of thought. But the Act does not require that the expression must be in an original or novel form, but that the work must not be copied from another's work – that it should originate from the author."[32]

31 [1916] 2 Ch 601.8
32 *Ibid* at 608.

It is this distinction of originality from uniqueness that must be understood and borne in mind constantly in any examination of the originality of a computer program. The computer program's functionality may be hackneyed, commonplace and offer no real difference from a hundred competitors on the market-place. Nevertheless, so long as the work is not copied from another's and originates from the author, that will suffice.[33]

The concept of "originality" has remained with us in section 1(1) of the Copyright, Designs and Patents Act 1988 since the Copyright Act 1911, but often the question in relation to computer programming technologies is how much "originality" needs to be injected by the programmer into his work before copyright arises in it? The question was considered by the Privy Council in the case of *Macmillan & Co Ltd v Cooper (K&J)*[34], in which it was alleged that there was copyright in a selection or abridgement of a non-copyright work. Lord Atkinson, in delivering the judgment of the Court, said: "What is the precise amount of the knowledge, labour, judgement or literary skill or taste which the author of any book or other compilation must bestow upon its composition in order to acquire copyright in it ... cannot be defined in precise terms."[35] It is here, as was pointed out by Maugham J in *Cambridge University Press v University Tutorial Press Ltd*[36], that the real difficulty arises. There is no guiding principle as to the quantum of skill and judgement required and it is contended that this problem is severely exacerbated by the new nature of computer programs and the requirement to have this question answered in some reasoned and reliable fashion. The tests set out in Chapter 3 attempt to address, in part, the problems arising here.

The exercise of literary taste and judgement

In *University of London Press Ltd v University Tutorial Press Ltd*, Peterson J gives us some pertinent help as to the degree of literary taste and judgement that must be applied in order for copyright to arise where he says:

> "It was said, however, that they [Prof Lodge & Mr Jackson – the authors of the works in dispute] drew upon the stock of knowledge common to mathematicians, and that the time spent in producing the questions was small. These cannot be tests for determining whether copyright exists. If an author, for purposes of copyright, must not draw on the stock of knowledge which is common to himself and others who are students of the same branch of learning,

33 This is subject to the concept that copyright may, in some circumstances, subsist in an infringing work. See Chap 6 and **ZYX Music GmbH v Chris King** [1995] FSR 566.

34 LR 51 Ind App 109,125. 93 LJ PC 113,121.

35 *Ibid* at 335.

36 (1928) 45 RPC 335.

> only those historians who discovered fresh historical facts could acquire copyright for their works. If time expended is to be the test, the rapidity of an author like Lord Byron in producing a short poem might be an impediment in the way of acquiring copyright, and, the completer his mastery of his subject, the smaller would be the prospect of the author's success in maintaining his claim to copyright."[37]

And later in the judgment goes on to say:

> "...there remains the rough practical test that what is worth copying is prima facie worth protecting."[38]

Accordingly it can be seen that those computer programmers who may have been formally taught in their science, may draw upon the common stock or knowledge of computer programming techniques and the doing so will not reduce the "originality" in their works; nor does it matter if they work swiftly. It is often a concern of the computer program developer that due to the fact that there might only be one or two ways in which to address a programming mechanism in a given operating system environment[39], the code they invent might have been invented and used before in another computer software product and thus their work will be infringing copyright. The dicta of Peterson J above are therefore helpful in showing that this fear or contention (broadly held in the computer programming community) is an erroneous one.

In *IBCOS Computers Ltd v Barclays Mercantile Highland Finance Ltd*[40] Jacob J commented usefully on these "aphorisms" and said:

> "I have set forth the tests which are taken directly from the statute because not only is this what the law requires but because by doing this one can avoid aphorisms such as 'there is no copyright in an idea' or 'prima facie what is worth copying is worth protecting'. The courts have used these in the past but they can only serve as a guide. There are dangers in departing from the Act too far. For instance the latter aphorism, taken literally, would mean that all a plaintiff ever had to do was to prove copying. Originality, appropriate subject matter for copyright and a taking of a substantial part would all be proved in one go. One would not need the Act if the aphorism represented the law. It proves too much."[41]

In commenting in this manner the learned judge is right, for no matter how many guidelines are offered by different judges, in differing times and in differing technological and historical contexts, one must always bear in mind that it is a true construction of the Copyright, Designs and Patents Act 1988 that genuinely matters. This view itself can also be overstated, for a proper

37 At 609.
38 *Ibid* at 610.
39 For an explanation of operating systems and other software environments, see Chap 4.
40 [1994] FSR 275.
41 *Ibid* 289.

balance must be struck between the words of the Copyright, Designs and Patents Act 1988 itself and the assistance previous applications of the law can give. The requirement of the exercise of taste and judgement by the author is a good example of this. In *GA Cramp & Sons Ltd v Frank Smythson Ltd*[42], which involved an action for the infringement of certain parts of a diary, the plaintiffs alleged that the tables in the diaries had been copied. In brief, it was held that copyright had not been established since the commonplace matter of the tables left no room for taste and judgement. Thus valuable insight is given into the possible lack of subsistence of copyright in data tables which leave no room for the exercise of taste and judgement in their construction.

Measuring the degree of knowledge, labour and skill

The exercise of knowledge, labour, skill and judgement as a criteria of paramount importance in bringing about the subsistence of copyright in a work cannot be overstated. But once again, the difficulty in measuring to what degree this criteria must be exercised is difficult in the extreme and has exercised some of the most outstanding minds in English legal history. Viscount Simon LC approved Lord Atkinson's observation in delivering the judgment of the judicial committee of the House of Lords in *MacMillan & Co Ltd v K&J Cooper* where he said:

> "What is the precise amount of knowledge, labour, judgement or literary skill or taste which the author of any book or other compilation must bestow upon its composition in order to acquire copyright in it within the meaning of the Copyright Act of 1911 cannot be defined in precise terms. In every case it must depend largely on the special facts of that case, and must in each case be very much a question of degree."[43]

Viscount Simon LC went on to say:

> "There was no evidence that any of these tables was composed specially for the respondent's diary. There was no feature of them which could be pointed out as novel or specially meritorious or ingenious from the point of view of the judgement or skill of the compiler. It was not suggested that there was any element of originality or skill in the order in which the tables were arranged."[44]

In the case of *Ladbroke (Football) Ltd v William Hill (Football) Ltd*[45], some useful dicta were made by the House of Lords with respect to the arising of copyright in betting coupons. Although dealing with compilations, it is submitted that the following dicta do add some valuable indications as to

42 [1944] AC 329.
43 At 335.
44 *Ibid* at 336.
45 [1964] 1 WLR 273

what elements are necessary for copyright to arise in a literary work. Per Lord Reid:

> "And it is not disputed that, as regards compilation, originality is a matter of degree depending on the amount of skill, judgement or labour that has been involved in making the compilation."[46]

And per Lord Evershed:

> "I conclude that there was present here the requisite degree of skill, judgment and labour, not only in selecting out of the vast possible total of wagers those which should be offered, but also in the way in which the result of the selection was presented to the customer, including particularly the arrangement of the document and of its component headings and the way in which such headings were described and were coloured and also in the way which, in the appropriate notes underneath the headings, the punter was informed of the possibilities open to him under each heading."[47]

These dicta are useful since they go to demonstrate that skill, judgement and labour are as much elements in the originality of a compilation as any other species of literary work. Computer software products, in so far as they may be collections of a large number of discrete but interacting computer programs, are compilations within the meaning of the Copyright, Designs and Patents Act 1988 and a great deal of development work goes into how the computer program is displayed to the end-user who could be unkindly referred to as a type of "punter". It should be noted, therefore, how applicable Lord Evershed's dicta seem to be to the display choices that are available to computer programmers. In this manner this work will go to show that cases which may have arisen when computer programming was in its infancy, can often have a direct and obvious allegory in computer programming technology.

Certainty

Regard ought to be made as to whether the author has expressed himself in terms which are sufficiently "certain". It seems that in works which are short and preparatory in some manner to a fuller treatment of the idea to be developed later from such preparation, the courts are wary of recognising the existence of copyright without the subject-matter of the work being expressed with "certainty".[48]

---

46 *Ibid* at 277.

47 *Ibid* at 282.

48 **Tate v Thomas** [1921] 1 Ch 503 and **Green v Broadcasting Corp of New Zealand** [1989] RPC 700 (PC).

Chapter 3

THE DEVELOPMENT OF COMPUTER PROGRAMS

INTRODUCTION

The subject of the development and manufacture of computer programs is a complex one and is the subject of substantial financial investment by the computer industry since it directly drives the existence, quality and commercial success of any computer software product. In 1993[1] the turnover in the United Kingdom of the computer services industry was £6,383 million. However, in simplistic terms a thread of commonality runs among all methods of developing commercial computer software. This chapter will attend to the different processes, recognised within the software industry, which bring the computer program into being in machine-readable form and not the stages of testing and market preparation (including such items as market surveys, direct mailing campaigns and advertising generally) that usually follow later, since these do not impinge directly on the copyright issues associated with computer software. This chapter will also review briefly the newer and alternative methods of computer programming, including structured methods and automated methodologies.

A SIMPLIFIED "NON-AUTOMATED" SOFTWARE DEVELOPMENT ENVIRONMENT

The stages in a simplified, but reasonably standard "non-automated" computer programming environment for examination are summarised directly below. By using the term "non-automated", it is meant that the computer programs themselves and the design material prepared prior to actually coding, is effected directly by human beings.

1 The latest year in which statistics were available from the Central Statistic Office of the DTI at the date of submission of this work.

The Stages are as follows:-

Stage 1 – The concept
Stage 2 – Describing and refining the concept
Stage 3 – Specification
Stage 4 – Flow-charting
Stage 5 – Coding

An examination of these stages will prove useful later so as to set down the factual matrix against which the law can be applied and so that through the application of the Copyright, Designs and Patents Act 1988 a determination can be made as to when copyright arises in the works that originate during the above stages and which species of copyright works arise in the development cycle of the computer programs.

Stage 1 – the concept

Every computer program begins with an idea or concept. The computer technician, marketing executive or entrepreneur will have a concept of what he sees the software doing, what problems it will solve and the utility of the program generally and perhaps its place in the market in which it will be designed to compete. It will be recalled from Chapter 2 that copyright protection is given to literary, musical, dramatic and artistic works and not to ideas *per se*.[2] The paraphrasing of part of the judgment of Pritchard J in *Plix Products Ltd v Frank M Winstone (Merchants)* into the context of the development of computer programs will be of benefit in analysing what species of concepts and ideas in computer programs are protected by copyright:

> "There are in fact two kinds of 'ideas' involved in the making of any work which is susceptible of being the subject of copyright. In the first place; there is the general idea or basic concept of the work. This idea is formed (or implanted) in the mind of the author. He sets out to write a computer program which will track and control the stock in a warehouse or design a computer program which can act as a form of encyclopaedia drawing information from databases or to make a computer game where futuristic space ships engage alien craft in combat – or whatever project he has in mind. While this 'idea' remains as a thought in the author's mind it is, of course, not copyright. It is accepted by the proponents of the 'copyright in ideas' theory that the mere act of reducing a general or basic concept of this sort to a tangible form does not result in a monopoly in the concept.

2 See Chap 2.

> Then there is a second phase – a second kind of 'idea'. The author of the work will scarcely be able to transform the basic concept into a concrete form, i.e. 'express' the idea – without furnishing it with details of form and shape. The programmer of the stock control product will think of the requirements of the system, the real-life processes it needs to account for, details of its screen displays and so forth. The programmer of the software encyclopaedia will think of the subject matter to be covered, the ease of use of its interface for users of different ages, the methods employed in searching a large database in response to simple and complex search criteria. The computer game maker will similarly design the shapes and forms of the space craft, the patterns in which they are to move whereby he believes he can most effectively express his basic idea in a colourful, compelling and attractive manner. Each author will draw on his skill, his knowledge of the subject, the results of his own researches, his own imagination in forming his idea of how he will express the basic concept. All these modes of expression have their genesis in the author's mind – these too are 'ideas'. When these ideas (which are essentially constrictive in character) are reduced to concrete form, the forms they take are where the copyright resides."[3]

Thus it can be seen that it is only when the concept comes to be described and refined (as set out in Stage 2 below) that the prospect of copyright commencing to subsist arises.

Stage 2 – describing and refining the concept

In this stage the computer programmer will usually set down on paper a narrative description of the various functions of the computer program and how he will seek to give voice to those functions through the application of various algorithms and other mathematical devices. Documentation will be produced, some of which will be literary works within the meaning of the Copyright, Designs and Patents Act 1988; others will be too short or simple to enable copyright to subsist within them. It is at this stage in the development of a computer program that once again the dicta made by Pritchard J in *Plix Products Ltd v Frank M Winstone (Merchants) supra* is most relevant where he said:

> "The way the author treats the subject, the forms he uses to express the basic concept, may range from the rude and simplistic to the ornate, complicated – and involving the collation and application of a great number of constructive ideas. It is in this area that the author expends the skill and industry which (even though they may be slight) give the work its originality and entitle him to copyright."[4]

---

3 Paraphrased at [1986] FSR 63 at 92–93.
4 At 92.

Testing for the creation of copyright

For copyright to arise in a preparatory design material and/or a computer program the human author must exercise his:

- Knowledge[5]
- Labour[6]
- Judgement[7]
- Programming Skill and Taste[8]

These cannot be defined in precise terms[9], but:

- it does not matter that the programmer drew upon the stock of knowledge common to programmers[10]; nor
- that the time spent in producing the code was small.[11]
- It must all depend largely on the special facts of the computer code in issue, and must in each case be very much a question of degree.[12]

However, one should always bear in mind:

- the rough practical test that what is worth copying is prima facie worth protecting;[13] but
- the work must not be copied from another's work – it should originate from the author;[14] and
- the author must express himself with certainty.[15]

It will be recalled from Chapter 2 that the definition of "literary work" in the Copyright, Designs and Patents Act 1988 was extended by the Copyright (Computer Programs) Regulations 1992 whereby a new section 3(1)(c) was added in which "preparatory design material for a computer program" was expressly protected as a literary work. Not every piece of preparatory design

---

5 **Macmillan & Co Ltd v Cooper (K&J)** .
6 *Ibid.*
7 *Ibid.*
8 *Ibid.*
9 *Ibid* at 335.
10 **University of London Press Ltd v University Tutorial Press Ltd.**
11 *Ibid.*
12 **Macmillan & Co Ltd v K&J Cooper** at 335.
13 **University of London Press Ltd v University Tutorial Press Ltd** at 610. It will be recalled from Chap 2 that although Jacob J usefully commented in what he describes as "aphorisms" in **IBCOS Computers Ltd v Barclays Mercantile Highland Finance Ltd**, it is submitted that these "aphorisms" are of greater worth than the learned judge would have, especially as Jacob J did not propound any new formula or series of tests that could be applied in their stead.
14 **University of London Press Ltd v University Tutorial Press Ltd** at 608
15 **Tate v Thomas** and **Green v Broadcasting Corporation of New Zealand.**

Material will be automatically protected, but will have to satisfy the ordinary tests for the subsistence of copyright as set out in this chapter and Chapter 2. However, it is likely that the documentation produced in describing and refining the concept meets the criteria for the subsistence of copyright[16] and it should therefore be possible to extract from the dicta set out in Chapter 2 the elements of originality that need to be present before copyright in preparatory design material arises and, furthermore, in what degree those elements need to be present.

The species of copyright works created in the development cycle

The real question that faces the legal advisers of producers of computer software is: what type of copyright arises in the different stages of computer software development and at what point does it come into being? The legal adviser then has to contend with the different methods of software development – initially manual methods verses automated methods (CASE). This process is further complicated by section 21(4) of the Copyright, Designs and Patents Act 1988 (which was averred to in Chap 2, but for the purposes of this analysis, is repeated here as a matter of convenience) which tells us that:

> "In relation to a computer program, a 'translation' includes a version of the program in which it is converted into or out of a computer language or code or into a different computer language or code."

We can see therefore that it is possible for a computer program to subsist in a form which is not either computer language or code. It can consequently be argued that detailed preparatory design materials are nothing more than translations of the computer program (or vice versa) and, if the position is that preparatory design materials are computer programs, then the further question arises at what point in the elaboration of these preparatory design materials does copyright subsist? Again further to this, if the computer programmer is not producing preparatory design material (say, *e.g.* he is applying himself to a short but discrete component part of the program during maintenance) and begins to write computer program code directly; at what stage does copyright subsist in this version of the work? The formulation set out on p 35 above goes some way to solving this problem.

This is a difficulty of serious proportions, especially for the commercial software producer who is perpetually concerned with ex-employees taking parts of computer programs in the earliest stages of development to competitors.

---

16 See Chap 2.

Stage 3 – specification

The hard work begins as the programmer sets down functional and technical specifications of each and every part of the program. Imagine here that the programmer has in mind a machine to build – and at this stage is working out the functions and dimensions of the various components which go to make up the machine as a whole. It may well be that certain problems to be solved in the context of the new program that the programmer is devising have been addressed and solved by him in previous computer programs he has written. Furthermore, there might be accepted solutions held in the general store of knowledge of computer programmers from which he might wish to draw. A new copyright will arise in the new computer program even if it contains computer programs, code or routines previously included in other computer programs so long as there was, overall in the new program, a sufficient amount of skill and labour exercised in its creation.

Thus, at this stage at which specifications of varying complexity are being drawn up, new copyright works will arise and pre-existing copyright works will be re-used. Literary works of a number of species will arise, including preparatory design material, tables and some compilations. Since it is also possible for computer programs to subsist in a form that is not computer language or code, computer programs themselves will also arise at this point. The question that therefore arises here is what factors distinguish between a computer program and preparatory design material since the Copyright, Designs and Patents Act 1988 distinguishes between them itself? No case law exists on this subject at all, but a sensible interpretation of the Copyright, Designs and Patents Act 1988 can be made by arguing that the individual specifications, tables and flow-charts which are produced as the constituent elements of a computer program (thus being developed in anticipation of the production of computer code) are preparatory design materials The totality of all of the preparatory design materials, in other words, the collection of all of the preparatory design materials except the computer code itself is, within the meaning of the Copyright, Designs and Patents Act 1988, the computer program itself but subsisting in a form outside of computer language or code. The processes that are given expression in the totality of the preparatory design materials and the processes that are given expression in the computer program are, it is submitted, identical. Merely the forms in which these processes are expressed are different – one can be directly executed by a computer, the other cannot.

Stage 4 – flow-charting

Although it could be quite properly said that flow-charting is not a separate activity from specification, it is divided apart since it involves a different set of skills and results in a manifestly different format.

The nature of flow-charts

Whereas in the specification stage the specifications produced are written in a narrative and mathematical form, flow-charts are something quite different. A flow-chart is set out in a graphical format, showing not only the constituent parts of the program, but also the order in which they are invoked and the alternative mechanisms that are available within the program itself which will be invoked only in certain sets of specific circumstances. It is in the flow-chart stage that the programmer can see not only what the program will be made of, but how it will work.

Flow-charts and CASE technology

Without wishing to investigate the new methodologies of automated computer program production techniques, it may be useful here to point out that at the moment, some computer application software known as "CASE Tools" (which are software tools designed to aid the programmer in the production of his own computer programs) produce flow-charts for the programmer. In brief, the programmer enters certain data and variables into the program during its operation and it will produce the flow-chart and other types of specifications. Some newer CASE tools enable the programmer to enter flow-charts into the product and then automatically generate fully executable computer code without further input from the programmer. The output it produces in minutes might very well represent many man hours of work if the programmer was to attend to the production of flow-charts or computer code himself.

Flow-charts as copyright works

Figure 3.1 is an example of a simple flow-chart and a reasonably complex program may, at specification stage, have many flow-charts produced to give expression to the structure of the program. It will be recalled from Chapter 2 that section 4(1) of the Copyright, Designs and Patents Act 1988 tells us that the term "artistic work" means :

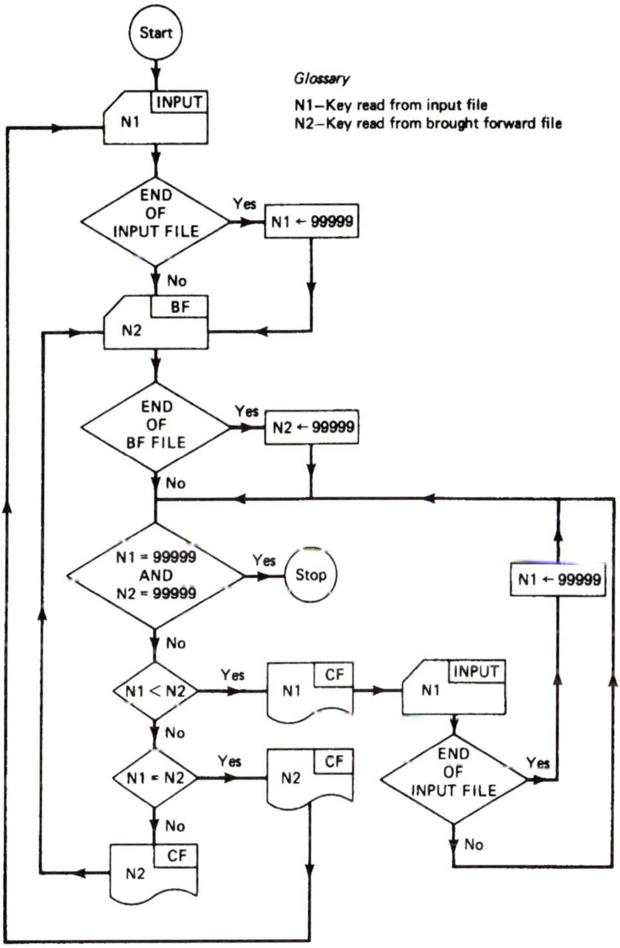

Figure 3.1

(a) a graphic work, photograph, sculpture or collage, irrespective of artistic quality;
(b) a work of architecture being a building or a model for a building; or
(c) a work of artistic craftsmanship.

Section 4(2) of the Copyright, Designs and Patents Act 1988 defines the term "graphic work" and tells us that it includes a "painting, drawing, diagram, map, chart or plan". Thus, within the meaning of the Copyright, Designs and Patents Act 1988, a flow-chart for a computer program is protected both as an artistic work as it is probably a drawing or a diagram in its own right, but also as a literary work as preparatory design material.

Bearing in mind that ideas, however original, are not protected by copyright; where a diagram (flow-chart) embodies an original idea, it is the diagram (flow-chart) and not the idea which is protected. However, a flow-chart is a great deal more than just a collection of lines, boxes and circles since it contains so much critical information with respect to the logic and flow of data throughout the computer program. In *Anacon Corporation Ltd v Environmental Research Technology Ltd*[17] Jacob J considered the nature of copyright that exists in circuit diagrams and held that they were artistic works within the meaning of the Copyright, Designs and Patents Act 1988.[18] However, the learned judge went much further and took the view that a circuit diagram is more than just visual information for it contains a great deal of writing. The circuit diagram, the learned judge reasoned, was also a list of the components in a circuit with details as to how they are connected. Thus, the judge held that the circuit diagram was not only an artistic work, but a literary work.[19] Jacob J commented with respect to the circuit diagram that:

> "My first thought was that it would be absurd to regard a circuit diagram as a literary work, but the more one thinks about the ambit of that expression, as used in the Act, the more one is driven to the conclusion that provided it is all written down and contains information which can be read by somebody, as opposed to appreciated simply with the eye, the more one sees that that is just what it is. Similarly musical notation is written down, but needs expressly to be taken out of the definition of 'literary work'. But that which is not expressly taken out remains within it. What one has here is electrical engineer's notation."[20]

Then what one may have here in the flow-chart is software engineer's notation. It is submitted that the learned judge's interpretation of the law is a sound one and therefore a flow-chart, if carrying sufficient notation, may also qualify as a literary work.

Degree of elaboration in flow-charts

Even though the idea embodied in the diagram (flow-chart) may be of profound significance and of great economic worth, if the diagram (flow-chart) is of very simple design, the protection afforded by copyright is relatively weak. In *Kenrick & Co v Lawrence & Co*[21] the plaintiff conceived the idea of printing and publishing cards bearing a representation of a hand

17 [1994] FSR 659.
18 *Ibid* at 662.
19 *Ibid* at 663.
20 *Ibid* at 664.
21 (1890) 25 QBD 99.

holding a pencil in the act of completing a cross within a square, with a view to its cards being used at elections by illiterate voters. The plaintiff procured an artist to make, under his directions, a drawing of the representation. Subsequently the defendant published similar cards with a hand holding a pencil, but the hand in the defendant's cards was in a slightly different position, though the idea was clearly taken from the plaintiffs cards. It was held that the defendant had not infringed the plaintiff's copyright. There was no copyright in the idea, the defendant's work was not an exact reproduction of the plaintiffs and the plaintiff was not entitled to prevent anyone from producing such a simple design as a hand in a square in any form. In *Commercial Signs v General Motors Products of Canada Ltd* Kingstone J commented that:

> "All that was done by the plaintiff firm, in so far as these five so-called artistic sketches are concerned, was to make an enlargement or copy of the original drawings with certain colouring and the use of certain letters which had the effect, by reason of the experience of the plaintiff firm in matters of this kind, of bringing out clearly the distinctive points that were necessary in these signs and banners. There was nothing original or inventive that would enable the plaintiff to claim that its artistic work was being copied or wrongly used by the defendant. The only conclusion is that there was no artistic skill, within the meaning of the Copyright Act, displayed by the plaintiff in the preparation of these cuts, but merely the mechanical work of putting the drawing in such a form as to enable the customer to view it from a proper perspective."[22]

It is therefore always important to bear in mind that even flow or logic diagrams need to be sufficiently elaborated and display more than the thresholds of originality and inventiveness to qualify for copyright protection.

Stage 5 – coding

It is at this stage that the programmer will begin to create the computer program in a form that can be read and executed by the computer. The programmer may write the program in a particular computer language such as "BASIC", "COBOL" or "C". The program written in such a language will be converted by the computer into a form it can execute directly during the running of the program.

One must remember at all times the computer programs such as the one set out in Figure 3.2, although often referred to as "*code*" are not encrypted in the sense of secret code which, once decoded, is converted into ordinary

22 [1937] 2 DLR at 313.

```
*/
#define ERROR 0
#define MAXTEXT 20000
#define MAXTEXT 200
#define MAXPTR 1500
#define MAXPTR1 1501
#define MRGORDER 7
#defineMRGORD1  8
#define LOGPTR 13
#defineLOGPTR1  14
#define EOF - 1
#define NULL 0
char name [13], name2[23];
int infil[MRGORDR1];
int infile, outfile, tmpfile;
unsigned linptr[MAXPTR1], nlines;
int temp;
char *linbuf, endext[MAXTEXT];

main(argc,argv)
int argc
char *argv[];
{
            unsigned high, lim, low, t;
            linbuf=endext;
            if (argc,3)
                  {
                  }
```

Figure 3.2

```
1  00001000    207C00001010
2  00001006    7200
3  00001008    611E
4  0000100E    4E4E
5  00001010    4E5554532020
6  00001018    000A
7  0000101A    0019
8  0000101C    424F4C545320
9  00001024    000F
10 00001026    0014
```

Figure 3.3

```
var i:integer;

begin
   gettop(presentpointer);
   writeln;
   while presentpointer<>nil do
         begin
               with presentpointer^.liststrang do
               for i=1 to count do write (symbols[i]);
               writeln;
               presentpointer:=presentpointer^.next
         end
end;
```

Figure 3.4

language. Rather, computer code is a language. A language that both computers and human beings are capable of "understanding".

Alternatively the programmer might choose to compile the program so that it is rendered into a form which can be more readily, and therefore more speedily, executed by the computer. Some computer programs do not resemble ordinary language at all. For example, the part of a computer program set out in Figure 3.3 is written in MC68000 Assembly Language; whilst the part of a computer program set out in Figure 3.4, which is written in the computer language known as "PASCAL", does, in the author's opinion, closely resemble ordinary English.

In any event, the programmer will store the program as he writes it. Of course, the programmer may choose to type or hand-write the program on paper. However, it is much more likely that he will type the program into the computer. As he does so the program is held in the computer's electronic memory. Computer memory is usually of a volatile type and will therefore be lost if the computer's power supply is disconnected.

The programmer will therefore store the program, in a form that the computer can register (often referred to as a "machine-readable" format) which is permanent. The programmer's choice will usually be either magnetic media or optical media.

In magnetic media such as cassettes, tapes or hard or floppy disks, the program will be written in machine-readable form by magnetically altering the arrangement of iron oxide molecules on a base plastic foundation in much the same way as an audio or video cassette.

Examples of the current standard disks are shown in Figures 3.5 and 3.6 – Figure 3.5 being a diagram of the standard $5^1/_4$ inch floppy disk and Figure 3.6 being a diagram of the higher capacity $3^1/_2$ inch floppy disk. Both disks being commonly used with micro or personal computers (often abbreviated to "PCs").

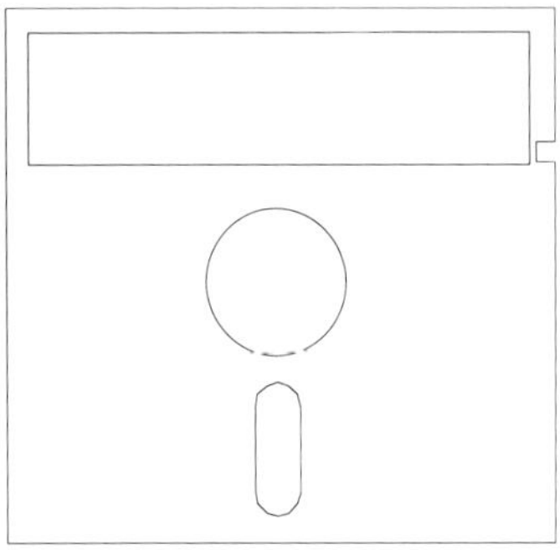

Figure 3.5

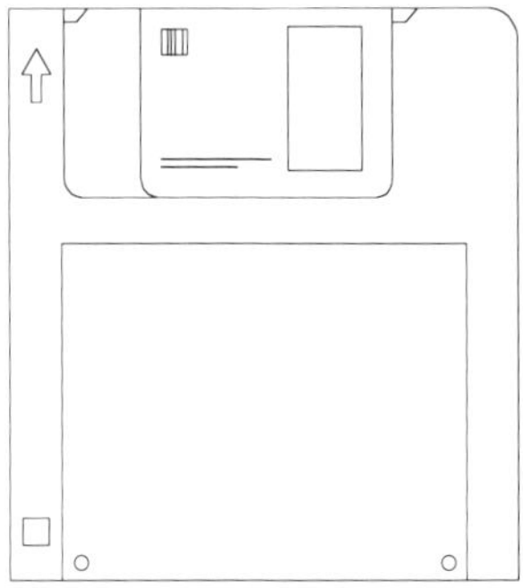

Figure 3.6

With respect to optical media, the program is stored by a laser making pits in an aluminium and plastic foundation also in the form of a disk, in much the same way as an audio compact disc is produced.

Optical media have the advantage over magnetic media disks as they have a very much larger storage capacity and tend to have a longer life as no working parts actually come into contact with the optical disk, whereas the "head" which reads the contents of a floppy disk or tape actually comes into direct physical contact with the medium itself causing a degree of wear. Optical disks look very much like the audio compact disk with which we have all become familiar.

Formal "Non-Automated" Software Development Environments

Formalised and generally accepted structure and procedures have been developed by the software industry which are often applied, in the modern development environment, to the construction of computer programs. A number of the more pre-eminent procedures will be examined here, such as "systems engineering", "traditional development" and the "divide and conquer" principle. Alternative and more radical and modern software engineering philosophies which are also in current usage will be examined, such as classical "Information Engineering Methodology" (IEM), "Business System Implementation" (BSI) and a technique which straddles non-automated and automated software development techniques – "Rapid Application Development" (RAD).

Systems engineering

A systems engineering modelling framework looks at a business model from five different "altitudes" or layers. Each layer serves as a platform from which to view application systems at different levels of detail.

Architectural layer

The architectural layer is a high-level, broad brush view of the organisation to be automated. It consists of three interlocking architectures that form a high-level blueprint for meeting the organisation's goals and objectives. As it is a description of the business to be modelled and not a description of a computer program (at whatever level of explanation) it may be argued that such a document will not qualify as preparatory design material. However, if sufficient literary taste, skill and originality has been exercised, it may qualify as being susceptible to copyright protection in its own right as a literary work.

Conceptual layer

The conceptual layer is a model of the data relationships, activities and business rules on which systems will be based. This model subdivides the concepts introduced at the architectural layer into subordinate pieces and describes them in much more detail. Once again, such a work may not qualify as preparatory design material as it is directed to explaining and describing the business upon which the computerised systems (computer programs) will be based; but at this stage of elaboration it is likely copyright would have arisen and the work would be classed as a literary work within the meaning of the Copyright, Design and Patents Act 1988.

External layer

The external layer is a model of system behaviour as experienced by an end-user of the system. It contains specialised information about the conceptual layer of particular interest to users, such as screen layouts and function key assignments. This model would qualify as preparatory design material. It may also contain complicated flow diagrams which would qualify for copyright protection in themselves, both as artistic works and as preparatory design material in their own right.

Implementation layer

The implementation layer is a specialisation of the external layer. It maps the external details about the system to a specific computer hardware and software environment. This layer would certainly be preparatory design material but, as always, the usual tests with respect to all species of literary works would still need to be applied.

Execution layer

The execution layer consists of databases and applications executing on specific computing equipment. This layer becomes the reality of the model that stands above it and is the computer program itself.

Thus the external layer and the implementation layer collectively are the computer program subsisting in a form outside of computer language or code.

The systems engineering framework consists of static set of layers through which developers move in different ways, depending on their objective. Top-to-bottom progress is only one of several alternative pathways and each pathway differs from the others based on its direction, starting-point and ending-point. Development, or **forward engineering**, is the general movement from the top to the bottom of the framework. **Reverse engineering** is the general movement from the bottom to the top of the framework. In one form of reverse engineering, **design recovery**, either the external layer, the implementation layer or both are populated from the bottom up to the top. In another form of reverse engineering, **current systems analysis**, the conceptual layer is populated from the bottom up to the top. **Re-engineering** is a combination of forward and reverse engineering: developers reverse engineer the existing application to the conceptual layer, then forward engineer it. **Modification**, or **maintenance**, is a pathway in which developers enter at the appropriate layer in the framework, make changes, then push those changes through to the execution layer. Maintenance comes from the side and pushes down.

The direction of movement through the framework determines the order of tasks, their structure, and their dependencies. For example, during forward engineering, developers design a system based on business rules. During reverse engineering, developers deduce business rules from an existing system.

Ultimately, the task structured depends on the pathway through the framework, the size and complexity of the problem, the project team's experience, their preferred order of work and common sense criteria. Companies can choose among alternative approaches based on ease of communication, degree of automation and cultural fit.

Traditional development

The layers correspond to deliverables from the five traditional development stages. These stages imply a forward direction of movement through the systems engineering framework. Each stage views data, activities and interactions in more detail than the preceding one. One should not confuse the modelling framework (the layers of systems engineering) with the development stages that populate it, since a consideration of these stages in consecutive order is helpful before changing the order or rearranging the tasks. The stages, in order, are:

Planning

During this stage planners gain a broad view of the information needs of the business. From this information, they create a blueprint for the future and sub-divide the blueprint into smaller segments. The chief deliverable from this stage is a model of the entire enterprise that includes subject areas and function diagrams. Planning populates the architectural layer. Once again as these works form a description of the business to be modelled and not a description of a computer program (at whatever level of explanation) it may be argued that such a document will not qualify as preparatory design material. However, if sufficient literary taste, skill and originality has been exercised, it may qualify as being susceptible to copyright protection. In other circumstances, this document may be of considerable size and undoubtedly qualify as a copyright work.

Analysis

During this stage analysts examine a particular segment of the business area. They develop a detailed, conceptual model of this business area based on its information needs. This model includes entity type and process diagrams. Analysis populates the conceptual layer. As in the case of the conceptual layer above, such a work may not qualify as preparatory design material; but it is submitted at this stage of elaboration it is likely copyright would have arisen and the work would be classed as a literary work within the meaning of the Copyright, Design and Patents Act 1988 and, indeed, contain artistic works.

External design

During this stage designers detail a business system within a particular business area. They consider how the user will interact with the business system without concerning themselves with the target environment. The model at this stage includes procedure diagrams and screen and window layouts. External design populates the external layer. At this level of elaboration a very great deal of time, taste and expertise would have been expended to produce this stage. This stage would constitute preparatory design material as the focus of the work has moved from an understanding of the business issues to the design of the computer program application. However, it is possible to say that since the only purpose of the previous stages is to bring about design documentation for the computer program in order to enable coding to commence, they are in fact stages conducted in preparation of the computer program and the works produced as a consequence are preparatory design material.

Internal design

During this stage designers tailor the results of external design to a target computing environment. They consider the hardware environment, operating system, teleprocessing monitor and database management system. The model at this stage reflects the physical details of specific computers. Internal design populates the implementation layer. This stage would certainly be preparatory design material but, as always, one must always have regard to the fact that the usual tests with respect to all species of literary works would still need to be applied.

Construction

During this stage developers generate all the executable components of a system, including programs, databases, job-control statements, screen formats and transaction definitions. These pieces enable an application system to be tested in the development environment and run in the target environment selected for implementation. Construction populates the execution layer and a computer program is produced. The computer programs are thus generated.

The "divide and conquer" principle

The traditional approach to systems engineering is based on the principle of "divide and conquer". Developers address smaller sections of the business model as the level of detail increases, thus reducing each task to a manageable size. For example, one planning project can produce 10 analysis projects, which can result in 100 external design projects.

Each project requires a project sponsor – a senior executive having overall authority and responsibility for the project. Project team members include a project manager and individual contributors having appropriate business skills. Members of the initial planning project team gather information to determine the mission, objectives, goals and critical success factors of the enterprise. They gather this information from interviews and from written material such as a business plan (possibly qualifying as a literary work but probably, it is contended, not preparatory design material). In addition, they develop an information strategy plan and high-level enterprise model. Subsequent analysis projects evolve from this initial model producing literary works at different levels of elaboration and of differing and often increasing levels of complexity.

Organisations having immediate needs in a particular business area can elect to bypass the planning stage and proceed directly with analysis. Each analysis project centres around a single business area. Because each enterprise is unique, each company must determine its own key business areas. Each analysis project team consists of analysts familiar with the business area under development. These analysts model business requirements at a conceptual level. The project manager can choose to apportion work by area of expertise. For example, he or she might assign data-administration specialists to the data model and applications specialists to the activities model. This division of labour can continue through subsequent development stages.

Each analysis project typically results in multiple external design projects. For example, the personnel business area might break down into payroll, benefits and recruitment business systems. Similarly, the finance business area might decompose into general accounting and forecasting. Each external design project team includes designers with appropriate knowledge of the business system under development. These designers take an external view, concerning themselves with how users will interact with the system and produce preparatory design material by virtue of this process. Potential end-users contribute heavily to design decisions at this point, since they will be the ultimate beneficiaries. The resulting business system model is completely portable and essentially independent of its target computer hardware environment.

External design projects combine to yield internal design projects based on database implementation considerations, packaging decisions and the number of target environments which produce yet more preparatory design material. Members of the internal design team have sufficient technical expertise to fine-tune the design to its intended hardware and software environment. Internal design decisions do not affect the end-user, except from a performance standpoint.

Each external design project typically results in construction being performed. While once the most time-consuming part of system development, construction in a CASE environment can be reduced to a few keystrokes. After this automatic translation and computer program generation takes place, the design is physically implemented in its target computer language and executes in its intended target computer hardware environment – the computer programs are thus generated.

Alternative Non-Automated Approaches

Three systems engineering variants from which developers typically choose as alternatives to those identified above are classical Information Engineering Methodology (IEM), Business System Implementation (BSI) and Rapid Application Development (RAD).

Classical IEM

Classical IEM includes seven stages: Information Strategy Planning (ISP); Business Area Analysis (BAA); Business System Design (BSD); Technical Design (TD); Construction Transition and Production. The first five stages correspond to the traditional system development stages already discussed. Two additional stages, Transition and Production, address the movement of executing applications into production and the monitoring of applications once the system becomes operational. Both operate on the execution layer.

During transition, developers move program modules between libraries, install online transactions onto production machines, install databases, decide about the speed of system introduction, decide how it will be phased, consider interfaces to existing databases that have not been re-developed and deal with operational documentation and initial training. During production, developers take backups, re-organise databases, handle emergencies, monitor and analyse the system, initiate minor course corrections in system performance, make modifications arising from changing business requirements and track issues and requests.

In theory, the seven stages execute like a waterfall cascading down, so that all of one stage is completed before another stage begins. In actual practice, this classical view rarely conforms to the realities of life. More often, one piece of a system is in the design stage while another piece is already in the construction stage undergoing system testing. Successful practice of IE relies on an understanding of both the framework and how it can be adapted to specific real-world situations. Those who practise classical IEM today do not necessarily assume a forward engineering sequence of tasks. They allow for different pieces of a system to iterate through the stages at different rates.

Business system implementation

An alternative approach, business system implementation, treats external design, internal design and construction as a single stage. During this stage, developers define an outline of the external and implementation layers, including the business systems and databases to be implemented thus producing the usual selection of preparatory design materials. Then they select a piece of the outline and immediately begin iterating through design, construction and testing, producing, in a sense, computer programs directly. They do the same for the next piece, and so on until a working system evolves. They therefore tend to produce planning documentation and descriptions (literary works), flow diagrams and design documentation (preparatory design material and artistic works) and computer programs (a species of literary work) in close order.

Rapid application development

A third approach, rapid application development, is a more radical departure from classical IEM because the duration and cut-off points of stages differ. RAD aims to build systems very swiftly by relying heavily on group development techniques. It begins with Information Needs Structuring (INS), an optional one-week definition by key senior executives of overall information needs and business areas thus producing a literary work or series of works in the ordinary sense.

Then developers perform Requirements Planning (RP) for a business area over a one- to three-week period, during which they outline data and activity models in group sessions, and scope design areas. Users then join developers in Joint Application Development (JAD) sessions over a three- to five-week period of User Analysis and Design (UD). This stage overlaps the last part of traditional analysis and the first part of traditional design. It relies extensively on prototyping (the direct production of computer programs) to allow users to verify screen designs and overall system structure. During the next stage, Construction, a "SWAT" team of programmers who are "Skilled With Advanced Tools" builds all the components required to complete the system from the external design. The final stage, Cutover, is equivalent to the transition stage of classical IEM. These "advanced tools" may be similar to CASE tools in their action which is discussed below.

Computer Aided Systems Engineering – "CASE"

A new technology has emerged for building application systems faster and better than ever before. Computer-Aided Systems Engineering ("CASE") tools are quickly transforming the workplace, as organisations apply the power of the computer to the task of computer programming itself. Using CASE tools, companies are making a quantum leap from traditional flow-charting and hand-coding to high-level, interlocking diagrams that translate into fully complete applications.

Most CASE tools are available on a variety of computer types and can generate systems to run on multiple platforms ranging from PCs, workstations to mainframes. As CASE tools generally generate code from flow charts and diagrams, a trend has developed whereby companies re-use large blocks of computer program code to a greater degree than ever before.

By clearly defining the relationships between diagrams and diagramming objects, CASE tools perform powerful automatic computations that speed up development. The more automatic connection made by the computer, the quicker developers can produce a working system. With the ability to design, generate and test applications at the same workstation, CASE tool users can prototype systems quickly without concerning themselves with the final target computer hardware environment. At the same time, CASE tools often also support a top-down approach to systems development. Companies can model their entire enterprise in diagrams first, then flesh out the pieces.

Over the past decade, systems developers have struggled unsuccessfully to keep pace with large advances in the computer hardware arena. Faced with growing application backlogs and increasing maintenance costs, the systems development community has sought productivity and quality improvements along two distinct yet converging paths.

One path has produced methods for visualising and organising systems and data. Examples include basic flow-charting; functional decomposition; modular programming; structured programming, design and analysis; data modelling; strategic data planning and object-oriented analysis and design. These emerging methods have created a rich framework for addressing problems and formulating solutions.

The other path has resulted in development tools for building systems more quickly, accurately and easily. The products of this path include assemblers, compilers, online editors, interactive debuggers, database management systems, teleprocessing monitors, fourth-generation language, diagramming tools and code generators.

CASE tools and computer-generated works

Where CASE tools have been used in the production and development of computer programs, it is submitted that one must have regard to section 9(3) of the Copyright, Designs and Patents Act 1988, which although already addressed in Chapter 2 is set out below for the convenience of the following analysis; where it says:

> "In the case of a literary, dramatic, musical or artistic work which is computer generated, the author shall be taken to be the person by whom the arrangements necessary for the creation of the work are undertaken."

Section 178 of the Copyright, Designs and Patents Act 1988 tells us that the term "computer-generated":

> "in relation to a work, means that the work is generated by computer in circumstances such that there is no human author of the work".

Considering the provisions of section 21(4) of the Copyright, Designs and Patents Act 1988, it can be strongly argued that at the current state of technology when CASE tools produce computer programs, the resulting computer programs are not, in fact, "computer-generated" within the meaning of the Copyright, Designs and Patents Act 1988. If the authoring computer programmer has produced flow-charts in which copyright subsists (in other words, in circumstances where he has exercised sufficient taste, labour, judgement, knowledge and programming skill), then the process of computer code generation by the CASE tool is one of translation. The computer-generated code can therefore be treated as a mere adaptation of the original program which did not exist in the form of either a computer language or code. Therefore, at the current state of technology, computer programs can never be computer-generated by CASE tools.

However, the learned authors of *Copinger and Skone James on Copyright*[23] take a differing view with respect to computer-generated works where they say:

> "...where, for example, a computer is employed to convert a program from one language to another, such as from assembly code to machine code, and no creative input is required from any human agency and nothing is required to be done other than to load the necessary programs and give the required commands, it is thought that the program thereby generated is properly to be regarded as having had no human author."[24]

It is respectfully submitted that the above interpretation is entirely inconsistent with section 21(4) of the Copyright, Designs and Patents Act 1988 since Assembly Code, Machine Code, Source Code or Object Code are all but translations of the same computer program. It is suggested that the preferred interpretation of the law is that compilers, assemblers, CASE tools and the like are all very sophisticated translators. In *Express Newspapers Plc v Liverpool Daily Post and Echo Plc*;[25] Whitford J (in addressing the issue of whether the author of a computer program which generated certain random numbers set out within tables also was the author of the product of the computer program) said:

> "The computer was no more than the tool by which the varying grids of five-letter sequences were produced to the instructions, via the computer programmes, of Mr. Ertel [the author of the computer program in question]. It is as unrealistic as it would be to suggest that, if you write your work with a pen, it is the pen which is the author of the work rather than the person who drives the pen."[26]

The correct interpretation of the law is that CASE tools and the like, in being extremely sophisticated automatic translators, are merely the tools of the computer programmer and do not give rise to computer-generated works or any other species of copyright work.

This view is not shared by David Bainbridge in his book *Software Copyright Law*[27] where he (when quoting from *Express Newspapers Plc v Liverpool Daily Post and Echo Plc*) says:

---

23 13th ed (Sweet & Maxwell, 1991).

24 *Ibid* at 78, paras 4-14.

25 [1985] 1 WLR 1089.

26 *Ibid* at 1093.

27 Butterworths, 1994.

> "Therefore, case law before the Copyright, Designs and Patents Act 1988 seems to contradict the very existence of computer-generated works. If a sequence of letters selected at random by a programmed computer has a human author, being the person who wrote the computer program used to select the random numbers, then what type of work could be described as being created by a programmed computer?"[28]

It is respectfully submitted that it is not a correct interpretation of *Express Newspapers Plc v Liverpool Daily Post and Echo Plc* to draw the conclusion that the decision contradicts the existence of computer-generated work. There is a presumption of statutory interpretation that "... in the absence of any clear indication to the contrary Parliament can be presumed not to have altered the common law farther than was necessary to remedy the 'mischief'"[29] it was directing itself to. The Copyright, Designs and Patents Act 1988 has not altered the common law as set out in *Express Newspapers Plc v Liverpool Daily Post and Echo Plc* but is supplementing it with the new concept of computer-generated works.

It may be at the current state of technology that programmed computers (in other words, computer programs) are not capable of generating computer-generated works within the meaning of the Copyright, Designs and Patents Act 1988. However, the technology in CASE tools is rapidly advancing, with CASE effecting more and more and the flow charts and diagrams entered into by the end-user becoming relatively less with respect to time and effort. CASE tools are drawing increasingly upon databases of rules and libraries of computer code within them so that eventually, one could speculate, CASE tools will be capable of producing computer-generated works. In addition to the foregoing, a discipline of computer programming concerned with "artificial intelligence" may, in the near future, be capable of constructing computer programs which generate truly original literary, dramatic and artistic works without the intervention of a human author.

Maintenance and modification

Due to the complexities of computer programming and the time and cost constraints placed upon computer programmers both by their employers and market forces, it is seemingly inevitable that commercial computer software products contain errors (referred to in the industry as **bugs**). The computer-software industry therefore often offers to the users of its products a

28 At 143.
29 **Black-Clawson International Ltd v Papierwerke Waldhof-Aschaffenburg AG** [1975] 1 All ER 810; per Lord Reid at 815.

maintenance or support service whereby, for a fixed annual fee the author or licensor of the product will continue the development of the product so that the known bugs are eradicated from it and the functionality enhanced (which, usually, introduces further bugs in the computer code). The vast majority of commercial computer software products are made up of large numbers of independent computer programs which are linked or compiled. As the user moves from one function of the software product to another, further computer programs within the structure are activated or de-activated. In this sense, therefore, it is submitted that in these circumstances and therefore in every commercial instance, the computer programs will not only be protected as literary works but their collection together as a computer software product will be protected as a "compilation" by virtue of section 3(1)(a) of the Copyright, Designs and Patents Act 1988.

When considering this point, the learned judge in *IBCOS Computers Limited v Barclays Mercantile Highland Finance Limited* turned his attention to the commercial computer program known as "ADS" with respect to its status as a compilation and said:

> "The ADS 'program' is in fact a complicated composite of interrelated programs, routines and sub-routines. Mr. Turner gives the following figures: 335 program files, 171 record layout files and 46 screen layout files. Mr. Howe submitted that not only each individual program has copyright (and perhaps several since each of these will have been modified and updated) but also the package as whole has a copyright – as a kind of compilation. The submission was that the program of all programs is an original program.
>
> This must be right. The Act specifically confers copyright on a compilation subject to its being original. The amount of skill, labour and judgment which went into the ADS package as a whole is very substantial, well above the threshold of originality accepted in other fields of copyright.
>
> Accordingly in my judgment the copyright works include not only the individual programs but the whole package. Moreover in every case where a program was revised or modified enough for a fresh copyright to be created, that copyright is also a relevant work."[30]

One can also see the learned judge directing himself towards the tests of originality and the degree of skill, labour and judgement discussed above. But as small parts of the computer software product are updated or corrected, unoriginal material (in other words, short pieces of programming code which do not pass the test for originality) may be included into the compilation. In *John Richardson Computers Ltd v Flanders and Chemtec Ltd*[31], Ferris J held, *inter alia*, when addressing this point with respect to a computer

30 At 289.
31 [1993] FSR 497.

software product to which he referred to as the "BBC Program" that the case of *Macmillan & Co Ltd v K&J Cooper*[31a] was on point, and quoted from the speech of Lord Pearce in *Ladbroke (Football) Ltd* [31b] in the following terms:

> "... For many compilations have nothing original in their parts, yet the sum total of the compilation may be original. ... In such cases the courts have looked to see whether the compilation of the unoriginal material called for work or skill or expense."[32]

Ferris J then went on to quote Lord Pearce further from this case:

> "Whether a part is substantial must be decided by its quality rather than its quantity. The reproduction of a part which by itself has no originality will not normally be a substantial part of the copyright and therefore will not be protected. For that which would not attract copyright except by reason of its collocation will, when robbed of that collocation, not be a substantial part of the copyright and therefore the courts will not hold its reproduction to be an infringement."[33]

Applying *Macmillan & Co Ltd v K&J Cooper* when considering whether a series of product type codes supplied with the product and held in data files within certain parts of the computer programs supplied could be protected as a compilation, Ferris J held:

> "I am satisfied that, although originality cannot be claimed for a good proportion of the codes supplied as part of the BBC program, the collection of codes as a whole is a compilation originally made by Mr. Richardson personally as a result of the expenditure of time and effort and imagination."
>
> "So far as the re-written program alone was concerned I find it difficult to see how this can have been an original work in which a separate copyright was capable of subsisting, particularly having regard to Section 21(4) of the 1988 Act (previously Section 1(2) of the 1985 Act) under which the conversion of a computer program from one computer language or code into another such language or code is to be treated as an adaptation of the first program."[34]

Ferris J further and importantly quotes from and applies *Ladbroke (Football) Ltd v William Hill (Football) Ltd*, and chooses a passage from the judgment of Lord Pearce:

> "In deciding therefore whether a work in the nature of a compilation is original, it is wrong to start by considering individual parts of it apart from the whole, as the appellants in their argument sought to do. For many compilations have nothing original in their parts, yet the sum total of the compilation may be original. (see, for instance, the case of Palgraves Golden Treasury referred to by the Privy Council in *Macmillan & Co Ltd v K&J Cooper*).

31a LR 51 Ind App 109, 125.
31b [1964] 1 WLR 273.
32 [1993] FSR 497 at 521.
33 *Ibid*, the speech of Lord Pearce at [1964] 1 WLR 273, 293.
34 [1994] FSR 275.

> In such cases the courts have looked to see whether the compilation of the unoriginal material called for work or skill or expense. If it did, it is entitled to be considered original and to be protected against those who wish to steal the fruits of the work or skill or expense by copying it without taking the trouble to compile it themselves."[35]

The learned judge goes on to quote Lord Pearce later in that case:

> "Whether a part is substantial must be decided by its quality rather than its quantity. The reproduction of a part which by itself has no originality will not normally be a substantial part of the copyright and therefore will not be protected. For that which would not attract copyright except by reason of its collocation will, when robbed of that collocation, not be a substantial part of the copyright and therefore the courts will not hold its reproduction to be an infringement ... They afford no justification, in my view, for holding that one starts the inquiry as to whether copyright exists by dissecting the compilation into component parts instead of starting it by regarding the compilation as a whole and seeing whether the whole has copyright. It is when one is debating whether the part reproduced is substantial that one considers the pirated portion on its own."[36]

The maintenance of computer software products and compilations

One can therefore see that one must look at the compilation of computer programs as a whole to determine whether the works are to be further protected as a compilation and that sufficient literary taste, judgement, expertise, imagination and effort have been expended to cause a new copyright to arise in the individual programs and a new copyright in the compilation itself. It may well be, therefore, that in the computer software industry where new updated versions of a product include substantial new concatenations of computer program modules, some of those being new with respect to the previous version, but some also containing new code: not only will the new modules be susceptible to copyright protection but the whole product (the whole new version) may be a new work as a compilation. Before closing on this particular subject, the decision in *Total Information Processing Systems v Daman*[37] could be argued to contradict the foregoing view. Jacob J in *IBCOS Computers Limited v Barclays Mercantile Highland Finance Ltd* himself took a different view and effectively disposed of the efficacy of this case where he said:

35 At 291.
36 At 293.
37 [1992] FSR 171.

"In connection with the whole package being a copyright compilation I should mention *Total Information Processing Systems v Daman* 1 [1992] F.S.R. 171, it was not a full trial the (page 16) matter concerned unusually being dealt with as a preliminary issue in an interlocutory motion, with the result that there was no testing by cross-examination of the evidence. The preliminary point was:
'whether there was an arguable case that the copying of the Field and Record specifications in a program called a Contract Costing Program is an infringement of copyright.'
His Honour Judge Paul Baker made a number of observations which, taken out of context could be misleading. He said at p.179:
'The mere linking of several programs is not in my judgement itself an original literary or artistic work in the way that the collective presentation of literary works by divers authors is. Nor could the compilation be regarded as a computer program separate from and in addition to the individual programs.'
Whilst that may be right on the facts of that case it cannot be correct as a general statement. Indeed no counsel before me accepted it as accurate. There is no reason why a compilation of computer programs should not itself acquire a separate copyright. Someone might, for instance, produce a selection of games on a disk. If there was enough originality in that selection it would surely be afforded copyright. The games might be wholly separated or they might have linking elements, e.g. common joystick control programs. In my view it is all a question of degree, just as it is in the case of any other compilation.
He went on to say:
'To accord it copyright protection (that is to say the compilation) would lead to great inconvenience. It would mean that the copyright owners of one of the components could not interface with another similar program to that of the other components without the licence of the compiler.'
No counsel supported this and I cannot agree. Of course the owner of the copyright in an individual program could interface his program with that of another. What he could not do is to put his program into an original compilation of another without that other's licence."[38]

This must be right and *Total Information Processing Systems v Daman* does not contradict the view given above. *Total Information Processing Systems v Daman* was not a full trial, but the point addressed was done so as a preliminary issue in an interlocutory motion. The point addressed was whether the copying of the field and record specifications in an application program could constitute an infringement of copyright. Jacob J in *IBCOS Computers Ltd v Barclays Mercantile Highland Finance Ltd* was right to hold that this reasoning in *Total Information Processing Systems v Daman* is highly distinguishable since the Court was addressing itself to a very specific set of facts where it held that the mere linking of several computer programs would not constitute a compilation and sets no general rule at all. It is, nevertheless, a lesson that the ordinary criteria of skill, judgement and taste

38 At 289.

have to be applied to compilations of computer programs in determining whether a copyright arises in the compilation separately from its constituent computer program parts.

Translation

It needs to be recognised, that when software producers or computer programmers wish to change their program from one computer language to another, this can be done either manually (in the sense that a professional translator might translate a document written in French into English) or another computer program, a translation software product, might be used to translate the code. In either event, it is usual for some new code to be introduced since one cannot produce a "word-for-word" translation from one computer language to another. Some of this new code might be too insignificant to acquire copyright in its own right, but it is submitted that:

(i) attention should always be given to the notion of new code being written in or with respect to the translation process; and
(ii) the tests described above with respect to the subsistence of copyright (including in compilations) will need to be applied to such new code to determine if any new copyright is arising.

Porting

The term "porting" is used to describe the process where a computer program is adapted so that it will execute within a different hardware or operating system environment. In this process, new code is almost always added to the existing programs and, indeed, some of the existing code will be modified. With respect to the process of porting:

(i) attention should always be given to the likelihood of new code being written as additions or modifications to the computer programs;
(ii) the tests described above with respect to the subsistence of copyright generally and especially with respect to compilations will need to be applied to such new code to determine if any new copyright is arising; and
(iii) in the event that a series of compiled (connected) programs are being ported (and in some cases new computer program modules may need to be written in replacement of existing modules which specifically address the machine/operating system environment in which the product operates) or in addition to existing modules, the tests described above will need to be applied to such new code to determine if any new copyright is arising and further the tests described above will need to be applied to determine if a new compilation has occurred and therefore whether a new copyright has arisen with respect to the work as a compilation.

Chapter 4

The Operation of Computer Programs

Introduction

Having evaluated the methodologies through which computer programs are generated and developed in Chapter 3, this chapter will assess the different levels of transformations and translations undergone by the computer program during its execution on computer hardware. In this context, the modes in which computer programs exist subsequent to the development cycle will be examined together with the manner in which fully-realised computer programs qualify as different species of copyright works. In doing so this chapter will introduce, for the first time, the very important component of computing known as the "operating system" which is a species of computer program which is directed not to the applications being processed by an end-user, but which is directed towards the computer hardware system itself. This chapter will also be directed to an analysis of the files that computer programs generate and use during their operation so as to identify the species of copyright works subsisting within them and consider, in depth, the "products" of different types of computer programs as they execute.

Computer Programs – Transformations and Translations

In understanding how a computer program is executed (or "run") by a computer, a short historical review of how computers were originally used in industry will be useful in understanding the modern-day machine and its interaction with the present-day computer program.

Consider as a starting-point the native and basic computer hardware consisting of one central processor, memory and various peripherals (such peripherals being, *e.g.* a printer and, in the beginning of computer technology, a card reader). In the absence of any other software (which will be averred to later), the operation of loading and running an application program would have to have been performed entirely under human control. Computer systems without such aids do not now exist, but were quite common in the late 1960s. Thus this somewhat historical computer with a batch system employing the use of punched cards for input and a printer for output will be taken as an example.

For each job, the computer operator would perform something similar to the sequence of tasks outlined below:

(i) place the punched cards containing the source code of the computer program into the card reader;
(ii) initiate a computer program to read the cards;
(iii) initiate a compiler to compile the source code (so as to produce object codes which can be directly executed by the computer);
(iv) place the data cards, if any, in the card reader;
(v) initiate the execution of the compiled program;
(vi) remove the results of the executed program from the printer.

The overall processing speed of this type of computer was obviously dependant on the rate at which the operator could press the appropriate buttons and feed the card reader with punched cards, and consequently the performance of this type of computer was limited by the speed and agility of the operator.

The first improvement to be made to this type of computer hardware configuration was to make the machine itself carry out automatically, without operator intervention, the sequence of steps necessary to read in, compile, load and execute computer programs. The operator's role was therefore reduced to loading cards into the card reader at one end of the machine and tearing off print-outs at the other. Throughput was consequently increased. However, it is necessary to understand that the price to be paid for the increasing of performance in this fashion, was the dedication of some computer resources (being memory and some processor time) away from processing the data itself and towards the execution of a program which performed the necessary job sequencing operations.

Since all jobs would not necessarily require the same sequencing operations (*e.g.* some jobs might not need compilation) the control program would need to infer from one or more control cards precisely which operations were to be performed in any particular case. In other words, the control program had to be capable of interpreting a **job control language**. In addition to this, the errors which inevitably occurred in some jobs could not be allowed to affect jobs later in the sequence, and so the control program had to be responsible for handling these errors as they occurred. Control programs with these features were, in fact, embryonic operating systems.

Operating systems

A system of this type was limited by the speed at which it could perform input and output (often referred to in the computer industry as "I/O") and the next stage in improving efficiency was to reduce this dependency. This was first achieved by the technique of **off-lining**, whereby all input and output tasks were performed to and from magnetic tape. The tasks of converting card input (or indeed from other input sources such as punched paper tape) to magnetic tape, and converting magnetic tape output to printed output (or punched paper tape) were relegated to an independent satellite computer of less power and cost with respect to the main computer itself. The transfer of magnetic tapes between satellite and main computers was conducted by hand by unloading the tape, for example, from the satellite computer and loading it up on the input devices of the main computer. Off-lining systems, notably the "IBM Fortran Monitor System", ran successfully from the late 1950s into the mid-1960s.

Off-lining

Off-lining reduced input–output dependency by ensuring that all input–output tasks were performed from magnetic tape, which was the fastest and cheapest available medium at the time. The price paid in terms of computing power was the addition to the embryonic operating system of further computer program routines for the coding and packing in magnetic tape, of the data eventually destined for some other peripheral (and conversely for input). It should also be noted that since magnetic tape is a serial information (information or data being recorded one after the other – thus data item 12 can only be accessed after data items 1 to 11 have been addressed) there was at that time no notion of scheduling jobs to run in any order other than that in which they were presented to the system from the magnetic tape.

Channels and interrupts

In order to eliminate input–output dependency rather than merely reduce it, techniques were developed whereby the processes of input and output could be overlapped with processing. This was made possible by the development of two very important hardware features – the **channel** and the **interrupt** – which are now in almost universal use in every computer of every description.

A channel is a device which controls one or more peripherals, performing data transfers between the peripherals and memory quite independently of the central processor. An interrupt is a signal which transfers control of the central processor to some fixed location, whilst at the same time storing the previous value of the program counter so that the central processor can effectively and accurately return to the computer program it was previously processing. Thus the computer program being executed at the time of the interrupt is temporarily abandoned by the central processor, but can be resumed later at the point at which it was interrupted. An interrupt from a channel acts as a signal to indicate that a data transfer has been completed. Hence it is possible for the central processor to initiate a peripheral transfer, to continue the processing of a computer program while the channel controls the transfer, and to receive notification by means of an interrupt when the transfer is complete. Due to the processing speed of modern computers, these interrupts occur in periods of time much less than one second and thus the impression is generated that the computer is actually performing many different tasks all at the same time when often a large number of tasks are being handled one after the other, but at high speed.

Using channels and interrupts, it became possible to read-in jobs onto some suitable storage medium (usually magnetic disk since disk as a magnetic medium for storage had become available by this time), and to execute them one by one at the same time as other jobs were being read in. The consequent additions to the rapidly growing operating system were software routines to handle the interrupts and further routines to decide which of the several jobs stored on disk was to be run next. This latter function, which became known as **scheduling**, derived from the introduction of disks (which are a medium upon which files can be accessed randomly or by choice rather than serially in the order they were stored) as a replacement for magnetic tape which is essentially a serial medium. A system working in this way was known as a **single-stream batch monitor** (single-stream meaning that only one job was executed at a time) and such systems were predominant in the mid-1960s.

Multiprogramming

The main disadvantage of the single-stream system was found to be the dedication of the entire computer to the execution of one single job at a time, no matter how large or small that job was. This disadvantage was overcome by the computer development industry by the introduction of what became known as **multiprogramming**. This technique involved the running of several programs in the computer at the same time. The concept and practice involved several programs (jobs) being held simultaneously in the computer's memory and the central processor dividing its time between them according to the resources (such as channels or peripherals) that each one needed at any one instant. In this way it was theoretically possible, by having a suitable mix of jobs held in computer memory at any one time, to achieve an optimum utilisation of the computer's processing resources. This included especially central processor utilisation, as whenever a job was waiting for an input–output transfer to be completed, the processor could switch to some other job then currently held in memory. The additional load on the operating system was the control of resources and the protection of one job from the activities of another. An operating system of this type was called a **multi-stream batch monitor**, and versions abounded on all large computers of the early 1970s.[1]

At this stage in the development of the computer and the parallel development of the operating system, one can see that at this time there existed reasonably sophisticated systems which made good use of the hardware available. The main disadvantage from the user's point of view was the lack of interaction between the user and the job as it passed through the computer. Interaction between the user and the computer program or job running is valuable and desirable in many situations, particularly for example in the development and debugging of a computer program, as debugging becomes easier if the programmer is immediately able to test the modifications he has made and thus see their effect, making further modifications as necessary. Similarly, many problem-solving programs require "steering" by the user; that is, the user directs the further action of the computer program after examining the results so far. In order for this type of interaction to become feasible, the multi-stream batch system (operating system) was developed so that it was able to accept input from users typing on the keyboards of remote terminals; in other words it became what was to be known as a **multi-access system**. In the early 1970s most manufacturers produced multi-access operating systems for their larger computers.[2] By the mid-1970s the batch and multi-access modes of operation had been combined into a single operating system.[3]

1 *e.g.* GEORGE 3 on the ICL (International Computers Limited) 1900 series of computers and OS/360 on the IBM (International Business Machines) 360 and 370 series of computers.

2 *e.g.* MINIMOP on the ICL 1900; TSS/360 on the IBM 360 and 370 series, and TOPS-10 on the DEC (Digital Equipment Company) DECSystem-10.

3 *e.g.* in such operating systems as MVS for the IBM 370, MCP on the Burroughs 6700 and 7700 series and VME on the ICL 2900 series of computers.

Later developments in operating systems have concentrated on the provision of more sophisticated facilities within the operating system designed to make better use of the increased power of modern hardware and the superior design techniques available to the modern software developer. Computer hardware manufacturers have provided systems on which more than one operating system or machine instruction set may be executed at the same time, thus providing their customers with a gradual path for upgrades[4]; where further facilities are available which permit the running of computer programs developed for earlier series of machines on later series of machines. The VM operating system (IBM 370 and descendants) allows the user to run any IBM operating system which can be run on the raw computer, but in parallel with other operating systems. Apart from the increased functionality that this offers, this also provides a useful testing environment where commercial work can be undertaken by the computer in one environment, whilst the same computer runs a newer environment separately (but contemporaneously) which can be thoroughly tested before the switch to the newer operating environment is made.

Networking

Another major development which is becoming increasingly important to the computer-using community has been the addition of better facilities for computer systems to communicate with each other – known as **networking**. Batch systems are now less important than they used to be, and the emphasis has shifted from externally submitted jobs which generate printed output, to jobs submitted from interactive terminals which generate output in a whole series of different alternatives, ranging from visual displays to printed output to files which may be examined later from a terminal or some other networked computer.

As one can see from the preceding parts of this chapter, a great deal of development effort, resources and money has been put by the computer industry in to that species of computer software product known as the operating system. The operating system is now, in the modern computer system, the *sine qua non* for running an application program on a computer. Let us therefore evaluate, in the context of an operating system being present and running on a computer, how an application program is executed upon it so as to evaluate and identify the translations and transformations through which the original program will pass through in order to be executed.

4 *e.g.* VAX/VMS by DEC and CME for the ICL 2900 series of computers.

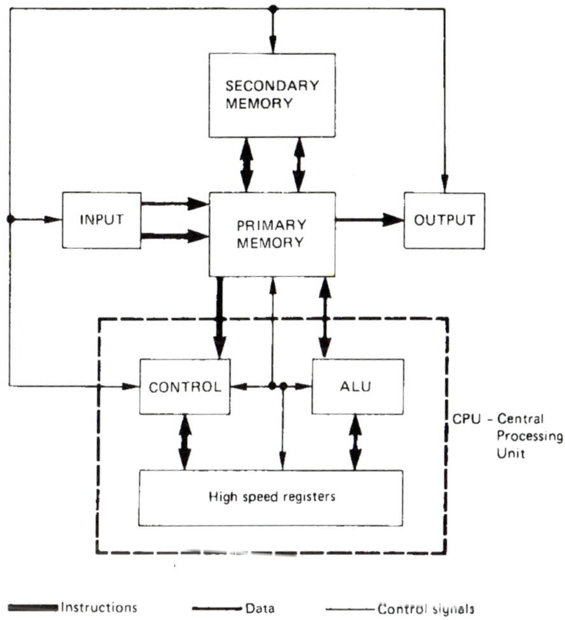

Figure 4.1

The central processor

As explained earlier, the application computer program will be stored on either some form of magnetic or optical medium.[5] For the purposes of this exercise, we will assume that the application computer program is in object-code form since it has been compiled by its developer from source code prior to being stored. An instruction will be given by the user either to or via the operating system to load the application computer program into the computer's memory so that it may be processed by the central processor. Figure 4.1 is a general diagram of the functional components of the computer with respect to the exercise under discussion. This diagrammatic representation shows the information and control flow within this part of the computer system. "Primary memory" connotes the random access memory held within the computer itself, whilst "secondary memory" connotes the storage medium being used. The "input" and "output" controllers are used by the operating system as described above. The central processor is composed of high-speed registers in which the execution of the application computer program is tracked, the "control unit" which has overall control of the computer system and the "ALU" (Arithmetic/Logic

5 See Chap 3.

Unit) which performs the computerised operations on numeric and other data. The operating system will cause the appropriate peripheral (be it a disk or tape drive) to find the application computer program on the medium and read the file in which it is contained. As the file containing the application computer program is read, a copy of it is made in the computer's primary memory and the copy of the application computer program on disk remains there unchanged. At this point, it is submitted that both a copy and a transformation of the application computer program is made. The issue of copying is an obvious one and since the object or executable code of the application computer program has been copied and that new copy no longer resides in the storage medium but as electric impulses in the computer's memory, the application computer program now exists in an electronic form within the meaning of the Copyright, Designs and Patents Act 1988, section 178.

The central processor of the computer can only process a computer program when it is in a binary format, and although in a sense the application computer program may now be in electronic object code form, it may need translating from this type of code by an ancillary part of the computer to the central processor into a binary code. This action will constitute a translation within the meaning of the Copyright, Designs and Patents Act 1988, section 21(4). As the application computer program is executed by the central processor, it will interact with the operating systems as calls are made to peripherals and displays are constructed on the computer's monitor or terminal. The central processor, as explained above, will execute the application computer program intermittently at high speed through the use of interrupts as it turns its "attention" to sending messages to input and output devices. The application computer program will cease to execute either in accordance with its own internal instructions (it may make one pass through a certain set of data and then cease executing) or when the user issues a command for it to do so.

Computer Programs – Species of Copyright Works

When executing, computer programs have the capacity to manifest themselves in a large variety of modes which sets the computer program apart from all other species of works which are susceptible to the protection of the law of copyright. For the purposes of evaluating the species of copyright works which are capable of being "generated" or "produced" by a computer program when executing, three broad types of computer programs will be assessed, being:

- Games programs – which, for the purposes of this chapter, are distinguished as being computer programs of a completely recreational nature with no serious or productive application (other than enjoyment).
- Business programs – which, for the purposes of this chapter, are distinguished as meaning applications computer programs (as opposed to operating systems) which are not recreational in purpose but can be put to a serious and productive application such as spreadsheets or wordprocessors.
- Multimedia programs – which are computer programs which effectively straddle the distinctions drawn between games programs and business programs made above. Multimedia programs are exclusively available on optical media (at the size of an audio compact disk and are known as CD-ROMs (being an acronym of Compact Disk – Read Only Memory)) and contain music, film footage, pictures and animation. Their application bridges the business and recreational areas since they often take the form of encyclopaedias or other types of reference material.

Games programs

Games programs are now very common in modern-day Western society. They principally take three forms:

(i) those that are executed on dedicated **arcade** machines which may cost many thousands of pounds sterling and which are not generally or usually available to members of the public.

(ii) Those which are executed on **games consoles**. Games consoles are small and relatively inexpensive (costing hundreds of pounds

sterling) computers dedicated to executing games programs which are stored in a **cartridge**. The cartridge is, in fact, a printed circuit board carrying the games program stored in an integrated circuit (computer chip). The edge of the printed circuit board has connectors which protrude through the cartridge's case and connect to the computer components in the games console.

It is this connection which loads the computer programs into the console. As indicated before, this stores the computer program in an *electronic form*[6] in a medium which is non-volatile memory. In other words, the contents of this memory does not disappear in the absence of power, but the memory can only be read; it cannot be written to in the normal course of events, hence its name Read Only Memory (or ROM). **Joypads** or **joysticks** are connected to connectors on the games console. These are hand-held devices containing buttons and or switches of various configurations through which the game is controlled by the player or players.

(iii) Those that are executed on **personal computers**. Compared to those games programs available on cartridge, computer games for personal computers tend to be much larger and more complex since they are inclined to take advantage of the personal computer's larger memory capacity, overall greater processing power and speed and the option of a hard disk being available to store data and programs not necessarily constantly stored in the computer's primary memory. Games programs are usually available on diskette for the personal computer but are increasingly available on optical media as the size of games programs has grown considerably (this is a trend which is currently not abating).

Modern games programs are further typified by having colourful and fast-moving graphics, playing music and sound effects generated electronically and containing what could commonly be described as a plot. To elucidate these concepts and further to identify and analyse the copyright works which are seen and heard during the execution of games program, a typical games console games program will be evaluated.

A typical games program

In the games program called "Mega Bomberman"[7] the instruction manual

6 Copyright, Designs and Patents Act 1988 s 178.
7 Produced by the Software Hose "Hudson Soft" in 1994.

which accompanies the cartridge describes the story upon which the game is set as follows:

> "Bomber Planet was a beautiful place, and its inhabitants lived in peace, protected by five spirits. But one day, invaders arrived; the Bagulaa and his Robot Army. In the battle that followed, the Spirit Pictures – the source of the Spirits' magical power – were destroyed. Without the special spirit power to protect it, Bomber Planet was thrown off balance and split into five pieces. But wait! All is not lost! Bomberman has arrived to restore the Spirit Picture and reassemble Bomber Planet! It won't be easy – the pieces of Bomber Planet are crawling with Bagulaa's robot minions and animals who've been brainwashed into helping the invaders. Bomberman has allies – called Louies – who can help, but only if Bomberman can find them.
> As Bomberman, use your bombing skills to save Bomber Planet in a normal game, or choose one of ten special courses and challenge up to three other players in a battle of strategy. Pack your bombs, hop aboard a Louie, and get ready for some explosive action!"

The player controls the movement of the "Bomberman" around the screen through a maze. The maze is populated by robots and animals, contact with which kill the "Bomberman". The player uses his skill in operating the "Bomberman" by placing bombs which on exploding modify the shape of the maze and/or kill the robots.

In this way the "Bomberman" makes his way through each stage collecting the pieces of the "Spirit Pictures" so that at the end of each section of a particular stage, the "Spirit Picture" is assembled. As each section of each stage is completed, a regular (and for each stage, identical and repeating) animated sequence appears – the "Bomberman" stands before the completed "Spirit Picture", a cloud of glowing blue and sparkling lights emanate from it (accompanied by a musical, tinkling sound effect), the cloud of lights circle the "Bomberman" and are thereafter absorbed by him. Indeed, before the game is played, an introduction appears. This looks like a film. It depicts the plot of the "Mega Bomberman" game as one sees a comet approaching a planet looking like earth. Comet splinters break off from the main body of the comet and when impacting the planet split it into several pieces – this animated sequence or film is accompanied by music and sound effects.

The playing of each stage is accompanied by music and each action – whether laying a bomb, kicking a bomb, mounting a "Louie" or the bomb exploding – is accompanied by a specific sound effect. In a games program such as "Mega Bomberman" there may be as many as 80 individual sound effects contained and used within the game. The bombs themselves once laid are animated. They pulse and swell rhythmically until they explode. The "Bomberman" himself may be represented in different styles.

The question therefore arises as to what species of copyright works, if any, are produced, contained or generated within the Games Program. In *John Richardson Computers Ltd v Flanders and Chemtec Ltd*, Ferris J held, *inter alia:*

> "As Sir Robert Megarry VC remarked in the Thrustcode Case (*Thrustcode Ltd v WW Computing Ltd* (1983) F.S.R. 502), if two things which are invisible are to be compared then normally they must be reproduced in visible form, or in a form which is in some way perceptible, before it can be determined whether one infringes copyright in the other. The two main ways, perhaps the only ways, in which a computer program can be made visible are by printing out the code on paper or by displaying on screen the prompts, entries, reports and other material which the program presents in visible form to the user. The latter is not, however, itself the program. It is a product of the program. The screen display is not itself the literary work which is entitled to copyright protection. A particular display may enjoy a separate copyright protection as an artistic work in the form of a photograph, or as a film, or as being a reproduction of an artistic work in the form of a drawing the copying of which will be, for copyright purposes the copying of the drawing."[8]

In the case of "Mega Bomberman" it is possible to extract the "products" of its execution. They are as follows:

- *(i)* music (being and including melodies and harmonies) which play during different sections of the game;
- *(ii)* sound effects which are played in association with certain events within the game;
- *(iii)* animated sequences which always appear in the same sections of the game and execute in the same manner each time the requisite part of the game is reached;
- *(iv)* visual backgrounds to the game action which always appear in an identical fashion no matter how many times the game is played;
- *(v)* the character of "Bomberman" in all of its variations;
- *(vi)* individual icons used within the game, such as the shape, design and motion of the pulsating bombs which "Bomberman" lays;
- *(vi)* the plot to the game as described in above.

Music

Section 3(1) of the Copyright, Designs and Patents Act 1988 vests copyright in musical works and defines them as "a work consisting of music, exclusive of any words or action intended to be sung, spoken or performed with the

8 At 527.

music". The term "music" is not defined in the Copyright, Designs and Patents Act 1988, but for the purposes of this work is taken to mean "sounds in melodic or harmonic combination, whether produced by voice or instruments".[9]

Although it is highly likely that in the development of the games program the music was originally written down in standard musical notation, if the music was "written down" directly in the form of the relevant routines in the games program this would not alter the subsistence of copyright in the music. This is so since section 3(2) of the Copyright, Designs and Patents Act 1988 tells us that "Copyright does not subsist in literary, dramatic or musical work unless and until it is recorded in writing, or otherwise" and it is contended that the recording of the music in computer code falls within the meaning of either "in writing" or "otherwise".

In consequence, the music recorded within a computer program (whether written in standard musical notation originally or not) constitutes a separate and distinct copyright work and will be protected as a musical work within the meaning of the Copyright, Designs and Patents Act 1988. Further to this, the musical work should not be seen as "a product of the program" in the manner that Ferris J viewed the screen displays under his consideration in *John Richardson Computers Ltd v Flanders and Chemtec Ltd*.[10] Rather, the musical work is the product of ordinary human effort, judgement, expertise and skill which has been exercised both in its composition and its reduction into a material form; the "material form" being a computer program.

Sound effects

It is often in the character of sound effects that they are neither melodic nor harmonic in nature and would therefore not qualify as music following the definition set out above. However, it is submitted that the sound effects produced by computer programs are protected with a separate copyright by the Copyright, Designs and Patents Act 1988 as sound recordings.[11] The sound effects are sound recordings which are "a recording of sounds, from which the sounds may be reproduced..."[12] and as this definition is to be construed "regardless of the medium on which the recording is made or the method by which the sounds are reproduced or produced"[13] it is suggested that these sound recordings are recorded within the medium of a computer

9 *Oxford English Dictionary* (2nd ed).
10 At 527.
11 S 5(1). See Chap 2 p 14.
12 S 5(1)(a).
13 S 5(1).

program. The notion of the sound recording being recorded in the medium of a computer program is to be preferred in this circumstance for two principal reasons. Firstly, since the computer program in **run-time** (in other words, directly during its execution) produces the sound effects and secondly, if one considers the recording medium to be the computer program itself, it becomes irrelevant which form the computer program is existing in at any one time – thus it becomes immaterial whether the computer program itself is recorded in magnetic media (on a disk), or existing electronically (in computer memory or on a ROM in a cartridge. This is not the case if the sound recording is regarded to have been recorded in the magnetic medium of a disk for instance. It is this problem, it is submitted, which was not overcome by David Bainbridge in his work *Software Copyright Law* when addressing the issue of whether screen displays (being the product of a computer program) could be "films" within the meaning of section 5(1) of the Copyright, Designs and Patents Act 1988.

He contends that since the definition of a film (being similar in essence to that of a sound recording) includes "a recording on any medium from which a moving image may by any means be produced" he argues that "[t]he display is a moving image, and a magnetic disk or other computer storage must come within the meaning of 'any medium', and 'any means' must include computer technology".[14] This automatically denies the existence of the recording when being processed in the computer's primary memory of its central processing unit. It must be the case that copyright should and does attach itself to every copy existing, whether on magnetic media, primary memory or during electronic processing.

Animated sequences

In certain sections in the game "Mega Bomberman", particular sequences of animation appear accompanied by music and sound effects. For example, the beginning of the game opens up with an animation of a comet approaching an earth-like world with shards of this comet detaching from the main body of the comet itself and thereafter striking the planet.

Other sequences include, for example, radiating and spiralling lights circling the "Bomberman" and being absorbed by him following the completion of the "Spirit Picture". It will be recalled from Chapter 2 that section 5(1) of the Copyright, Designs and Patents Act 1988 defines a film as "a recording on any medium from which a moving image may by any means

14 *Ibid* at 100.

be produced". On page 72 above, some *obiter dicta* of Ferris J in *John Richardson Computers Ltd v Flanders and Chemtec Ltd*, were averred to, specifically where Ferris J said:

> "...The screen display is not itself the literary work which is entitled to copyright protection. A particular display may enjoy a separate copyright protection as an artistic work in the form of a photograph, or as a film, or as being a reproduction of an artistic work in the form of a drawing the copying of which will be, for copyright purposes the copying of the drawing."[15]

The learned judge is correct when he holds that the screen display is not itself a literary work which is entitled to copyright protection. However, the learned judge has erred where he takes the view that a screen display may enjoy a separate copyright protection as it may be a film; for the screen display represents the visual playing of the recording which is being produced by the computer technology from the medium of a computer program in the same way, for example, that the moving images on a television represents the visual playing of the recording which is being produced by household video recorder technology from the medium of magnetic tape in a video cassette. The copyright subsists, consequently, in the recording and not the display and it is this assertion which is the proper match between the technology employed and the action of the Copyright, Designs and Patents Act 1988.

Not all animation on games programs takes place in a regular and repeating, predetermined fashion. Some areas of games programs run in an identical fashion each time, and therefore lend a further similarity to what one would, in common sense, describe as a film. However, many games programs produce animated figures on the television screen which are under the direct control of the game-player and, on a cursory examination, therefore do not repeat long animated sequences in a completely regular or repeatable fashion. However, on a more detailed examination, it can be seen that the movement of the character on the screen is achieved by the sequential knitting together of a large number of different animated sequences at a speed in real-time that only computer technology can achieve. For example, a computer program routine which takes a character from "Stand Still" to "Take Aim and Fire" will produce approximately 20 "frames" (*i.e.* separate drawings of the character displayed on the computer screen) to produce the one fluid movement of drawing the gun and taking a firing stance.

In this way it can be seen that the screen movement which seems to be generated afresh each time a games program is played is nothing of the sort. Rather, the computer program in response to a certain button being pushed on the joypad is selecting a routine from a large library of routines, generating

15 At 527.

the image on the computer screen and then moving to the next command issued by the player. However, the speed at which this takes place (moving smoothly from standing still to a drawn gun may take the character no more than one second) tends to give the impression that something is being generated afresh. This concept can be illustrated by imagining the computer program contains a library of hundreds of short pieces of film, each holding the image of a certain type of action in the same perspective. A whole film of a character eating, moving, running, jumping etc could be produced by knitting these short pieces of film together seamlessly. This is, in fact, what the computer program is doing. However, it is doing this in real-time and at high speed in response to different input from the player each time; thus producing a game which, on the face of it, plays differently each time it is played. The question then arises as to whether these short pieces of animation, which may be no longer than one second in length when "played", are capable of being a copyright work in themselves. This is an intractable problem which cannot be answered with certainty. A tentative submission may be advanced though that although the single frame of the computer animation cannot be protected as a photograph (since the Copyright, Designs and Patents Act 1988 excludes a single frame of a film from being protected as a photograph[16]) it may be protectable as part of a film.[17]

In the light of these sequences of animation being very short in length (including the length of the computer program code required to generate them and especially their short duration when executing in real-time) recognition ought to be made of the fact that although the Copyright, Designs and Patents Act 1988 places no restriction on the simplicity or length of a literary work in order for copyright to subsist within them; the courts have regularly refused protection for very short works. It was held in *Exxon Corporation v Exxon Insurance Consultants International Ltd* that despite a considerable amount of original effort over many months and a great deal of money being exercised over the formation of the word "Exxon"; it could not qualify as a literary work.[18] The questions that arise from this line of cases cannot be answered with any certainty, nor can any useful proposition be posed empirically and based on something other than pure opinion with respect to it since no decision exists on this point nor raises the matter at all. However, having said this, it is

16 S 4(2).

17 **Spelling Goldberg Productions Inc v BPC Publishing** [1981] RPC 283. It should be borne in mind that this case addressed a film being considerably longer than the few seconds of animation in a computer program.

18 The courts have declined to protect the titles of magazines and books: see **Rose v Information Services Ltd** [1987] FSR 254 and the useful dicta of Graham J in **Exxon Corpo v Exxon Insurance Consultants International Ltd** at 79.

argued that it is likely that the courts would strongly favour an argument, based on the line of cases of which *Exxon Corporation v Exxon Insurance Consultants International Ltd* is one of the most notable, that copyright could not subsist in very short and discrete pieces of computer code. It is further suggested that the courts would, as an alternative, consider the large numbers of discrete code "fragments" as being a compilation within the meaning of the Copyright, Designs and Patents Act 1988. Nevertheless, it is suggested that this position, if actually adopted by the courts, would be an unsatisfactory one; for if the Court of Appeal in *Exxon Corporation v Exxon Insurance Consultants International Ltd* was correct where it held that it is sufficient for a work to be a literary work if it was intended to afford information and instruction[19], and thus the courts have permitted copyright protection for the most pedestrian of subject-matter notwithstanding the simplicity of the action and lack of skill required to construct the work such as a catalogue of type[20], tallies for bridge parties[21] and in tables comprising grids of five-letter sequences for a monthly newspaper competition;[22] then it follows that a short discrete piece of computer code would fall in line with the definition of a literary work adopted by the Court of Appeal in *Exxon Corporation v Exxon Insurance Consultants International Ltd* and may very well require a degree of literary taste, skill, judgement and effort that would far exceed such input into the examples of literary work just given above. Rather, it is suggested that size should not be a pertinent or deciding factor, in the assessment of a work as a literary work in which copyright subsists, where the work in question is computer code.

Visual backgrounds

Many games programs employ the use of static backgrounds against which the moveable images (known in computer programming terminology as **sprites**) are migrated. It is submitted that these static visual backgrounds are artistic works, perhaps in some circumstances being a copy of a drawing produced in the first instance without the assistance of computer technology. Once again, the dicta of Ferris J in *John Richardson Computers Limited v Flanders and Chemtec Limited*, is useful to consider where he said:

19 Approving the definition of a literary work given by Davey LJ in **Hollinrake v Truswell** [1884] 3 Ch 420 at 427–428 as one which "is intended to afford either information and instruction or pleasure in the form of literary enjoyment".

20 **Masson, Seeley & Co Ltd v Embosotype Manufacturing Co** (1924) 41 RPC 160.

21 **Stevenson (A) v Crook (HF)** [1938] Ex (Can) 299.

22 **Express Newspapers v Liverpool Daily Post** [1985] FSR 306.

> "...The screen display is not itself the literary work which is entitled to copyright protection. A particular display may enjoy a separate copyright protection ... as being a reproduction of an artistic work in the form of a drawing the copying of which will be, for copyright purposes the copying of the drawing."[23]

Characters

A great many modern games programs contain characters in the sense that the game may very well include a "plot" in which characters of an identifiable nature and appearance which are associated with behavioural attributes are involved. In preceding paragraphs the character of "Bomberman" was alluded to. In fact, the principal character of a games program may form the basis of "sequel" games programs on the same theme as the earlier ones including the same character.

A well-known example of this would be, it is submitted, "Sonic the Hedgehog".[24] "Sonic the Hedgehog" is a cartoon-type characterisation, often expressed in the form of an artistic work, being a blue hedgehog who wears red boots and who is able to run at high speeds. The concept of copyright protection for cartoon characters is well accepted by the courts of law. It is submitted that one of the preferred authorities on this point is *King Features Syndicate Incorporated v O & M Kleeman Ltd*.[25] Although dealing with an issue of infringement, the facts of the case involved the plaintiffs owning the copyright in a strip cartoon picture showing "Popeye" the sailor standing on a pier with a large bollard in the background and in the far distance a suggestion of cottages.

The defendants imported a quantity of "Popeye" brooches which were manufactured in Japan. They offered no evidence as to how the brooches came to resemble or contain what appeared to be the "Popeye" character. The House of Lords held that the brooches resembled the cartoon picture closely enough to constitute an infringement of copyright. Lords Russell of Killowen and Porter found that the brooches reproduced "the salient features" of the cartoon of "Popeye"; being principally the sailor's cap, the nose, the chin, the mouth, the swollen forearms upon which were tattooed ship's anchors, the baggy trousers, the pipe and the enlarged feet. Viscount Maugham pointed out that as the reproduction was not exact, the Court was obliged to examine the degree of resemblance. It is submitted that the learned Viscount Maugham thought that the test developed by Lord Shand in

23 At 527.
24 Produced by Sega Enterprises Limited in 1991.
25 [1941] AC 417, HL.

Hanfstarengl v Baines & Co was appropriate and applicable. Lord Shand took the view that:

> "The question of the infringement of the right depends on the degree of resemblance. It must be solved by taking each of the works to be compared as a whole and determining whether there is not merely a similarity or resemblance in such leading feature or in certain of the details, but whether, keeping in view the idea and general effect created by the original, there is such a degree of similarity as would lead one to say that the alleged infringement is a copy or reproduction of the original or the design – having adopted its essential features and substance."[26]

The Court took further notice that the drawing of "Popeye" was novel and exceptional (at the time in question nothing like "Popeye" had been seen before and it was not a case of a drawing of some hackneyed or common place subject-matter) and in applying Lord Shand's test, Lord Maugham was careful to make due allowance for the reference to a substantial work contain in the then new Act.

Copyright will therefore, in the ordinary course of things, subsist in the drawings of characters to be used in a games program as artistic works, especially if they are of exceptional novelty and are not common-place. The likes of "Sonic the Hedgehog" contain sufficient distinguishing features; the blue spines, red shoes, the thin arms, the gestures and the large ears to be protected on exactly the same basis as "Popeye" the sailor.

Game icons

As mentioned before, like many other games programs of its genre, "Bomberman" lays bombs which throb and pulsate until they finally explode. Games program characters may also be required, in the course of playing the games, to pick up, acquire or use certain icons. These icons are usually small symbolic drawings and it is in the nature of these icons that they are simple in design but suggestive as to their function so that the game-player can easily and more readily assimilate their action and purpose within the game. However the idea that may be embodied within the icon design, no matter how original, is not protected by copyright. Consequently, where a very simple diagram embodies an original idea, it is the diagram and not the idea which is protected. The protection afforded by copyright is relatively weak in such icons taken individually.

26 [1895] AC 20 at 31.

The plot

It is suggested that the description of the game program "Bomberman" given on page 74 represents a plot in the ordinary sense in which this word has been used with respect to dramatic and literary works. So long as a sufficient amount of independent skill, labour and expertise has been effected – whether it be of a literary, dramatic, musical or artistic character (as the case may be) – the courts have found that copyright will subsist in the plot involved. It should be borne in mind, however, that where the copying complained of is directed to ideas which are of an insubstantial or hackneyed character, even taken collectively, the courts will generally not find infringement. In *Hanfstaengl v Baines* the plaintiff's pictures (in which copyright subsisted) were represented on stage in the form of *tableaux vivants* and an artist in the audience sketched what he saw; these sketches being later published in a newspaper. The question therefore arose whether the newspaper had infringed the copyright in the original pictures.

The plaintiff's pictures were based on hackneyed themes (*e.g.* "Love at a stile") and their real merit, it was found, lay in the details of their execution. However, most of this detail had been lost in the process of transforming the pictures into a stage representation and from thence to the defendants' newspaper; what remained were the hackneyed themes. The House of Lords held that there was no infringement of copyright.[27] Thus it is argued that the use of hackneyed themes in games programs such as:

- a horizontally scrolling game featuring a space-ship given only vertical movement where the player shoots oncoming opponents;[28] or
- a cannon station moving horizontally beneath oncoming lines of alien space ships[29]

would reduce the likelihood that a plot within a new games program would receive protection.

Conversely, where a substantial amount of the detail of a plot or scenario are copied, the misappropriated material being original, there will be infringement even though the original author's language is not taken. In *Holland v Vivian van Damm Productions Ltd*[30] Oscar Wilde had composed a short story in which a nightingale allows her breast to be pierced by a thorn in order that her blood may stain a white rose red, thus enabling a young

27 See also **Dagnell v British & Dominions Film Corp** [1928–35] MacCC 391.

28 Originally seen in the late 1970s as the game "Defender" by Namco for Atari Corporation.

29 Originally seen in the late 1970s as "Space Invaders" by Atari Corporation.

30 [1936–45] MacCC 69.

man to satisfy the whim of a capricious girl. The court held that even though the defendants had represented the story as a ballet on stage and thus had not copied any of the words or language of the story, copyright had, nonetheless, been infringed. The Court of Appeal held in *Sutton Vane v Famous Players Film Company Ltd*[31] that although the concept or motive of a play could not be copyright, that dramatic incidents and action could have the capacity to be susceptible to copyright. In *Corelli v Gray*[32] the defendant's music hall act contained six scenes, five of which were taken from the plaintiff's book. The Court held that the taking of a combination of incidents in a copyright novel for the purposes of producing a dramatic work was an infringement of copyright even though none of the words were taken or copied. The Court went on to say that a combination of stock incidents (which, in themselves, may be hackneyed) may arrive at such a degree of complexity as to amount to an original work. Although there has been no case law in the United Kingdom on the matter of whether a plot may subsist in a games program, some assistance may be drawn from the judgment of Jacob J in *IBCOS Computers Ltd v Barclays Mercantile Highland Finance Ltd.*

It should be borne in mind that this case concerned the alleged infringement of copyright of a business applications program and could be argued to be highly distinguishable on that point since the computer program under scrutiny in *IBCOS Computers Ltd v Barclays Mercantile Highland Finance Ltd* was not graphics orientated and therefore did not show the depth of picture-orientated activity that a modern games program would. However, having said this the judgment of Jacob J is a seminal one since it is addressed to the structure of the software under consideration and when considering the dicta of Ferris J in *John Richardson Computers Ltd v Flanders and Chemtec Ltd* on this point Jacob J said:

> "I thoroughly agree with what Ferris J. went on to say: 'Consideration is not restricted to the text of the code...' That must be right: most literary copyright works involve both literal matter (the exact words of a novel or computer program) and varying levels of abstraction (plot, more or less detailed of a novel, general structure of a computer program)."[33]

It is accepted that the learned judge here has not held that a plot may subsist in a computer program; but it is a very strong indication that there is more protected in a computer program by the law of copyright than merely the code and that the judiciary are prepared to consider computer programs as being like any other form of literary work. Accordingly it is possible to argue

31 [1923–28] MacCC 374 and [1928–35] MacCC 6.
32 (1913) 29 TLR 570; affirmed 30 TLR 116, [1911–16] MacCC 107, CA.
33 At 302.

from a justifiable stand-point, without it being mere speculation, together with the authority previously cited, that the plot in a computer game program is protectable as a copyright work. The producers of distinct and original plots for games programs may protect them as such and effectively prevent their inclusion by competitors into other games programs. Further to this, the plots to games programs may not be appropriated into other forms of artistic works, such as cartoons, plays or films, without the authorisation of the copyright owner or authorised licensor.[34]

Business programs

Business Programs as defined above are also capable of generating, during and through their execution, products which are very similar in nature to the icons produced by games programs as described above. These are also referred to as "icons" and a selection of icons are illustrated in Figure 4.2.[35] The legal status of graphical devices such as the icons discussed on page 79, and their standing as part of a graphical user interface and its connection with the "look and feel" of a computer software product will be considered fully in the following chapter. However, the nature of an icon as a separate copyright work will be considered here.

It can be observed in Figure 4.2 that icons in business programs serve very much the same function as those to be found in games programs. The user of the business program uses a pointing device such as a mouse[36] to activate the icon by moving the pointer on the monitor screen of the computer over the icon to be chosen and selecting it by depressing one of the buttons (most often the left) on the mouse.

Icons such as those illustrated in Figure 4.2 will sometimes "move" when selected in as much as they will give the impression that they have been depressed. In this way, the producers of graphically orientated business programs have sought to give the impression of a "virtual desktop" containing series of buttons; some of which have been depressed by the user to achieve a desired configuration or activation of the software product. As

34 In fact the successful computer game "StreetFighter" produced by Nintendo for the SNES games console system is to be released in the UK in 1995 as a film.

35 Reproduced from part of a "Button Bar" from the word processing application software product "WordPerfect" for the Windows graphical environment.

36 A mouse is a hand-held device usually connected to a personal computer. Most usually carrying two buttons (one on the left and one on the right) the mouse is moved by the operator's hand. The movement of the mouse is tracked by a rolling sphere within the base of the mouse which is translated into a similar and proportional movement of a pointer on the computer screen.

Figure 4.2

the developers of business programs have sought to make the interaction between the operator of the program and the program itself more intuitive – so that operators can more easily acquire the skills to operate the program effectively – the use of icons has become more prevalent.

It is submitted that a good example of a typical icon employed in a Business Program is the "Keyboard" icon in Figure 4.2 (being the second from the top). It represents a "button" which when depressed will activate a menu system for configuring the keyboard of the personal computer. It is designed to be suggestive of its application, simple to understand and, in a sense, almost self-explanatory. Icons may not necessarily be accompanied with text. Due to the purpose of the icon being simplicity and suggestiveness, the icon design will ordinarily be simple. It is because of this very fact that copyright will not subsist within individual icons within the rule best expounded in *Kenrick & Co v Lawrence & Co*. It may be arguable that significant collections of individual icons (often referred to a **button bars** or **tool bars**) may be protected as the literary and artistic levels of skill, taste and judgement involved may pass the requisite threshold for copyright protection.

Multimedia programs

The advent of CD-ROM technology has meant that the developers of computer software products can now supply their offerings on an inexpensive medium which is capable of a very large storage capacity. A by-product of such media being available to developers at an economic cost together with the further development of graphical user interfaces has been the development of multimedia programs.

In order to explain the nature of multimedia programs, an example will be taken whereby the constituent parts of this species of product may be examined and explained with greater clarity. The product to be considered is entitled "Encarta".[37] Encarta is a CD-ROM encyclopaedia. When executing on a multimedia personal computer (being a personal computer configured with a CD-ROM drive, high-resolution colour graphics monitor, a sound card and speakers) Encarta is a computer software product through which information can be retrieved just like a standard encyclopaedia. So, for example, if an inquiry concerning a musical instrument was made to Encarta, it would display a digitised photograph of the musical instrument together with, perhaps, a diagram of the construction of the musical instrument in question. The Encarta user would also be able to hear some music being played on the instrument and see some digitally recorded footage of the instrument actually being played. The multimedia product will contain a number of discrete elements which, it is submitted, are as follows:

Computer programs

The multimedia programs produce the graphic user interface, allow searches to be executed on individual words or strings or combinations of words so that the user can quickly "look-up" the item or subject in which they are interested. Other linked computer programs will recall images (whether moving or stills) whilst others will be mechanisms through which the music or sound is generated. In a real sense, the multimedia program is the mechanism which knits the text, visual images and sounds produced by the product together as a whole.

Text

Like standard encyclopaedias in book form, products such as "Encarta" will contain and display a very great deal of written text. The text which is to be

37 Produced by Microsoft Corporation in 1994 and updated in 1995.

retrieved in association with other subject-matter are held in discrete files which are accessed and displayed by the text retrieval and display routines of the multimedia program.

Music and sounds

Music and sounds, whether it be a string quartet or the sound of an elephant trumpeting, are digitally recorded and held in digital format in files held on the CD-ROM. As in the case of Text, above, retrieval routines in the multimedia program will retrieve these files and play them through the multimedia personal computers appropriate peripherals.

Diagrams and pictures

Diagrams and pictures, whether it be a diagram of an internal combustion engine or the picture of a cartoon character are digitally recorded (**scanning** is another term for the digital recording of images) are also held in digital format in files held on the CD-ROM. As in the case of Text, above, retrieval routines in the multimedia program will retrieve these files and display them through the multimedia personal computer on its monitor.

Moving pictures

Moving pictures, whether it be a film or an animated cartoon are also digitally recorded and held in digital format in files held on the CD-ROM. As in all of the cases above, retrieval routines in the multimedia program will retrieve these files and display them through the multimedia personal computer onto its monitor.

Photographs

Photographs are digitally recorded (scanned) and are held in digital format in files held on the CD-ROM. As in the foregoing cases retrieval routines in the multimedia program will retrieve these files and display them through the multimedia personal computer onto its monitor.

Accordingly multimedia programs are a type of "compilation"[38] containing discrete copyright works including computer programs, standard literary

38 The term "compilation" not being used in the sense employed in the Copyright, Designs and Patents Act 1988.

works (text), artistic works (digitised paintings, pictures and diagrams), sound recordings, photographs and films. A true compilation, in the statutory sense of section 3(1) of the Copyright, Designs and Patents Act 1988 is a specie of literary work; yet it is through this vehicle that the courts have permitted individual pieces of works or individual works which are too short or unoriginal to be worthy of copyright protection in their own right, when collected together, to acquire copyright protection. It does not seem possible, however, for a compilation within the meaning of section 3(1) of the Copyright, Designs and Patents Act 1988 to include "collections" of different species of copyright works – sound recordings, artistic works, photographs etc. Thus, the current position of copyright law is that if a multimedia program contains materials which are too short or unoriginal to be capable of carrying copyright, then the effort, taste and judgement in combining these elements together where they include drawings, sound recordings or photographs cannot be protected by copyright. Indeed, instead of logically treating multimedia programs as a special class of compilation, so that the totality of the work is protected by copyright, the law of copyright chooses to fragment the aggregate work into its constituent parts and protect those parts which pass the ordinary tests for the subsistence of copyright. This illogicality is not in the best interests of the concept of copyright protection, and that copyright should subsist separately in the totality of the multimedia program separate from its constituent parts as it does in a compilation, so that the expertise, effort, skill and judgement in knitting very large numbers of disparate parts into a cohesive whole may be effectively protected.

Chapter 5

The User Interface and Command Structure

Introduction

The importance of the user interface

The manner in which the user of a computer program interacts with the computer program through what is generally known as the "user interface" is of extreme importance to the producer of computer software products. The most able, ingenious and efficacious computer program product would fail miserably in the market-place if the manner in which it forced the user to interact with it was burdensome, difficult or overly complex. Interfaces which are hard to use not only encourage users to seek alternative computing methods of achieving their objective, but also lend themselves to a higher incidence of user error. The user interface is therefore perceived in the computer software product industry as one of the most important and key areas of a computer program's functionality. Computer software products often succeed or fail on the merits of their user interface alone. A less functional computer software product with a good or attractive user interface might well be preferred to a more functional computer software product which contains a user interface which is less attractive or more difficult to use. This is the crux of the matter. As software houses are intent on jealously protecting the "look" of their products they seek to restrain competing software houses from producing computer software products with user interfaces similar to their own. Thus the concern of software house A is that if copyright protection of computer programs only extends to the literal content of the programming code, then competing software house B, subsequent to seeing software house A's user interface, may begin programming from scratch, without copying the code behind software house A's computer software product but basing the exercise of their taste, skill and expertise and on the innovative idea of software house A's user interface, and thereby produce a user interface identical to that of software house A. Here lies, in a sense, the essential nature of the computer program which distinguishes it from all other types of copyright work. The computer program, dependant on its state, has the capacity to manifest itself in a variety of modes. Inert, and separate from a computer, the computer program gives the appearance of being a standard literary work in the form of software engineer's notation. When active, the computer program manifests itself as if it is was a film, a picture or a piece of music.

Understanding the "look" of the user interface

How a computer program displays its interface information to the user is generally described as the "look" of the product. Some manufacturers of proprietary computer software products deem it of great importance that their product has the correct "look"; not only so that their product is easy to learn and use, but also to provide a functional similarity between their products so as to encourage the end-user to purchase their products over another's when already using one product from their product line. The computer software industry has also built a type of commercial goodwill akin to that of "brand loyalty". Thus, an end-user of product "ABC" produced by the "ACME Software Company" will have become accustomed to the look of the "ABC" user interface and associate that look with the "ACME Software Company". When selecting their next application program, the end-user (it is claimed by the computer software industry) will wish to stay with the "ACME Software Company" interface look so that they will need to learn less overall and acquire the ability to use the next computer software product more easily than if they start with a competitor's product which would have an interface look with which they are unfamiliar.

Understanding the "feel" of the user interface

The user interface, however, has aspects which go far beyond the mere look of a computer program. The purpose of the interface is primarily to enable the interactive use of the computer program by the end-user. All computer programs, whether of a graphic or text type, are issued **commands** by the end-user to initiate the functionality held within or expressed by the computer program. How the designer of the computer program has arranged and fashioned these commands represents what is known as the "feel" of the computer program and is generated by the **command structure** of the computer software product. One could analogise this in the same manner in which one could describe the "feel" of a motor vehicle when being driven. How the designers of the motor vehicle have fashioned the steering and suspension geometries and how the ergonomics of the instrument panel of the vehicle have been contrived all lend themselves to how the motor vehicle "feels" to the driver. The "feel" of a motor vehicle when being driven is, it is generally accepted in the motor vehicle industry, a highly important factor in the general level of satisfaction that the motor vehicle delivers to the driver or owner. So it is, it is submitted, with computer software. Many computer software products are large, complex and intricate, containing many hundreds of commands which, when interacting with the end-user, may lend to a distinctive "feel" through its operation.

The look and feel of computer software has therefore become, in more recent years, of very great importance to the largest of computer software houses. Since the largest of computer software product manufacturers originate in the United States, it is accordingly not surprising (it is contended) that more case law has been generated in the United States than in the United Kingdom.

In this chapter therefore, the subsistence of copyright in the user interface and its look and feel will be examined in detail and in this instance, due to the quantity of persuasive authority originating from the United States, case law from that jurisdiction will be considered alongside of English authority.

Textual User Interfaces and Command Structures

The text-based user interface

The illustration set out in Figure 5.1 is an example of a simple and standard textual user interface.[1] The user is reminded of the command structure at the right-hand side of the screen and commands are entered into the computer program through the keyboard by using combinations of the "Ctrl" and "Alt" keys. At the top right of the screen, one can see what are generally referred to as "pull-down menus". In this instance, when the user wishes to back up the data (save or conserve the data by making a duplicate of the data

1 A labelled screen-shot from the Organiser Link II software produced by Sharp Corporation.

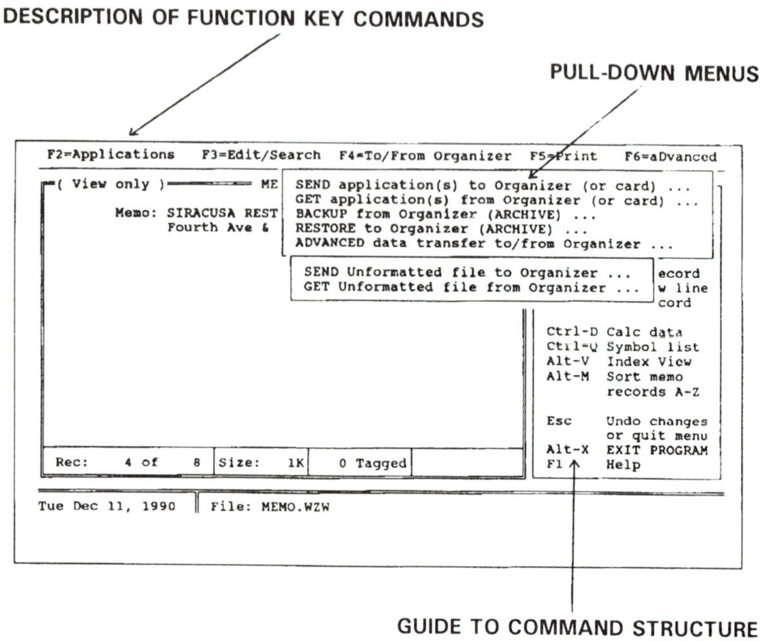

Figure 5.1

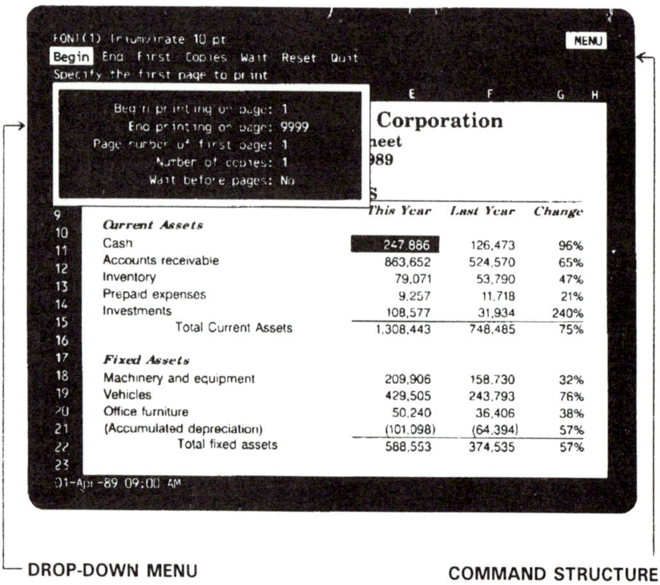

Figure 5.2

on separate media so that it cannot be lost) held on a personal organiser[2] to the personal computer using this particular piece of software, the user would select (or press) function key number four (F4) to engage the command "To/From Organiser". Once the F4 key had been depressed, a new menu would appear on the screen which would have appeared to emerge or drop down from the area on the screen inviting function key F4 to be depressed. The user would then select "BACKUP from Organiser (ARCHIVE)" from the menu and so on, until all of the choices have been made and the computer program executes the task set selected. This is therefore not only an example of a textual user interface but also an example of command structure.

Figure 5.2 depicts the user interface of one of the premier spreadsheet application computer software products known as Lotus 1-2-3.[3] The user interface of Lotus 1-2-3 can be simply described as being a grid headed with letters at the top and numbers on the left-hand side. Above this grid sits a selection of commands.

These commands change so that further command selections can be made with, sometimes, drop-down menus appearing at appropriate stages. The user interface, as with many modern computer software products, can be modified within certain limits by the end-user. In this context it appears that the grid-lines are, in fact, optional, amongst other facets of the interface, which can be controlled and set-up to the user's particular preference, including colours, font types and sizes. Nevertheless, it is submitted that it is important to note that the command structure remains set at all times.

Command structures

A depiction of part of the command structure to the user interface of Lotus 1-2-3 is given in Figure 5.3. Although not part of the user interface appearing visually in the same way as that set out in Figure 5.2, Figure 5.3 sets out part of the Lotus 1-2-3 command structure in a type of flow-chart or tabular format. It is submitted that the sequence of commands and the effects that they produce are of paramount importance to the way in which Lotus 1-2-3 feels through use to the user. This is, of course, part of the "look and feel" proposition for users to become strongly familiar with the command structure and memorise large sections of it. The protection of the command structure by copyright is therefore, it is submitted, of critical importance to the

2 An electronic personal organiser is a small computer (usually powered by batteries) designed to hold personal information such as names, addresses, telephone numbers, a diary and schedules.

3 Produced by Lotus Development Corporation of the United States.

The Print Commands

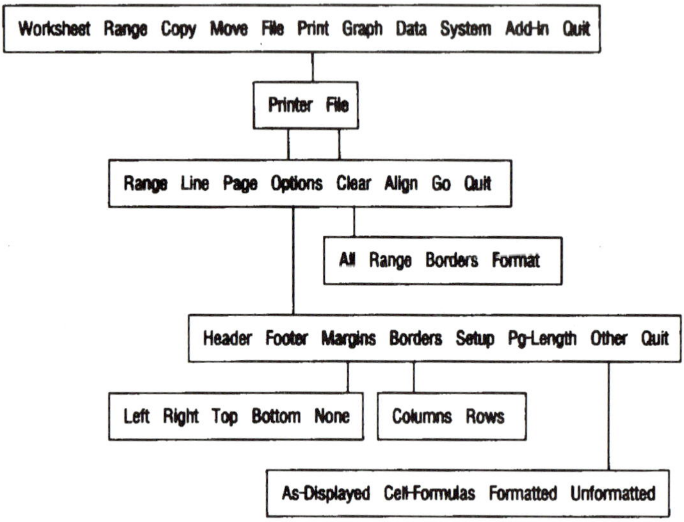

The Range Commands

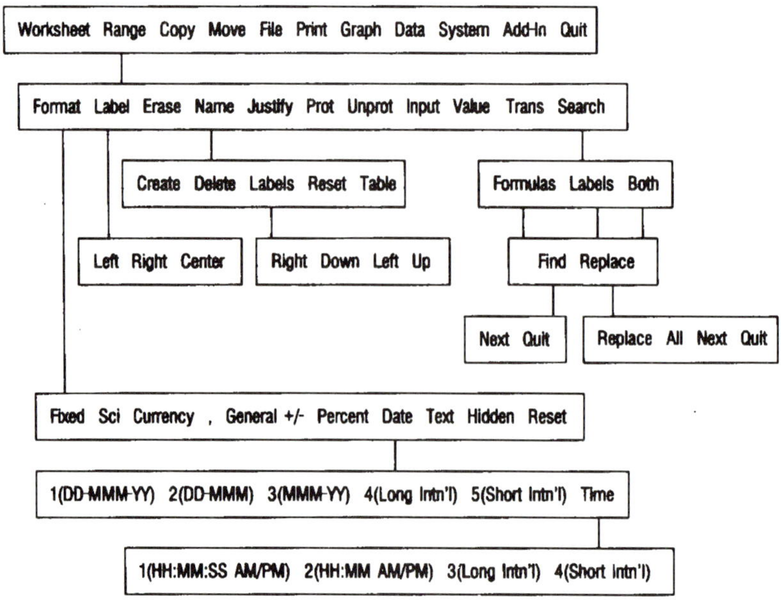

Figure 5.3

protection of the user interface overall and, in this sense, one cannot really divide one away from the other.

Evaluating useful US law

Unusually, in the area of what can be termed the law of software copyright, an actual precedent exists from the United States which is principally directed to establishing what copyright exists in the user interface of Lotus 1-2-3. This is *Lotus Development Corporation v Paperback Software International*;[4] but it is contended that an evaluation of this case from the contextual perspective of English law (to which this work is directed) would be overly burdensome without first examining the nature of copyright protection for computer programs in the United States. In this manner, it is contended, *Lotus Development Corporation v Paperback Software International* may be examined in its correct jurisdictional context so that its applicability to the English law jurisdiction can be properly tested and evaluated.

Defining the computer program under US law

The United States Copyright Office, consistent with its policy to resolve questions of copyright in favour of the party seeking to register, has accepted computer programs for registration since the early 1960s;[5] but it is contended, the status of computer programs as a copyright work was, at that time, uncertain. The legislative history of the United States of America Copyright Act of 1976 clearly stated that computer programs could properly be the subject of copyright, but this Act specifically preserved the then existing law concerning the use of copyright works in computers.[6] Congress adopted this temporary measure until the submission of the final report of the "National Commission on New Technological Uses of Copyrighted Works" in July 1978, which led to the enactment of the Computer Software Copyright Act of 1980. The Computer Software Copyright Act 1980 added a new definition to the Copyright Act 1976[7] in section 101, which is repeated, as a matter of convenience, from Chapter 2 above.

4 740 F Supp 37 (D Mass 1990).
5 Copyright Registration for Computer Programs, Announcement from the Copyright Office, 11 *Bull. Copyright Society* 361 (1964).
6 17 USC § 117 (1976).
7 See Chap 2 p 13.

> "A 'computer program' is a set of statements or instructions to be used directly or indirectly in a computer in order to bring about a certain result."[8]

The Computer Software Copyright Act 1980 further repealed, *inter alia*, section 117 of the US Copyright Act and substituted a new section 117 specifying certain limitations on the rights of the authorised licensee under the copyright in computer programs. The Computer Software Copyright Act 1980 permits the licensee under the copyright in a computer program to make another copy or adaptation to facilitate its use or guard against damage or destruction. Adaptations of the original copy of the computer program may only be transferred with the authorisation of the owner of the copyright in the computer program. Making only two exceptions, the Computer Software Copyright Act 1980 implicitly made any other copying or the making of adaptations of a computer program an infringement of the copyright owner's exclusive right to reproduction.

Eligibility for copyright protection

To be eligible for copyright protection, the computer program under US law must be fixed in a tangible form of expression.[9] For the purposes of the Computer Software Copyright Act 1980, the work is fixed in a tangible medium of expression when it is sufficiently permanent or stable so that it can be perceived or received for more than a transitory period, with or without the aid of a machine.[10] The manner in which this requirement for fixation applies to computer input was considered in *BellSouth Advertising and Publishing Corp v Donnelly Information Publishing Inc*[11] where the court held that the act of keying information into a computer and storing it on magnetic tape is a physical act of copying. Whilst the court did not have to consider whether storage on a hard or floppy disk would meet the fixation requirement, it is submitted that the court's analysis indicates that the medium of storage is irrelevant for this purpose.

Term of copyright protection

The protection afforded by copyright in the United States extends for the life of the author plus 50 years, or 75 years from the time of the work's first

8 17 USC § 101.
9 *Ibid*, § 102(a).
10 *Ibid*, § 101.
11 933 F2d 952, 958, 91-1 Tr Cas Par 69, 468, 19 USPQ 2d 1345, 3 CCH Comp Cas Par 46,490 (11th Cir 1991).

publication if the work was made for hire.[12] However, in June 1993, the European Commission approved Directive 93/98/EEC to harmonise the term of copyright in European Union members' jurisdictions at 70 years; thus requiring implementing legislation in European Union Member States by 1 June 1995.[13] In view of and as a response to this action, the United States Registrar of Copyright is re-examining the term for all US copyright works and may recommend a change in current US law.[14]

Publication and registration

Publication and registration are not prerequisites for copyright protection. As described above, copyright protection in the United States automatically attaches to a work which is considered to have been "fixed in a tangible medium of expression".[15] However, statutory incentives for the recording or registration of copyright ownership do exist. Registration is essential to maintain the right to seek judicial intervention in copyright infringement except for actions for infringement of copyright in works subject to the Berne Convention on Copyright where the country of origin was not the United States and where the cause of action arises on or after 1 March 1989.[16] If registration is to be made, computer programs can be registered in either their published or unpublished forms.[17] In order to gain maximum protection

12 17 USC § 302(a) and (c).

13 See Chap 10 with respect to EU law with respect to computer software technology.

14 58 Fed Reg 40838, 54378 (1993).

15 17 USC § 301(a).

16 17 USC § 411(a). In the US, a copyright work is considered to be subject to the Berne Convention if:

(a) in the case of an unpublished work, one or more of the authors is a national of a nation adhering to the Berne Convention, or in the case of a published work, one or more of the authors is a national of a nation adhering to the Berne Convention on the date of first publication;

(b) the work was first published in a nation adhering to the Berne Convention, or was simultaneously first published in a nation adhering to the Berne Convention and in a foreign nation that does not adhere to the Berne Convention;

(c) in the case of an audiovisual work:

  (1) if one of more of the authors is a legal entity, that author has its headquarters in a nation adhering to the Berne Convention; or

  (2) if one or more of the authors is an individual, that author is domiciled, or has his or her habitual residence in, a nation adhering to the Berne Convention.

17 The US Copyright Office will also accept the registration of databases – see 37 CFR §§ 202.3, 202.19 and 202.20. Registration requires the deposit of the "best edition" of a work and databases which are available in a CD-ROM format are generally considered by the Copyright Office to be best editions and software houses are encouraged to deposit them together with the computer programs supplied with the database which are used to search it (along the lines of multimedia packages as described in Chap 4 above) and the user manuals (see 37 CFR Part 202.19).

from the Copyright Office, producers of computer programs in the United States deposit two copies with the Copyright Office.[18] It should be noted that several statutory incentives intended to encourage authors to continue to register their copyright works in a timely fashion exist. For example, prima facie weight is given by a registration certificate in establishing the existence of a valid copyright in an action for infringement of copyright and is further used in the recovery of statutory damages and attorney's fees.

The degree of analysis to be conducted

An in-depth analysis of all of the US case law involving the copyright protection of computer programs would be beyond the scope of this work. However, now that the basis for copyright protection in the United States has been made out, a review of what are submitted to be the more important lines of cases in the United States will prove very useful in measuring the degree of protection afforded to user interfaces and command structures in the United Kingdom under the Copyright, Designs and Patents Act 1988.

Copyright protection for computer software

Apple Computer Inc v Franklin Computer Corp[19] is the first significant and far-reaching decision on the copyright protection of computer software in the United States. The court held that the object code of a computer program is protectable by copyright, including when it is embodied in a ROM. The court determined that the operating system[20] is entitled to copyright protection as a copyright work even if the computer program implements methods, processes, ideas and systems. The court reasoned that, if only one or a few other expressions are possible for a particular idea, the expression is "necessarily dictated by the underlying subject matter", and therefore, the idea and expression have merged and are therefore not capable of being protected by copyright. If, however, "other programs can be written or created which perform the same function as ... Apple's operating system program, then that program is an expression of the idea and hence copyrightable."[21]

18 17 USC §§ 407–410. In June 1988, the Copyright Office determined that all expression capable of carrying copyright owned by the same depositor and embodied in a computer program, or first published as a unit with a computer program, including screen displays (and thus user interfaces) is considered a single work and should be registered on a single application form (53 Fed. Reg. 21817 (1988)).

19 714 F2d 1240 (3d Cir 1983).

20 As described in Chap 4 above.

21 At 1253.

Following this decision, the Ninth Circuit held in *Apple Computer Inc v Formula International Inc*[22] that all computer programs, fixed in any medium, are protected under the law of copyright regardless of their purpose or function.[23] The Court also stated *obiter* that all computer programs stored in ROM or disk are designed to operate a machine in such a manner as to ultimately produce some useful communication to the end-user, whether the computer program communicates directly with the end-user or directs certain computerised machine functions which eventually result in communication.[24] The court further held that there was no authority for the proposition that the US copyright concept and doctrine of protectable expression must be an expression which is directly communicated to the computer user. Further to this case and along much the same lines and in accordance with the trend of authority by then established, the decision in *NEC Corp v Intel Corp*[25] held that computer program microcode (being very short computer programs held in an integrated circuit which controls the method by which integrated circuits operate) known as microcode fixed in a microprocessor (or integrated circuit) was "a set of statement or instructions used directly or indirectly on a computer to bring about a certain result" and that the function of the microcode or that the fact that microcode was programmable by the end-user did not affect its status as being a computer program in law and thus a copyright work.

Following these decisions, most commentators and academics in the United States agreed that all significant issues of the subsistence of copyright in computer programs had finally been resolved and that secondary issues, such as the degree of substantial similarity to establish infringement of copyright, would require the court's collective attention.

In *Whelan Associates Inc v Jaslow Dental Laboratory Inc*[26] a federal court of appeals held that the copyright that subsists in a computer program goes beyond just the lines of programming code contained in the computer program. The Court ruled that the copyright subsisting in a computer program may extend to the computer program's structure, sequence and organisation. The federal Court of Appeals approved the dicta of the judge in the District Court where he stated: "The expression of the idea in a software computer program is the manner in which the program operates, controls and regulates the computer in receiving, assembling, calculating, retaining, correlating, and

22 562 FSupp 775 (CDCal 1983) affirmed 725 F2d 521 (9th Cir 1984).

23 Also see **Williams Electrics Inc v Arctic International Inc** 685 F2d 870 (3d Cir 1982); and **Tandy Corp v Personal Micro Computers Inc** 524 FSupp 171 (NDCal 1981).

24 At 778-780.

25 645 FSupp 590 (NDCal 1986).

26 797 F2d 1222 (3d Cir 1986).

producing useful information either on screen, print-out or by audio communication."[27] The Court of Appeals in *Whelan Associates Inc v Jaslow Dental Laboratory Inc* supported its position by reference to the decision in *SAS Institute Inc v S&H Computer Systems Inc*[28] where the Court ruled that the structure of a program may be protected by copyright even where the actual lines of computer code are different. The Court held that to the extent that the defendant modelled its computer program after the source code to the plaintiff's computer program, such copying was of expression and not merely of ideas. The Court specifically held that: "At every level, the [programming] process is characterised by choice, often made arbitrarily, and only dictated by necessity. Even in the case of statistical calculations, there is room for variation, such as in the order in which the arithmetic operations are performed."[29] The decision in *Whelan Associates Inc v Jaslow Dental Laboratory Inc* has been much criticised, it is contended, by academics and it is further contended that following it, a trend emerged of disregarding its analysis of the law (except in the Third Circuit, where it represented the controlling precedent).

The Court of Appeals for the Fifth Circuit determined in *Plains Cotton Cooperative Assoc v Goodpasture Computer Service Inc*[30] that the structure, sequence and organisation of the computer program under scrutiny was dictated by considerations of functionality rather than considerations of original authorship. This case may be explained in the sense that the Court seemed to adopt the argument that the similarities between the computer programs of the plaintiff and the defendant existed because both computer software systems conveyed the same standardised information that was to be contained on a "cotton recap sheet" and because of the unique aspects of the cotton market.[31]

The "abstraction – filtration – comparison" analysis

In June 1992 the Court of Appeals for the Second Circuit[32] generated the

27 609 FSupp 1307 (EDPa 1985).

28 605 FSupp 816 (MD Tenn 1985).

29 At 825.

30 807 F2d 1256 (5th Cir 1987).

31 See also **Synercom Technology Inc v University Computing Co** 462 FSupp 1003 (NDTex 1978).

32 The judgments of this court are, it is submitted, generally thought to be of a high standard and thus persuasive authority with respect to the determination of issues of copyright as much of the publishing industry in the US is located in the city of New York, which is under the court's jurisdiction. However, it is submitted that it should also be borne in mind that since much of the US computer industry is located in the state of California, the Ninth Circuit, which includes that state, has rendered a number of important opinions and decisions on computer law issues.

decision in *Computer Associates International Inc v Altai Inc.*[33] The Court stated that "[I]t is now well-settled that the literal elements of computer programs, i.e. their source and object codes, are the subject of copyright protection." The Court further directed itself to the scope of copyright protection for non-literal elements such as flow-charts, inter-modular relationships[34], parameter lists and macros.[35] The Court of Appeals affirmed the trial judge's view that *Whelan Associates Inc v Jaslow Dental Laboratory Inc* oversimplified the dichotomy between ideas unprotected by the law of copyright and expression which ought to be so protected; especially in the light of advances in computer programming technology. The Court of Appeals suggested a three-step approach to determining the existence of infringement of copyright subsisting in non-literal elements; as follows:

1. Abstraction

The two computer programs under investigation are examined to determine if there is substantial similarity between them. "Initially, in a manner that resembles reverse engineering on a theoretical plane, a court should dissect the allegedly copied program's structure and isolate each level of abstraction contained within it."

2. Filtration

"This process entails examining the structural components at each level of abstraction to determine whether their particular inclusion at that level was 'idea' or was dictated by considerations of efficiency, so as to be necessarily incidental to that idea; required by factors external to the program itself;[36]

33 982 F2d 693 (2d Cir), 3 Comp Cas (CCH) ¶ 46,666.

34 The relationship between different computer programs (known as modules) within a computer software product, which make calls to one another and distribute data between each other. So, *e.g.* one module may deal with the collection of data being input, which then communicates that data to a second module (being a computer program) which performs calculations using that data; which then communicates the data being the product of such calculations to a third module (another discrete, but interrelated, computer program) which presents the new data to the end-user. The production of modules within such a computer software product is encouraged in the software production industry as it promotes good programming style and decreases programming errors as bugs are more easily identified.

35 A macro can be two types of programming. Associated with a particular application; it can either be a recording of keystrokes which the application "play-back" so that a complex sequence of key-strokes can be executed by the application at speed in response to one command from the end-user or, in more sophisticated software applications, macros can be created by the end-user in a macro language. This is a type of programming language particular to a specific application and able to modify the execution of the application in question.

36 Such as the need to use certain standard programming techniques or to use certain standard commands with respect to the operating system or hardware the computer program is to execute upon.

or taken from the public domain and hence in nonprotectable expression."

3. Comparison

When the court has sifted and dissected out ideas, efficiency aspects, external factors and material in the public domain, "there may remain a core of protectable expression ... [T]he court's substantial similarity inquiry focuses on whether the defendant copied any aspect of this protected expression, as well as an assessment of the copied portion's relative importance with respect to the plaintiff's overall program."[37]

Exclusive rights of the copyright owner in the United States

The exclusive rights of the copyright owner in the United States are set out in section 106 of the Copyright Act 1976; and one of these is the exclusive right to prepare and authorise others to prepare "derivative works"; which is a term defined in the Act which includes works based on a pre-existing work, and, in general, without regard to the form of the new work.[38] In *Lewis Galoob Toys Inc v Nintendo of America Inc*[39] the court considered whether the computer programs stored in a cartridge that a player could insert into his games console[40] to alter certain features of the games programs produced by Nintendo of America Incorporated was a derivative work. The court held that the computer programs were not derivative works since "the device merely enhances the audiovisual displays (or underlying data bytes) that originate in the Nintendo game cartridges." The court in *Lewis Galoob Toys Inc v Nintendo of America Inc* also considered the defence that the device did not infringe the copyright in the Nintendo of America Incorporated games programs because it was "fair use". This "allows a holder of the privilege to use copyrighted material in a reasonable manner without the consent of the copyright holder".[41] The court's review of the trial judge's

---

37 The abstraction – filtration – comparison approach was applied in **Autoskill Inc v National Educational Support Systems Inc** 994 F2d 1476 (10th Cir 1993) and **Gates Rubber Co v Bando Chemical Industries Inc** 28 USPQ 2d 1503 (10th Cir 1993).

38 This concept, it is submitted, is substantially akin to the notion of adaptation as set out in s 21 of the Copyright, Designs and Patents Act 1988.

39 964 F2d 965 (9th Cir 1992).

40 See Chap 4 for an explanation of this technology.

41 At 969 (quoting **Narell v Freeman** 872 F2d 907 at 913 (9th Cir 1989)). The doctrine of fair use was originally developed in the US by the common law but is not codified in s 107 of the Copyright Act 1976 as follows:
"Notwithstanding the provisions of sections 106 and 106A [moral rights], the fair use of a copyrighted work ... is not an infringement of copyright in determining whether the use made of a work in any particular case is a fair use the factors to be considered shall include –

findings on this question led it to agree that Lewis Galoob Toys Incorporated's device constituted fair use.

Another court of the Ninth Circuit considered the application of fair use in *Sega Enterprises Ltd v Accolade Inc.*[42] The plaintiff, Sega Enterprises Limited was a Japanese manufacturer of computer games. The defendant, Accolade Incorporated, reverse engineered or decompiled[43] the Sega object code to determine the functionality of the games console software interface. Having thus discovered the architecture, procedures and functionality of the machine interface, Accolade Incorporated then caused an internal company manual to be written explaining the technical functionality of the interface in question so that the Accolade Incorporated computer games programmers could produce and develop new games programs which would execute on the Sega Enterprises Limited games console. The judge at first instance held on the plaintiff's motion, that decompiling was prima facie an infringement of copyright, and could not be fair use. However, on appeal the injunction was vacated (lifted) and the case remanded.[44]

The Court of Appeal, based on the facts found by the trial judge (which included findings of fact that an unlicensed competitor could not under any circumstances determine the function of Sega Enterprises Limited software interface without using decompilation techniques) held that even though Accolade Incorporated was a direct commercial competitor to Sega Enterprises Limited, its use of the decompiled source code was permissible and not an infringement of copyright. As to the second factor set out in section 107 of the Copyright Act 1976 (nature of use), the Court of Appeals held that Accolade Incorporated's limited use also favoured its position, commenting that "[i]f disassembly of copyrighted object code is per se an unfair use, the owner of the copyright gains a de facto monopoly over the functional aspects of his work – aspects that were expressly denied copyright

---

41 *(cont.)*

(1) the purpose and character of the use, including whether such use is of a commercial nature or is for nonprofit educational purposes;

(2) the nature of the copyrighted work;

(3) the amount and substantiality of the portion used in relation to the copyrighted work as a whole; and

(4) the effect of the use upon the potential market for or value of the copyrighted work. The fact that a work is unpublished shall not itself bar a finding of fair use if such finding is made upon consideration of all the above factors."

The last sentence in factor #4 above was added by Pub L No 102–492, 106 Stat 3145 (Oct 24, 1992). The software industry in the US at the time opposed this change, since source code is usually unpublished and the reverse engineering of object code has been held, as discussed below, to be fair use.

42 785 FSupp 1392 (ND Cal 1992).

43 Obtaining source code from object code.

44 977 F2d 1510 (9th Cir 1992).

protection by congress." Since Accolade Incorporated disassembled entire interface programs written and owned by Sega Enterprises Limited, the third factor in section 107 of the Copyright Act 1976 factor favoured Sega Enterprises Limited but, under these circumstances, the Court of Appeals held that this would be given "very little weight" although the Court made no comment as to why it took such a view. As to the fourth factor under section 107 of the Copyright Act 1976, the Court held that whilst this conduct by Accolade Incorporated might cause some economic loss to Sega Enterprises Limited, the effect of competitive games to those produce by Sega Enterprises Limited would only be minor.

Shortly before the decision in *Sega Enterprises Ltd v Accolade Inc*, the Court of Appeals for the Federal Circuit in *Atari Games Corp v Nintendo of America Inc*[45] reached a similar conclusion on the fair use of reverse engineering a software interface designed to keep commercial competitors from producing games programs to operate on the plaintiff's games console. The Federal Circuit had jurisdiction over the case since a patent infringement claim was involved. However, in determining issues concerning the law of copyright, the Federal Court applied the law of the circuit in which the case commenced; in this case, that of the Ninth Circuit. Following the giving of the judgment in *Sega Enterprises Ltd v Accolade Inc*, the court noted that its opinion was consistent with the decision of the Federal Court in *Atari Games Corp v Nintendo of America Inc.*[46]

Rulings of lower courts with respect to screen displays

It is submitted that a short analysis of some decisions of lower courts in the United States would be useful in giving an overall perspective on the protection of look and feel in this jurisdiction, before moving on to one of the seminal cases in this area which directly relates to the interface depicted in Figure 5.2 above. A district court in California in the case of *Broderbund Software Inc v Unison World Inc*[47] held that the screen displays produced by computer programs are part of the overall structure of the computer program itself and are protected in consequence by the copyright in the computer program. Consequently the substantial copying of the menus of the interface constituted an infringement of the copyright in the computer program. However, in *Digital Communications Assoc Inc v Softklone Distribution Corp*[48], this view was rejected.

45 975 F2d 832 (Fed Cir 1992).
46 977 F2d 1510 at 1524, fn7 (9th Cir 1992).
47 648 FSupp 1127 (NDCal 1986).
48 2 USPQ 2d 1385 (NDGa 1987).

The court held that user interfaces and screen displays generally are not direct copies of the literal or substantive content of the underlying computer program, because the same screen can be created by a variety of separate and independently created computer programs. According to the court's decision, an individual screen display may be the subject of copyright protection as a "compilation". The court held that by granting such "copyright on the arrangement and design of the status screen, the court is not granting the plaintiff control over the idea of a command drive program, a 'status' screen depicting the status of the program's operations, or the use of particular command terms or symbols".

The lack of consistency in rulings on this matter continued in the inferior courts of the United States until the Court of Appeals for the Fourth Circuit concluded in *M Kramer Manufacturing Co Inc v Andrews et al*[49] that a copyright in an audiovisual game program[50] protects the underlying computer program to the extent that the program embodies the game's expressions. The Court of Appeals specifically held that "the fact that the computer program could have been separately copyrighted does not mean that the audiovisual copyright may not protect the computer program which implements the audiovisuals any more than the issuance of a patent will not necessarily render a work non-copyrightable"; and further stated that the "computer program or 'memory device' is the form in which the audiovisuals are 'permanently embodied' and are fixed in a tangible medium of expression 'capable of being' reproduced or otherwise communicated, 'either directly or with the aid of a machine or device'. The 'memory device', or computer program, is an essential element of the audiovisual copyright, satisfying the 'fixation' requirement for the issuance of a copyright and, as a 'copy', within the statutory definition, it is specifically protected from infringement under the audiovisual copyright."[51] It may be noted that the proposition advanced by the Court of Appeals in this case that a separate copyright subsisted in the audiovisual aspects of the computer program and that they were "fixed" in the medium of the computer program is similar to the argument advanced above with respect to the music (the "audio" in "audiovisuals") in a games program[52] that because it is highly likely that in the development of a games program the music was originally written down in standard musical notation, it was submitted that if the music was "written down" directly in the form of

49 783 F2d 421 (4th Cir 1986).

50 The subject of the action being a game program which, like most others, produced both melodies, tunes, sound effects and moving screen displays and was therefore dubbed "audiovisual" by the Court of Appeals.

51 At 443.

52 See Chap 4.

the relevant computer programming routines in the games program, this would not alter the subsistence of copyright in the music itself.

The argument made out above continued with the submission that since section 3(2) of the Copyright, Designs and Patents Act 1988 tells us that "Copyright does not subsist in literary, dramatic or musical work unless and until it is recorded in writing, or otherwise"; it was contended, in much the same way as the Court of Appeals in *M Kramer Manufacturing Co Inc v Andrews et al,* that the recording of the music in computer code falls within the meaning of either "in writing" or "otherwise". It was therefore argued, in consequence, that the music recorded within a computer program (whether written in standard musical notation originally or not) constitutes a separate and distinct copyright work and will be protected as a musical work within the meaning of the Copyright, Designs and Patents Act 1988. Further to this, it was argued[53] that the musical work should not be seen as "a product of the program" in the manner that Ferris J. viewed the screen displays under his consideration in *John Richardson Computers Ltd v Flanders and Chemtec Ltd.* Rather, the musical work is the product of ordinary human effort, judgement expertise and skill which has been exercised both in its composition and its reduction into a material form; the "material form" being a computer program. So far as the "visuals" in the "audiovisuals" are concerned, it was argued above[54] that, in English law, the screen display of a games program is not itself a literary work which is entitled to copyright protection; but it was contended that the screen display represented the visual playing of the recording which was being produced by the computer technology from the medium of a computer program in the same way, for example, that the moving images on a television represents the visual playing of the recording which is being produced by household video-recorder technology from the medium of magnetic tape in a video cassette. The copyright subsists, consequently, in the recording and not the display and it is this assertion which is the proper match between the technology employed and the action of the Copyright, Designs and Patents Act 1988.

Regard also ought to be made to the decision of the Court of Appeals for the Ninth Circuit in *Apple Computer Incorporated v Microsoft Corporation*[54a] in 1994 where Microsoft was accused of exceeding some of its rights under a licensing scheme with Apple and infringing Apple's copyright in some aspects of its Macintosh computer's graphical user interface. The Court of Appeals held that where the accused works include both licensed and unlicensed features, the establishment of copyright infringement will depend on whether the unlicensed features are entitled to copyright protection; and thus in establishing whether the copyrightable elements of a graphical user interface were infringed, works were required to

53 See Chap 4, p 72.

54 See Chap 4, p 75.

54a 35 F3d 1435 (9th Cir 1994).

be compared for "virtual identity", rather than "substantial similarity". This notion, it is submitted, represents an interesting area of divergence between US and English copyright law where the US court looks to see if the "original" and "infringing" works are virtually identical.[54b] The court commented that the ideas embodied in the graphical user interface a computer generates, including, for example, the use of windows to display multiple images, the manipulation of icons to convey instructions to the computer, and the use of menus, were not entitled to copyright protection.

In June 1990 Judge Keeton of the federal court in Massachusetts handed down the judgment of the court in *Lotus Development Corp v Paperback Software International*[55] in which it was held that menu screens and other parts of the user in the computer software product "Lotus 1-2-3" and the command structure therein[56] was "copyrightable expression" and had been infringed by the defendants. Judge Keeton, a law-school professor before being appointed to the bench, set out his decision in a 113-page judgment in which he reviewed the law of copyright of the United States from its constitutional basis that "The Congress shall have the Power. ... To promote the Progress of Science ... by securing for limited Time to Authors ... the exclusive Right to their Writings ..." to the enactment of the first Copyright Act in 1790 and on through the many changes made by the 1980 amendment that specifically defined a computer program and revised, *inter alia*, section 117 of the Copyright Act 1976.[57]

Rather than placing its decision that the defendant's user interface infringed the copyright in the plaintiff's computer program on the basis of the copying of the "look and feel" of Lotus 1-2-3; the court developed a three-part test, analogous to the "structure, sequence and organisation" concept suggested in *EG Johnson Controls Inc v Phoenix Control Systems Inc.*[58] It is submitted that the test laid down by the court in *Lotus Development Corp v Paperback Software International* can properly be summarised as follows:

1. Copyright does not subsist in ideas, only in original expression. The court must first of all define the idea in a copyright work so that it can be distinguished from the expression.
2. The court must determine whether the allegedly infringing expression of the idea is the only way (or one of the very few ways) in which the idea can be expressed; or does the criticised expression include identifiable elements that are not essential to the expression?
3. If the court has determined the presence or existence of such non-essential element, the court must then determine whether they are a substantial portion, from a qualitative perspective, of the copyright work.

54b 35 F3d 1435 (9th Cir 1994) at 1446.
55 740 FSupp 37, 15 USPQ 1577, 2 CCH Computer Cas ¶ 46,310 (D Mass 1990).
56 See Figs 5.2 and 5.3 above.
57 See p 94 above.
58 886 F2d 1173 at 1175 (9th Cir 1989).

The court held that there were a number of ways in which the user interface of "Lotus 1-2-3" could have been written and therefore was a copyright work. The court further held that the user interface of the marketed version of the defendant's computer software product known as "VP-Planner" was almost identical to that of "Lotus 1-2-3", that the user interface was a substantial portion of the work, and therefore infringing.

Very shortly after the decision in *Lotus Development Corp v Paperback Software International*, Lotus Development Corporation filed similar infringement actions against two of its principal commercial competitors in California, Borland and Santa Cruz Operation. Both of these two software houses filed suit in the Federal Court in California against Lotus Development Corporation for a declaratory judgment that their competitive judgments did not infringe the copyright in "Lotus 1-2-3" – these actions were dismissed. Later, Santa Cruz Operation settled with Lotus Development Corporation and withdrew the software product under contention from the market-place; however, the action against Borland continued in the state of Massachusetts. Amicus briefs were filed by several interested organisations, one by the Register of Copyright, another by several law-school professors. In an opinion handed down in March 1992, Judge Keeton denied motions by both parties for summary judgment, holding that neither had demonstrated the absence of a dispute as to the material facts of the case.[59] The learned judge also proposed possible jury questions for special verdict, and asked counsel to prepare comments thereon. In a manner particular to the rules of civil procedure in the United States, without a full hearing and yet having taken judicial notice of the opinions of several eminent academics, Judge Keeton revised the first test that he laid down in *Lotus Development Corp v Paperback Software International*, so the test may be summarised as follows:

1. Copyright does not subsist in ideas, only in original expression. The court must first of all define the idea, system, process, procedure or method in a copyright work so that it can be distinguished from the expression.
2. The court must determine whether the allegedly infringing expression of the idea is the only way (or one of the very few ways) in which the idea can be expressed; or does the criticised expression include identifiable elements that are not essential to the expression?
3. If the court has determined the presence or existence of such non-essential element, the court must then determine whether they are a substantial portion, from a qualitative perspective, of the copyright work.

59 788 FSupp 78 (D Mass 1992).

In July 1992, almost contemporaneously with the Court of Appeals for the Second Circuit giving its decision in *Computer Associates International Inc v Altai Inc*[60], and after hearing further submissions, Judge Keeton partially granted Lotus Development Corporation's motion for summary judgment, holding that "it cannot be genuinely disputed that a large part of the structure and arrangement of the menu commands is not driven entirely by functional considerations. There are sufficient non-functional aspects that at least hundreds and perhaps thousands of different expressions of the function were possible when Lotus chose the particular structure of menu commands incorporated in Lotus 1-2-3." After concluding that Borland did infringe the copyright in "Lotus 1-2-3", the court concluded that a jury should decide whether the amount of copying by Borland "was greater than the minimum essential to constituting a substantial part of the Lotus 1-2-3 work".[61] In March 1995 the Court of Appeals for the First Circuit finally considered the issue between Lotus Development Corporation and Borland International.[61a] Circuit Judge Stahl, delivering the major opinion of the Court, crystallised the task before it when he said:

> "This appeal requires us to decide whether a computer menu command hierarchy is copyrightable subject matter. In particular, we must decide whether, as the district court held, plaintiff-appellee Lotus Development Corporation's copyright in Lotus 1-2-3, a computer spreadsheet program, was infringed by defendant-appellant Borland International Inc, when Borland copied the Lotus 1-2-3 menu command hierarchy into its own Quattro and Quattro Pro computer spreadsheet programs"[61b]

Accepting that it was "navigating in uncharted waters"[61c] the Court first distinguished *Computer Associates International Inc v Altai Inc*[61d] on the ground that the Court was not confronted with alleged nonliteral copying of computer code[61e], and held, reversing the inferior court's decisions, that the Lotus menu command hierarchy could not be subject to copyright as it was a "method of operation" excluded by the action of the US Copyright Act USC S102(b).[61f]

60 For a discussion of this case, see Wilkins in (1994) 104(2) YLJ 435.

61 799 FSupp 203 (D Mass 1992).

61a **Lotus Development Corp v Borland International Inc** 49 F 3d 807 (1st Cir 1995).

61b *Ibid* at 809.

61c *Ibid* at 813.

61d 982 F 2d (2nd Cir 1992).

61e 49 F 3d 807 (1st Cir 1995) at 814.

61f S102(b) states: "In no case does copyright protection for an original work of authorship extend to any idea, procedure, process, system, method of operation, concept, principle or discovery, regardless of the form in which it is described, explained, illustrated, or embodied in such work."

US decisions in the context of English law

When juxtaposing the decisions in *Computer Associates International Inc v Altai Inc* and *Lotus Development Corp v Paperback Software International*, it is not possible to extract a definitive exposition of the law in the United States with respect to the subject to hand. However, Ferris J in *John Richardson Computers Ltd v Flanders and Chemtec Ltd* adopted the approach of the Court of Appeals in *Computer Associates International Inc v Altai Inc* where he said:

> "There is thus nothing in any English decision which conflicts with the general approach adopted in the Computer Associates case. I think that in preference to seeking the 'core of protectable expression' in the plaintiff's program an English court will first decide whether the plaintiff's program as a whole is entitled to copyright and then decide whether any similarity attributable to copying which is to be found in the defendant's program amounts to the copying of a substantial part of the plaintiff's program. This was the approach which was held to be correct in the William Hill case. But at the stage at which the substantiality of any copying falls to be assessed in an English case the question which has to be answered, in relation to the originality of the plaintiff's program and the separation of an idea from its expression, is essentially the same question as the United States court was addressing in Computer Associates. In my judgement it would be right to adopt a similar approach in England. This means that consideration is not restricted to the text of the code..."[62]

The learned judge reaches the right decision in English law for the wrong reasons. He is right, in principle, where he observes that there is nothing in any English decision which conflicts with the general approach adopted in *Computer Associates International Inc v Altai Inc*, but does not take account of the fact that the decision in this case is founded on the basis that the tribunal involved was immersed in the culture and tenets of the law of copyright of the United States and that, in modern times, the law of copyright in England is fundamentally a different creature of process than that of the United States.[62a] In any event, Ferris J is right to take the view that a court's consideration is not restricted to the text of computer program code and this view is consistent with previous English decisions. Cases of the United States are frequently cited by counsel in English copyright cases concerning computer programs on the basis that they either illuminate English law or fill the lacunae which are perceived to be present in the English law of copyright. Some judges are persuaded by these arguments, hearing debate on American

62 [1993] FSR 497 at 526.

62a It is suggested that it should be noted that the Court in **Lotus Development Corporation v Borland International Incorporated** 49 F 3d 807 (1st Cir 1995) often made reference to the US Copyright Act of 1976 and the intention of Congress (see, for example and in particular, 815, 817, and the concurring judgment of Circuit Judge Boudin who referred to the "tradition of copyright law, and the likely intent of Congress" at 820).

copyright law and even adopting American tests in their reasoning – as did Ferris J. However, it is contended that this is wrong in law. Jacob J supports this view in *IBCOS Computers Ltd v Barclays Mercantile Highland Finance Ltd* where, when addressing the issue of the distinction between an idea and its expression with respect to the originality of a computer program display, he said:

> "In this context there was some appeal to US cases on copyright. The fact is that US copyright law is not the same as ours, particularly in the area of copyright works concerned with functionality and of compilations. The Americans (many would say sensibly) never developed copyright so that functional things like exhaust pipes could not be copied. This is partly due to their statute, which is different from our Act. The US Copyright Code itself sets the law against protecting function."[63]

The learned judge then sets out paragraph 102 of the US Copyright code and continues:[64]

> "Moreover US case law has, ever since Baker v Selden 7 (1879) 101 U.S. 99, 25 L. Ed 841 been extremely careful to keep copyright out of the functional field, either by saying there is no copyright in, or that copyright cannot be infringed by taking, the functional. In Baker a design of ledger sheets which had a particular function was refused copyright. I doubt that would have happened here. That is not to say that American case law on copyright is never of assistance. But I do not think it assists me in relation to the subsistence of copyright."[65]

The question therefore arises as to the status of user interfaces and command structures under English law. Jacob J was prepared on principles of the law of copyright of England to hold that the subsistence of copyright in a computer program went beyond the text of the program code where he said:

> "The consequence of regarding ADS [the computer program in question] as a whole as a copyright work is that it is right to consider .... the program structure

---

63 At 292.

64 "102. Subject matter of copyright: In general

(a) Copyright protection subsists, in accordance with this title, in original works of authorship fixed in any tangible medium of expression, now known or later developed, from which they can be perceived, reproduced, or otherwise communicated, either directly or with the aid of a machine or device. Works of authorship include the following categories:
(1) literary works;
(2) musical works, including any accompanying words;
(3) dramatic works, including any accompanying music.
(4) pantomime and choreographic works;
(5) pictorial, graphic, and sculptural works;
(6) motion pictures and other audiovisual works; and
(7) sound recordings.

(b) In no case does copyright protection for an original work of authorship extend to any idea, procedure, process, system, method of operation, concept, principle, or discovery, regardless of the form in which it is described, explained, illustrate, or embodied in such work."

65 At 292.

> as a whole and the design features as a whole as part of the work, in addition to the literal bits of code and the program structure within an individual program."[66]

It has been already contended above that the introduction of American case law into the English legal process as was the case of Ferris J in adopting the mechanisms propounded in *Computer Associates International Inc v Altai Inc* in the case of *John Richardson Computers Ltd v Flanders and Chemtec Ltd* is inappropriate. It may well be that Jacob J was trying overly hard not to criticise or differ from his learned colleague Ferris J when he said that "Ferris J. in John Richardson Computers v Flanders found the American approach of some assistance at the later stage of considering whether a substantial part of a program had been taken."[67]; for it is submitted that Ferris J. was, in fact, directing himself to the question of the subsistence of copyright in the computer program that he had before him and especially the non-literal elements of the user interface. It is contended that where Ferris J said that "The United States authorities appear to place much reliance upon the principle that there is no copyright in ideas, only in expression of ideas. This principle is now enshrined in statute in the United States, It is, of course, recognised and applied in English Law too..."[68]; this caused the learned judge to accept the American authority that followed in his judgment, especially with respect to *Computer Associates International Inc v Altai Inc*, on face value where it was inappropriate so to do.

The status of the user interface and command structure in English copyright law

It is argued that there is a well-developed and pre-existing doctrine within the English law of copyright that the court may find and protect non-literal elements within a literary or dramatic work;[69] and in the light of the Copyright, Designs and Patents Act 1988 specifically providing that computer programs may exist outside of computer language or code[70] and preparatory design material is also a literary work.[71] Taken together, with the reasoning of the learned judge in *IBCOS Computers Ltd v Barclays Mercantile Highland Finance Ltd*, user interfaces and command structures, so long as they satisfy the usual tests as to originality, and are protected as either copyright works in their own right, or as part of the non-literal structure of the computer program that embodies them. With respect to the

66 *Ibid.*
67 *Ibid.*
68 [1993] FSR 497 at 523.
69 For example, see **Corelli v Gray**.
70 S 21(4).
71 S 3(1).

protection by the law of copyright of textual user interfaces in particular, case law may be found in lines of authority pre-dating modern computer programming technology which can properly be considered to be of, at the very least, purposeful and persuasive authority. In *Ladbroke (Football) Ltd v William Hill (Football) Ltd* the court considered the similarity in betting coupons (made up of grids in much the same fashion as a spreadsheet application program is such as "Lotus 1-2-3") and in deciding whether there was an infringement of copyright, their Lordships first had to decide whether a copyright subsisted within the plaintiffs' coupon before deciding the issue of infringement. The court held that there was copyright in the respondents' compilation and that it did not follow that because the fragments of the compilation, taken separately, would not be copyright, the whole could not be copyright.

The dicta of Lord Evershed is of assistance in the analysis of this matter so as to bring about some empirical and justifiable conclusion with respect to the ambit of copyright protection in this area. Lord Evershed said:

> "I conclude that there was present here the requisite degree of skill, judgment and labour, not only in selecting out of the vast possible total of wagers those which should be offered, but also in the way in which the result of the selection was presented to the customer, including particularly the arrangement of the document and of its component headings and the way in which such headings were described and were coloured and also in the way which, in the appropriate notes underneath the headings, the punter was informed of the possibilities open to him under each heading."[72]

This dicta of Lord Evershed could be strongly suggestive of the manner in which the "Lotus 1-2-3" user interface works. Paraphrasing, the following possible and hypothetical judgment could have been given by the learned judge in favour of Lotus Development Corporation in an action considering the subsistence of copyright in the "Lotus 1-2-3" user interface:

> "I conclude that there was present here the requisite degree of skill, judgment and labour, not only in selecting out of the large possible total of commands those which should be offered, but also in the way in which the result of the selection was presented to the user, including particularly the arrangement of the screen and of its component headings and the way in which such headings were described and were coloured and also in the way which, in the pull-down menus and help screens underneath the headings, the user was informed of the possibilities open to him under each heading."

As can be seen, little change has to be made to make His Lordship's judgment seem directly applicable to the issue under analysis.

72 At 282.

Graphic User Interfaces and Command Structures

A typical modern graphic user interface is set out in Figure 5.4.[73] It can be argued that the purpose of the graphic user interface is no different than any other type of interface; its purpose is to act as the medium through which the end-user can interactively associate with the computer program allowing for the giving of commands to the computer program on the part of the end-user and the giving of status, computing and resultant information to the end-user on the part of the computer program. The graphic user interface was developed to provide a more intuitive methodology and framework for this interaction. This would, it was argued, provide a more enjoyable and natural experience for the end-user, decreasing user error and increasing the end-user's ability to learn the functions of the computer program and thus increase the productivity and increase the rate of return generally made in it. In Figure 5.4, the end-user would not enter a series a suggestive but arbitrary commands as in "Lotus 1-2-3", but would use a pointing device to highlight text or make choices from the button bar. The button bar can be seen in Figure 5.4 as the set of icons at the top of the interface beneath the words "Netware Printer Connections".

An extract from the "Netware Printer Connections" user interface is set out in Figure 5.5. The capacity for icons such as those set out in Figure 5.5 to be susceptible as separate copyright works was examined in Chapter 4 above; but copyright will also subsist in a graphic user interface and original parts thereof in the same manner as a textual graphic interface as a non-literal component of the computer program itself or as part of original preparatory design material. Due to the wish of software producers to produce graphic user interfaces which are intuitive, in other words which suggest their function to the end-user in an obvious and direct fashion, the icons they construct are often simplistic in design and rudimentary. Care must therefore be taken over the possibility that a court of law may not see these non-literal aspects of the computer program as being original, or in the alternative, may not see them as being sufficiently substantial (from a qualitative point of view) to merit protection in an infringement action.

Behind any user interface is a command structure and a graphic display of part of a command structure is set out in Figure 5.6. Thus we can see that command structures are common to all types of application computer programs – it is the final method by which the end-user interacts and controls

73 A screen shot from the network software "Netware" produced by Novell Corporation of the US.

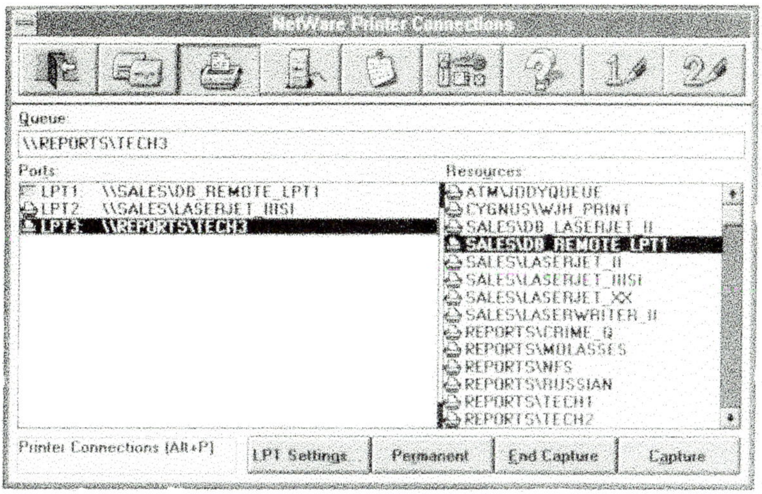

Figure 5.4

Figure 5.5

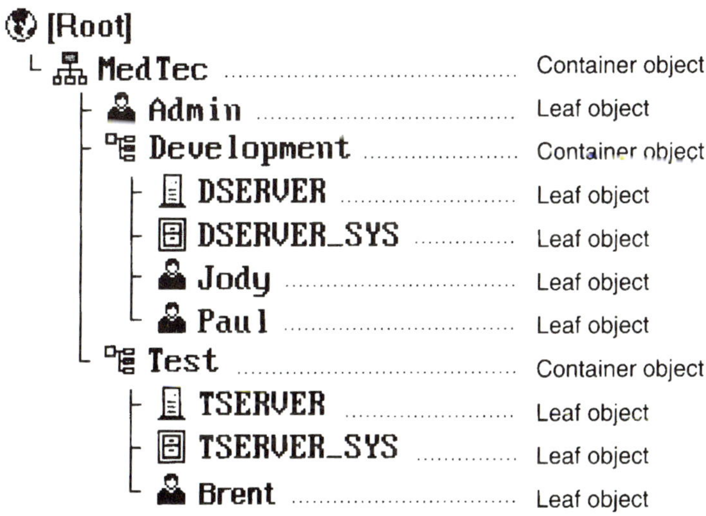

Figure 5.6

the functions and, broadly speaking, the general sequence of functions executed in the computer program.

Copyright in non-literal elements of a work

Further to the argument advanced above, the English courts of law have been willing to recognise the subsistence of copyright in non-literal elements in works other than literary works. It is well-established law that a dramatic work may be infringed by a second dramatisation which reproduces dramatic incidents without using or imitating the language employed in the first dramatic work. It is not necessary that the words in the second dramatisation should be identical or substantially identical to those used in the first dramatisation, for the situations, incidents and episodes, and the mode and methodologies in which the ideas are worked out and presented, may constitute a material portion of the whole work. The court will have regard to non-literal elements of the dramatic work such as the dramatic value and importance of what has been taken, even though the portion may in fact be quantitatively small and the actual language not copied. On the other hand, the fundamental idea or concept behind the two plays may be the same; but if worked out separately and on independent lines they may be so different as to bear no meaningful resemblance (from the perspective of copyright) to one another.[74] In the same way, the incidents in common between the first dramatisation and the second dramatisation may be drawn from common stock and common knowledge. On the other hand, the fact that a dramatic work prepared for performance in one medium is performed in another should make no difference to the issue of subsistence of copyright nor, for that matter, any issue of infringement. The question will always remain as to whether substantial use has been made of the series of dramatic incidents in which copyright subsists.

The activity of the courts in copyright infringement actions has not been limited to a review of non-literal aspects of literary and dramatic works. In actions for the infringement of copyright in musical works, the courts have unerringly directed themselves to whether the alleged infringement has made use of a substantial part of the skill and labour exercised by the original composer.[75] The courts will often determine whether this has been done or not without using a note-for-note comparison of the two works but may

74 **Rees v Melville** [1911–16] MacCC 96 and 168; **Sutton Vane v Famous Players Film Co Ltd; Bolton v British International Pictures Ltd** [1936–45] MacCC 20; **Poznanski v London Film Production Ltd** [1936–45] MacCC 107; **Ahmore v Douglas-Home** [1987] FSR 553.

make a more subjective judgment by the use of the ear;[76] or may hear expert witness evidence to assist the court in recognising the similarities or differences which may exist between the two works in a non-literal sense. The courts have further accepted that the copyright in a musical work may be infringed by copying without the taking of a single note directly from the original.[77]

Thus, the same principles of finding copyright in the non-literal aspects of a copyright work extend across the mainstream of works: literary, dramatic, musical – and artistic. With respect to artistic works, the fact that the plaintiff's work may have been the inspiration for the defendant's work will not of itself make the defendant's work an infringement[78], although if the "feeling and character" of the plaintiff's work has been taken this will be relevant, but not conclusive or decisive, consideration.[79]

Conclusion

In conclusion, the subsistence of copyright in non-literal elements of copyright works has been recognised by the English courts of law in literary, dramatic, artistic and musical works for a very considerable time. As with so many aspects of the application of the law of copyright to computer programming technology, the consensus in the legal and technical communities is that computer programs are so novel and unique in character, they demand the application of the law of copyright in a completely novel fashion. This is not so and is the wrong approach to take for there is a wealth of case law originating within the jurisdiction of the English courts of law which, when properly applied through reasoned argument and a fitting process of analogy, will and does protect the copyright in the "look and feel" of computer programs, together with their interfaces and command structures so long as they are sufficiently original and have had sufficient degrees of taste, expertise and judgment invested in them. Beyond this, unlike the United States, certain aspects of the computer program user interface may be properly regarded as films or artistic works recorded within the medium of the computer program.

---

75 **Francis Day & Hunter Ltd v Bron** [1963] Ch 587.

76 **Austin v Columbia Gramophone Co Ltd** [1917–23] MacCC 398; **Francis Day & Hunter Ltd v Bron** [1963] Ch 587

77 **Austin v Columbia Gramophone Co Ltd.**

78 **Baumann v Fussell** [1978] RPC 485.

79 **Brooks v Religious Tract Society** (1897) 45 WR 476.

Chapter 6

Ownership and the Computer Program

Introduction

This chapter will introduce an examination of the legal notion of the ownership of the copyright in computer programs and further examine how ownership arises. Further, it will consider who is first author with special reference to the use of consultant programmers by software houses and the commissioners of computer software generally, and the development of computer programs by the employees of limited companies including an examination of the generation of trusts with respect to the ownership of commissioned bespoke software. Modern computer programs and computer software products[1] due to their size and complexity are often not the product of one person's literary skill, taste, judgement and endeavour. Rather, a large number of individuals may have contributed to the development of the computer software product. For example, with respect to a CD-ROM based (multimedia) computer games program; the development team may include designers, computer programmers, artists, scriptwriters and actors whose voices and actions are recorded.[2] With respect to a large business-oriented computer software product, the development team may include management executives, business analysts, computer programmers and marketing executives. Finally, in the case of a computer software product produced in the context of a bespoke development by a software house for its customer, the foregoing list may be supplemented by the staff of the customer itself. Thus, it is argued, it is important to be able to apply the law with clarity so that it becomes clear as to "who owns what" in the development cycle.

The vast majority of important business computer programs are developed by employees and thus it is considered to be a proper exercise to evaluate the manner in which copyright is owned between employer and employee. It is also the case that little attention is paid in the computer software industry to

1 Especially multi-media products where a large variety of copyright works might be knitted together to form the whole work.

2 In the multimedia base personal computer games program "Star Trek: The Next Generation – A Final Unity" produced by Spectrum Holobyte in 1995, the credits list six designers, fifteen computer programmers, sixteen artists, five scriptwriters, one script editor and the voices of over forty actors.

the relationship between the person/company that commissions the development of bespoke computer software and the commissioned developer of such software with respect to the ownership of that which is produced. Indeed, an increasing number of commercial software houses are using freelance or contract programmers to supplement their in-house development teams without any consideration as to the title to the copyright works these "non-employees" produce. Thus, an investigation of the status of the legal ownership of such software would be, it is submitted, valuable. As argued above, modern computer programs may contain or be a number of copyright works contemporaneously[3] and indeed, may exist both as computer programming code and as certain classes of preparatory design material.[4] Consequently, this chapter will examine the concepts of authorship and ownership for the species of copyright works susceptible of existing in or as computer programs.

OWNERSHIP AND THE FIRST AUTHOR

Copyright as the property of the author

Copyright is a property right[5] and is in the nature of personal or moveable property.[6] Section 11 of the Copyright, Designs and Patents Act 1988 provides that the "author" of a work is taken to be the first owner of the copyright in the work with some exceptions which are described later in this chapter. The Copyright, Designs and Patents Act 1988 defines the expression "author" as meaning the person who creates the work.[7] However, it is submitted that this definition has not altered the law in relation to the classes of copyright work under consideration in this chapter and that decisions predating the Copyright, Designs and Patents Act 1988 are still good authority.[8]

3 See Chaps 3 and 4 above.

4 See Chap 3, p 37 above.

5 Copyright, Designs and Patents Act 1988, s 1(1).

6 *Ibid*, s 90(1).

7 *Ibid* s 9(1).

8 Authority is sought for this contention from s 172 Copyright, Designs and Patents Act 1988. S 172(2) states that "A provision of this Part which corresponds to a provision of the previous law shall not be construed as departing from the previous law merely because of a change of expression" and s 172(3) provides that "decisions under the previous law may be referred to for the purpose of establishing whether a provision of this Part departs from the previous law, or otherwise for establishing the true construction of this Part."

Under normal circumstances it will not be a difficult task to determine who is the person who is the author of the work in so far as they are the person who created it. Thus it is clear that a person who merely suggests the plot of a novel to a writer or suggests the subject of a picture to an artist, is not the author of the novel or the picture.[9] In the same way the person who merely suggests the idea behind a computer software application or the plot for a computer games program will not be, in the ordinary course of events, the author of the resultant work. Thus in a co-operative forum, where an entrepreneur with an idea brings together computer programmers to build the games program on the idea he suggests, he will not be the author of the work in the absence of some agreement to the contrary. In considering the question of authorship, it should be constantly borne in mind that copyright is capable of subsisting in the expression of an idea but not the idea itself.[10] On the one hand, if an author employs a short-hand writer to take down a story word for word, or a computer program designer employs a short-hand writer to take down word for word his specification for a computer program, it is the computer program designer who is the owner of the copyright in the work and not the short-hand writer. Therefore the author of a literary work is the person who originates the language[11] used, and the author of an artistic work is the person who actually executes the design. Thus if the computer programming code written by programmer A is de-bugged and improved by programmer B, it will be a question of the quality and quantity of the corrections and improvements as to whether the author is programmer A, programmer B or whether they are joint authors of the work.

Composite works

In the case of collective or composite works, such as multimedia encyclopaedias, modern CD-based games programs and other multimedia works, there will be a number (possibly a very large number) of distinct copyrights, being the copyright in the various contributions that are the constituent parts of the work, and a copyright in the entire work. The person who gathers together and arranges or codes the entire work will generally be the author of the whole work which will be a compilation within the meaning of the Copyright, Designs and Patents Act 1988. As to the separate constituent parts of the work, the author will be the persons who wrote

9 **Shepherd v Conquest** (1856) 17 CB 427; **Tate v Thomas.**

10 **Donoghue v Allied Newspapers Ltd** [1938] Ch 106.

11 Whether computer programming language or a natural language.

them, designed them, filmed them etc. In so far as it has been suggested previously in this work that a plot is capable of subsisting within, for example, a computer games program[12], it is important to note that where a person who contributes suggestions for the plot and arrangements of a musical play of which others are the authors of the music and lyrics, that person is not a joint author with them, and will have no right in the resultant copyright work.[13] Again, where persons have provided incidents from their own lives as the basis of articles or stories in which these incidents have been written up by others, the person providing the incidents is not the author of the written matter since he did not take sufficient part in the production of the expressed material which constitutes the original literary work, and which will be the subject-matter of the copyright.[14] In the case of artistic works, other than photographs[15], it will be the person whose hands fix the picture upon the canvas, paper or computer software medium which is the author. Accordingly where one person conceives of an idea for an artistic work but, being unable to draw, employs another under his direction, to execute the idea, the former will not be the author of the work.[16] The Copyright, Designs and Patents Act 1988 contains no special provisions as to the authorship of photographs so that, in relation to photographs made after the commencement of the Copyright, Designs and Patents Act 1988[17], the general principle will apply and the author of a photograph will be the person who creates it.[18]

It is generally assumed that this person will invariably be the photographer, but this obvious inference is one that can become blurred in the context of the application of computer technology. Many "photographs" may now be taken digitally by means of an electronic camera "photographing" the scene onto a type of CD-ROM. This data can then be manipulated by computer software and quite different effects produced from the "original photograph". Thus if the original image is taken by artist A and is manipulated and extended by artist B, it will be a question of the quality and quantity of the changes and improvements as to whether the author of the

12 See Chap 4.

13 **Tate v Thomas.**

14 **Evans v E Hulton and Co Ltd** [1923-28] MacCC 51; **Donoghue v Allied Newspapers Ltd; Housden v Marshall** [1959] 1 WLR 1.

15 Which in the context of computer programs may include the following: flow-charts and diagrams in preparatory design materials; icons in computer games programs and commercial software products; visual backgrounds in computer games programs; the characterisations in computer games programs.

16 **Kenrick and Co v Lawrence and Co; Nottage v Jackson** (1883) 11 QBD 627.

17 1 August 1989.

18 Copyright, Designs and Patents Act 1988, s 9(1).

resulting work, which may no longer be a photograph at all but some other species of artistic work, is artist A, artist B or whether they are joint authors of the work.

Computer-generated works

The ownership of the copyright subsisting in computer-generated works will not be addressed here, but has been addressed elsewhere in this work[19] and it is submitted is best presented in direct relation to the technology currently being applied to the development of computer programs.

Ownership of the Copyright in Works Created by Employees

The importance of the contract of service

Section 11(2) of the Copyright, Designs and Patents Act 1988 provides that where a literary, dramatic, musical or artistic work is made by an employee in the course of his employment, his employer is the first owner of any copyright in the work, subject to any agreement to the contrary. The expressions "employee", "employment" and "employer" all refer to employment under a contract of service or of apprenticeship.[20] Whether a person is engaged under a "contract of service" is a question of law depending upon the facts of the case[21], and the legal distinction between the two concepts of "contract of service" and "contract for services". Apart from the difficulties which the use of these expressions creates in relating to the determination of the ownership of copyright, in many cases there may be other difficulties: for example, questions that arise even where the author was employed under a contract of service relating to whether he was employed to produce the works in question or whether the works were produced in the course of his employment. In every such situation, the

19 See Chap 3.

20 Copyright, Designs and Patents Act 1988, s 178.

21 **O'Kelly v Trusthouse Forte plc** [1984] QB 90; **Lee Ting Sang v Chung Chi-Keung** [1990] 2 AC 374 (PC).

question as to whether there was an agreement to the contrary needs always to be answered. The two expressions "contract of service" and "contract for services" indicate the distinction between, for example, the case of a person engaged to do some specific work under a considerable measure of control, extending not only to the work which he does but also to the way in which he does it, on the one hand, and that of a person engaged in the capacity of an independent contractor on the other.[22] One aspect of the difference between these two concepts is that under a contract of service, the person employed is part of the business, and the work is done as an integral part of it; whereas under a contract for services, the work, although performed for the business, is not integrated into it but is an accessory to it.[23] The fundamental test has been said to be in answering the question of whether the person who performs the services is performing them in business on his own account.

If the answer is an affirmative one, the contract under consideration is a contract for services and not a contract of service.[24] It is considered that the foregoing is a good test and can be easily applied to the computer software industry, even in cases where freelance computer programmers may be engaged on projects by the same software house for extended periods of time, even years. However, it is submitted that no exhaustive list can be compiled of the considerations which are relevant in determining this question. Previously the concept of the exercise of "control" was a very important one but is no longer, it is submitted, the single most important determining factor.[25] Although parties cannot alter the relationship by labelling it in a particular fashion, where the situation is in doubt or ambiguous, so that it can be brought under one type of relationship or the other, it is always open to the parties to agree what the legal relationship between them ought to be.[26]

In order for the copyright in a work produced under a "contract of service" to vest in the employer, it is not sufficient for the work merely to have been written by the employee, but it further must have been made "in the course of his employment". Thus the court will seek to test the extent and ambit of the author's employment. Thus, for example, where a translation was made by a person on the regular staff of a newspaper, but during his spare time, the court held that the copyright remained with the employee and did not vest in the

22 **Stevenson Jordan and Harrison Ltd v Macdonald & Evans** [1952] 1 TLR 101 per Lord Evershed MR.

23 *Ibid* per Denning LJ.

24 **Market Investigations Ltd v Minister of Social Security** [1969] 2 QB 173.

25 *Ibid.*

26 **Massey v Crown Life Insurance Co** [1978] 1 WLR 676.

employer.[27] Again, where an accountant prepared and wrote lectures for delivery to universities and societies dealing with the business in which he was employed, it was held that this was not done in the course of his employment.[28] This was so notwithstanding that the giving of these lectures was useful in a marketing sense to the employer and, on that basis, the accountant's expenses were paid for by the employer. On the other hand, where the work is done outside office hours, but is the type of work which the employee might be expected to undertake for the employer and the results of such work might be used in competition to the employer, it is thought that the copyright in the new work would vest in the author but he would hold the copyright in a constructive trust for the employer or that the employee would be estopped, because of a breach of his fiduciary duty to his employer, from asserting that the work was not produced in the course of employment.[29] As identified above, section 11(2) of the Copyright, Designs and Patents Act 1988 provides that these provisions with respect to employment are always subject to an agreement to the contrary. Such an agreement may be express, oral, written or implied from the conduct of the parties or the circumstances of the case.[30]

Sound recordings and films

With respect to the making of sound recordings which often form part of multimedia works, the general rule is that the person who creates the work is the "author" of it. This is taken to mean the person by whom the arrangements necessary for the making of the recording are undertaken.[31] In relation to films, the Copyright, Designs and Patents Act 1988 makes almost identical provision for their authorship. The author of a film is the person by whom the arrangements necessary for the making of the film are undertaken.[32] This will normally be the producer of the film and not, for

27 **Byrne v Statist Co** [1914] 1 KB 622.

28 **Stevenson Jordan & Harrison Ltd v Macdonald & Evans.**

29 **Missing Link Software v Magee** [1989] FSR 361. Although this case deals with the software industry (in so far as it arose from the employees of a software house writing software competing with their employer's in their own time and on their own equipment) it deals with an application for interlocutory relief only and is therefore of little value save to be, it is submitted, an illustration of how difficult it can be for a court to make clear findings with respect to the ambit of an employee's employment even in circumstances where the computer programming department's manager is writing computer programs in his spare time.

30 **Massine v De Basil** [1936–45] MacCC 223; **Christopher Bede Studios Ltd v United Portraits Ltd** [1958] NZLR 250.

31 Copyright, Designs and Patents Act 1988, s 9(2)(a)

32 *Ibid.*

example, the camera operator.[33] However, this rule may have less applicability where computer technology is being used to generate the film. In other words where the computer graphics artist is operating computer software, making wire-frame drawings within the medium of computer programming files and thereby animating them. He is not merely pointing an optical recording device (camera) at a subject but is injecting a far higher level of taste, judgement and skill into the exercise. This is, unfortunately, yet another lacuna in the law of copyright in the context of computer software technology which seems impossible to address from a logical or empirical standpoint.

Equitable Ownership

Since copyright is a property right[34] in the nature of personal or moveable property;[35] it is possible for a person to have an equitable interest in a copyright work without being the legal owner. As it is a matter of equity, there are no set rules for determining the equitable ownership of a copyright work and, therefore, it is submitted that the appropriate course of action is to consider some of the leading cases on this subject where an equitable interest has been held to subsist. It seems that an equitable interest may be created, in the sense of holding the copyright in trust for another, where, for example, drawings are prepared by the managing director of a company to whom the general provisions of the Copyright Acts do not apply.

Thus, in *Antocks Lairn Ltd v I Bloohn Ltd*[36] it was held that the managing director would hold the drawings he made in trust for his company and would have to assign the copyright in them to the company if and when he was called upon to do so. In a case under the Copyright Act 1956, it was held that the draughtsman of a drawing who was a contractor and had been paid to make the drawings for the plaintiffs, claimed no ownership in them but in law owned the copyright in them; could be called upon to assign the copyright in the drawings to the plaintiffs on the ground that the plaintiffs were the owners of the equity in the copyright.[37] In *John Richardson Computers Ltd v Flanders and Chemtec Ltd*, Ferris J held, *inter alia*, with respect to the

33 **Adventure Film Productions Ltd v Tulley** *The Times* 14 Oct 1982.

34 Copyright, Designs and Patents Act 1988, s 1(1)

35 *Ibid*, s 90(1).

36 [1971] FSR 490. It is submitted that it is important to distinguish this case from circumstances where works are made by a director of a company in the course of his employment under a contract of service; for in these circumstances (in the absence of an agreement to the contrary) the copyright works will belong to the company.

37 **Merchant Adventurers Ltd v M Grew and Co Ltd** [1973] RPC 1.

copyright arising in computer programs written by an independent contractor:

> "...where the author of a work creates that work in the course of his engagement as an independent contractor to another, any copyright in that work belongs in law to the author and not to the party to whom he engaged himself to supply services. But in appropriate circumstances it may appear that the author is to be regarded as holding the copyright in trust for the person to whom he engaged himself. Thus in Massine v. De Basil a question was raised as to the ownership of the copyright in a ballet, for which the plaintiff, while working for the defendant, had contributed the choreography. It was held that he did so while employed under a contract of employment which disposed of the issue. But the Court of Appeal went on to say:[38]
> 'But even if the plaintiff could rightly be regarded as an independent contractor the Court was of the opinion that it ought to be implied as a term of the agreement that any work done by the plaintiff would be done on the basis that the defendant who had paid for the work should be entitled to such rights as might arise from that payment, and that he should not be deprived of the benefit of it merely on the ground that the person whom he paid was an independent contractor. It was important, they said, to remember that the subject of the copyright which was claimed was the ballet as a whole. The defendant had paid the money under the agreement for the supplying to his ballet of a part which was necessary for its completeness, and unless he was entitled to the copyright in that part of the ballet he would not be getting that benefit from the contract which must have been the intention of the parties. It was a necessary implication from all the facts of the case that the right to the choreography and the libretto in those cases where the plaintiff was responsible for them should in equity be the property of the defendant and that he should be entitled to have the rights assigned to him.'"[39]

In this respect, *John Richardson Computers Ltd v Flanders and Chemtec Ltd* is an important case. As indicated above, a great many software houses employ independent contractors to supplement their in-house development team. Consequently it seems clear that in circumstances where, for example, the software house has paid money under an agreement to the independent contractor for supplying computer code for the software house's computer software product which is necessary for its completeness, it is highly likely that the software house will be the owner in equity of the copyright in the work produced and should be entitled to have the rights assigned to them. This rationale will also apply in other circumstances where computer software is commissioned from a third party. Such a rationale may have far-reaching implications in an industry where a great many software houses earn their living by designing and writing bespoke applications for end-users

38 [1936–45] MacCC 223 at 226.
39 At 516.

in circumstances where the commissioning agreement is silent as to ownership.

Joint Authorship and Ownership

Development teams and joint authorship

Due to the size and complexity of modern computer programs it is likely, it is proposed, that works of joint authorship will arise. This issue is not only directed to a number of individuals joining together to develop a work, but in recent times, a trend has been established where companies join together to produce a computer software application. Two or more software houses may be involved or, indeed, two or more development teams will be involved, each employed by different employers where one might be the in-house development team of the end-user itself. It will certainly not always be the case that the end-user will wish to own the whole copyright outright since the software house might certainly wish to maintain their rights in the code so that it can be used for future projects and further, it is just as likely that no express written agreement is reached on the subject of ownership at all. For the purposes of the Copyright, Designs and Patents Act 1988, a work of joint authorship means "a work produced by the collaboration of two or more authors in which the contribution of each author is not distinct from that of the other author or authors".[40] The definition in the Copyright Act 1956 was the same except that the word "separate" was used in place of the word "distinct"[41] and it is consequently submitted that this change in wording has not effected any change in the law on this point.[42]

Joint tenants and tenancies in common

Co-authors will usually hold the copyright as joint tenants[43], although the circumstances of a particular case might indicate otherwise. In the absence of

40 S 10(1).
41 S 11(3).
42 This is a necessary exercise in order to test the validity of cases arising under the Copyright Act 1956 when considering the effect of the Copyright, Designs and Patents Act 1988.
43 **Lauri v Renad** [1892] 3 Ch 402.

an agreement to the contrary the shares in a tenancy in common will usually be equal[44] but, again, the special circumstances of a case may indicate otherwise; as where a publishing agreement provides for payment of differing proportions of royalties to the joint authors.[45] Upon the death of one joint tenant his interest in the copyright will pass to his co-owners by survivorship.[46] Upon the death of one tenant in common his interest in the copyright passes to his personal representatives as part of his estate.

The rights of joint authors

One of several owners of a copyright work cannot grant a licence to publish it which will be binding upon the others[47], nor can one of several owners of copyright grant to a third party an exclusive licence within the meaning of the Copyright, Designs and Patents Act 1988 since he cannot prevent the other owners from doing any of the acts restricted by copyright.[48] However, one of the joint owners can sue in respect of an infringement of the jointly owned copyright and obtain an injunction and his share of the damages without joining the other owners as co-plaintiffs[49], and one of several owners can obtain an injunction to restrain a joint owner from publishing the joint work without his consent.[50]

Qualifying provisions for joint works

If the subsistence of copyright in a work depends upon the authors satisfying the qualifying provisions of the Copyright, Designs and Patents Act 1988, then if any one of the authors satisfies those requirements the work will qualify for copyright protection.[51] However, where a work of joint authorship qualifies for protection under this provision, only those authors who satisfy such requirements are to be taken into account in deciding who is the first owner of the copyright and determining the duration of copyright. Under the

44 **Acorn Computers Ltd v MCS Microcomputer Systems Pty Ltd** (1985) 57 ALR 389; **Redwood Music Ltd v B Feldman and Co Ltd** [1979] RPC 1.

45 **Prior v Landsdowne Press Pty Ltd** [1977] RPC 511.

46 **Mail Newspapers plc v Express Newspapers plc** [1987] FSR 90.

47 Copyright, Designs and Patents Act 1988, s 173(2).

48 **Mail Newspapers plc v Express Newspapers plc** [1987] FSR 90.

49 **Lauri v Renad; Prior v Landsdowne Press Pty Ltd; Acorn Computers Ltd v MCS Microcomputer Systems Pty Ltd; Waterlow Publishers Ltd v Rose** [1995] FSR 207.

50 **Cescinsky v George Routledge & Sons Ltd** [1916] 2 KB 325.

51 Copyright, Designs and Patents Act 1988, s 154(3).

Copyright, Designs and Patents Act 1988, where copyright subsists only because one or more of the joint authors satisfy the qualifying provisions of the Copyright, Designs and Patents Act 1988, then only those authors are to be taken into account in determining the duration of copyright.[52] Care will therefore have to be taken by the computer software developing community when entering into agreements across a number of countries for the production of joint works that these provisions of the Copyright, Designs and Patents Act 1988 are carefully observed.

OWNERSHIP OF INFRINGING WORKS

There is nothing, either in the general tenets of the law of copyright or in the Copyright, Designs and Patents Act 1988 which prohibits the subsistence of copyright in a work which is an infringement of a pre-existing work, which is not a slavish copy, but involved in its creation the expenditure of skill, judgment and effort.[53] In *Redwood Music Ltd v Chappell and Co Ltd*[54] Goff J approved *Wood v Boosey*[55] and firmly rejected the argument that copyright could not subsist under the Copyright Act 1956 in an infringing work. *Redwood Music Ltd v Chappell and Company Ltd* was cited with approval in *ZYX Music GmbH v Chris King* by Lightman J where he said, going on to address whether the copyright in an infringing work is unenforceable:

> "It is established that the fact that the plaintiff's work, even if it infringes the copyright in another work, may nonetheless enjoy copyright (see Redwood Music Limited v. Chappell & Co. Limited [1982] R.P.C. 109 at 120); and the fact that the plaintiff's work does so infringe does not constitute a defence to proceedings by the plaintiff (see British Leyland Motor Corporation v. Armstrong Patents Co Limited [1982] F.S.R. 481 at 502). But the defendants contend that the fact that the plaintiff's work does infringe the copyright in another work renders the plaintiff's copyright unenforceable or at least unenforceable until the plaintiff has cured the infringement. The defendants for this submission pray in aid of section 171(3) of the Act [the Copyright, Designs and Patents Act 1988] which provides as follows:
> 'Nothing in this part affects any rule of law preventing or restricting the enforcement of copyrights on grounds of public interest or otherwise.'
> This issue does not appear to have been judicially determined..."[56]

---

52 *Ibid.*

53 **University of London Press Ltd v University Tutorial Press Ltd** at 608.

54 [1982] RPC 109.

55 (1866) LR 2 QB 340; (1867) LR 3 QB 223.

56 At 576.

After considering some academic writing on this matter, Lightman J took the view that the existence of the infringement of the copyright of a third party is not sufficient to bring this jurisdiction of the court into play.[57] Overall therefore, a new and fresh copyright may arise in an infringing copyright and the courts may be reluctant to exercise their discretion as a matter of public policy to restrain the full exercise of the rights in such copyright. Due to the high degree of cross-fertilisation that is conducted by employed computer programmers as they move from employer to employer, the likelihood of infringing works containing a high degree of new taste, judgment and expertise is high. This line of cases, therefore, has an obvious and direct applicability to the computer software industry.

57 At 577.

Chapter 7

Transmission of Title and Licensing

Introduction

This chapter will evaluate the mechanisms in which the copyright itself in a work is transmitted from one party to another and will further consider the mechanisms by which rights subsisting under a copyright are transmitted. Computer programs, programming technologies and computer software products are acquired and disposed of in the computer software industry frequently as software houses purchase each other and each other's products. This often takes place when software house A wishes to supplement its portfolio of computer software products and therefore acquires the copyright in products of software house B. Software houses generally produce revenue through licensing the use of their computer software products to end-users and accordingly it is contended that an examination of the legal nature of licensing and the restraints placed upon licensing strategies by the European Union will be pertinent.

Transmission of Title – Assignment

Distinguishing between the work and its medium

The ownership of the copyright in a work is distinct from the ownership of the physical material in which the copyright work is fixed. The transfer of title to the physical material does not necessarily transfer the title to the copyright, any more than the assignment of the copyright necessarily transfers the title to the physical material. Thus ownership of the magnetic or optical medium in which a computer program is recorded does not necessarily connote ownership of the copyright in the computer program itself. The main provisions of the Copyright, Designs and Patents Act 1988 that deal with the transfer of title are contained in sections 90 and

91.[1] By section 90(3) of the Copyright, Designs and Patents Act 1988 it is provided that an assignment of copyright is not effective unless it is in writing and signed by or on behalf of the assignor. The combined effect of section 90 of the Copyright, Designs and Patents Act 1988 and section 53(1)(c) of the Law of Property Act 1925 is that any assignment of copyright, whether it is of a legal or equitable interest[2], must be in writing.[3] Further, if the assignment is signed on behalf of the assignor, the person actually signing must have the authority of the assignor.[4] It should be borne in mind, having regard to the comparative youth of many computer programmers, that infants[5] can own and dispose of the copyright in computer programs (and, of course, copyright generally) in the same way as adults, but subject to the usual rules concerning the making of contracts by infants.[6]

Assignment in writing

The expression "writing" includes any form of notation or code, whether by hand or otherwise and regardless of the method by which, or medium in, or on which, it is recorded.[7] In the case of a body corporate the requirement that the assignment should be signed by or on behalf of the assignor is satisfied by the affixing of the company seal.[8] Section 90(2) of the Copyright, Designs and Patents Act 1988 deals with what is known as a "partial assignment". An assignment or any other transmission of rights subsisting under copyright may be limited so as to apply to one or more, but not all, of the things that the copyright owner has the exclusive right to do; and to part, but not the whole, of the period for which copyright is to subsist.[9] It is submitted that it is therefore of the utmost importance when effecting an assignment to determine, in any given situation, what person is, at the relevant time, the owner of the particular right comprised in the copyright of a certain work.[10] Consequently, where different persons are the owners of different

1 In the Copyright Act 1956, the main provisions addressing the transmission of title were to be found in ss 36 and 37 and did not differ in substance from the provisions now held in the Copyright, Designs and Patents Act 1988.

2 See Chap 6 for a discussion of the nature of equitable interest in computer programs.

3 **Performing Right Society Ltd v London Theatre of Varieties Ltd** [1924] AC 1; **Roban Jig and Tool Co Ltd v Taylor** [1979] FSR 130; **Wah Sang Industrial Co v Takmay Industrial Co Ltd** [1980] FSR 303 (CA of Hong Kong).

4 **Murray v King** [1986] FSR 116 (Federal Court of Australia).

5 See Family Law Reform Act 1969.

6 **Chaplin v Leslie Frewin (Publishers) Ltd** [1966] Ch 71.

7 Copyright, Designs and Patents Act 1988, s 178.

8 *Ibid*, s 176(1).

9 *Ibid*, s 173(1).

10 **J Albert & Sons Pty Ltd v Fletcher Construction Co Ltd** [1976] RPC 615 (SC of New Zealand).

aspects of copyright under partial assignments, the "copyright owner" is taken to be the person who is entitled to the aspect of copyright relevant for the purposes of the action or matter arising under the Copyright, Designs and Patents Act 1988.[11]

The Copyright, Designs and Patents Act 1988 does not state that an assignment of copyright needs to be in any particular or special form, other than it needs to be in writing[12], and signed by or on behalf of the assignor. An agreement may constitute an assignment of copyright even though the expression "copyright" is not employed in the drafting;[13] for example an effective assignment of copyright would occur if the drafting employed used the expression "the assets of the business" if the copyright formed part of those assets. In every case the scope and effect of an assignment of copyright depends upon the true construction of the document or documents which have been signed. Once the assignment has been made, the assignor may, like any other person, be restrained by the assignee from reproducing or authorising others to reproduce the work[14] except to the extent that is permitted by section 64 of the Copyright, Designs and Patents Act 1988.[15]

Assignment of the copyright – not style employed

It may be a difficult task to prove infringement by an author of his own work which he has assigned, because mere similarity is not, in itself, an infringement of copyright. It is generally accepted that such similarity is natural and does not raise any necessary inference of the improper use of previous works.[16] An artist who assigns the copyright in one of his works does not thereby assign

11 S 173(1).

12 S 178.

13 **Murray v King.**

14 **Rooney v Kelly** 14 Ir Com Law Rep. 158; **Colburn v Simms** (1843) 2 Ha 543; **The Educational Co of Ireland Ltd v Fallon Brothers Ltd** [1919] 1 IR 62.

15 The Copyright, Designs and Patents Act 1988 provides in s 64 that where the author of an artistic work is not the copyright owner, he does not infringe the copyright by copying the work in making another artistic work, provided that he does not repeat or imitate the main design of the earlier work. It should be borne in mind, it is submitted, that flow-diagrams are obviously artistic works and are a critical work in the development of a computer program since they represent the actions, reactions and logical flow of the computer program – in other words, the flow diagram can effectively be used to map the high-level functionality of a computer program. This right of an assignor with respect to artistic works is therefore, it is argued, an important and interesting one in the context of computer programming technology, especially when CASE tools are often driven by the input of flow-diagrams.

16 However, this assertion received little attention in **Francis Day and Hunter Ltd v Bron** nor in **Industrial Furnaces Ltd v Reaves** [1970] RPC 605 at 624.

his style or method of portraying similar subjects.[17] This rule is also of considerable interest to the computer programming community since it goes to the issue of style and methods of presentation in artistic works which are often included in computer software products, both commercial and entertainment. The computer programmer or computer graphics artist who might have assigned the copyright in interface icons in a commercial computer program or in characterisations in a games program can still proceed with their own particular style and continue to employ their own methodologies in treating similar subjects in the artistic works that they produce subsequent to previous assignments. Where an author has created a second work by using material from an earlier work, questions may arise as to whether there are separate copyrights capable of being vested by assignment in different persons. It is submitted that, if the derivative work has been produced by employing sufficient skill and labour it will be constituted as a new original work and thus the copyright in the first work and the copyright in the derivative work are capable of being separately assigned.[18]

Assignment of future copyright

The Copyright, Designs and Patents Act 1988 contains provisions under which an agreement may be made before a work is created which will have the effect of vesting the copyright initially in the person with whom the agreement is made as soon as the work is created.[19] The provisions in the Copyright, Designs and Patents Act 1988 are similar in effect to those contained in section 37 of the Copyright Act 1956. The provisions only deal with assignments of future copyright by a written agreement and leave oral assignments of copyright to be dealt with by the equitable jurisdiction of the courts of law.[20] Section 91(2) of the Copyright, Designs and Patents Act 1988 defines the expression "future copyright" as meaning copyright which will or may come into existence in respect of any future work or class of works or on the occurrence of a future event; and further provides that the expression "prospective owner" is to be construed accordingly and includes a person who is prospectively entitled to copyright by virtue of the type of agreement mentioned in section 91(1). The Copyright, Designs and Patents Act 1988 then provides in section 91(1), that where, by an agreement made

17 **Preston v Raphael Tuck etc Ltd** [1926] Ch 667.
18 **Redwood Music Ltd v Chappell & Co Ltd.**
19 S 91.
20 **Wah Sang Industrial Co v Takmay Industrial Co Ltd.**

in relation to any future copyright, and signed by or on behalf of the prospective owner of copyright, the prospective owner purports to assign the future copyright (wholly or partially) to another person, then if, on the copyright coming into existence, the assignee or another person claiming under him would be entitled as against all other persons to require the copyright to be vested in him, the copyright then vests automatically in the assignee or his successors in title by virtue of this subsection.

Thus section 91 of the Copyright, Designs and Patents Act 1988 contemplates not only a simple and single agreement between the author and one individual or company, as a result of which the copyright, when it comes into existence, will vest in that individual or company; but also a chain of assignments put into place before the copyright itself comes into existence. In the latter case, the copyright, when it comes into existence, will vest in the person or persons who, as a result of such chain of assignments, will then be the person or persons entitled to it.[21] It is important to note for software houses who may operate multinationally, that these provisions of the Copyright, Designs and Patents Act 1988 do not apply to works where the copyright arises in countries outside the United Kingdom; so that a form of confirmatory assignment made after the foreign copyright comes into existence may, it is submitted, be necessary and, at least, desirable.

Licences

Licences in general and non-exclusive licences

Licences are referred to in various sections of the Copyright, Designs and Patents Act 1988. Section 16(2) of the Copyright, Designs and Patents Act 1988 provides that copyright is infringed by a person who without the licence of the copyright owner, does or authorises another to do any of the acts restricted by such copyright. Accordingly it can be seen that a licence is a permission to do those acts or authorise those acts which otherwise would be an infringement of copyright.[22] Section 90(4) of the Copyright, Designs and Patents Act 1988 provides that a licence granted by the copyright owner is binding on every successor in title to his interest in the copyright, except a

21 **Chaplin v Leslie Frewin (Publishers) Ltd.** This result also flows from a construction of s 91(2) of the Copyright, Designs and Patents Act 1988 which defines "prospective owner" as including a person who is prospectively entitled to copyright by virtue of the type of agreement referred to in s 91(1).

22 See especially the dicta of Tindal CJ in **Muskett v Hill** (1840) 5 Bing NC 694.

purchaser in good faith for valuable consideration and without notice (actual or constructive)[23] of the licence, or a person deriving title from such a purchaser. It is little understood in the software industry that the continuance of a licence is not dependant on the continuing capacity of the grantor nor dependant upon the grantor of the licence retaining the copyright. Rather, the continuance of the licence is entirely dependant on the capacity of the grantor at the time of the granting of the licence only. In much the same way with respect to future copyrights, section 91(3) of the Copyright, Designs and Patents Act 1988 provides that a licence granted by a prospective owner of copyright is also binding on every successor in title to his interest (or, in such circumstances, his prospective interest) in the right, except a purchaser in good faith for valuable consideration and without notice (actual or constructive) of the licence or a person deriving title from such a purchaser. The licensee under a copyright, or under a prospective copyright, therefore, to the extent of the licence, can do acts restricted by the copyright.

Licences – oral, implied

Except in connection with exclusive licences, there is no requirement that a licence should be in writing. It can, therefore, be either oral, or implied from conduct, implied as a term of an agreement, or implied from trade practice or custom.[24] A licence will not be implied merely because it would be reasonable between the parties: it is submitted that the test is whether it is necessary to give effect to the intention of the parties and to give business efficacy to their relationship;[25] and the test overall of an implied licence is an objective one.[26] A licence which is no more than a consent cannot confer any interest in the right;[27] for if it did, nothing would remain in the licensor out of which to grant subsequent licences.[28]

A licence may be personal to the licensee, unless the circumstances of the granting of the licence and the terms of the licence justify the conclusion that it was intended to be assignable. A licence is not assignable where it appears that the licence was granted to the licensee because of the licensee's personal reputation.[29] A licence, if coupled with an interest in the right, would seem to

23 Law of Property Act 1925, s 199.

24 **Express Newspapers plc v News (UK) Ltd** [1990] FSR at 368.

25 **Shell UK Ltd v Lostock Garage Ltd** [1976] 1 WLR 1187 at 1197 and 1200; **Sport International Bossum BV v Hi-Tec Sports Ltd** [1988] RPC 329.

26 **Redwood Music Ltd v Chappell & Co Ltd** at 128.

27 **Neilson v Horniman** [1905–10] MacCC 234.

28 **Rundell v Murray** (1821) Jac 311; **Warne v Routledge** (1874) LR 18 Eq 497; **Chaplin v Leslie Frewin (Publishers) Ltd.**

29 **Dorling v Honnor Marine Ltd** [1964] Ch 560 at 568.

be *prima facie* irrevocable;[30] but a revocable licence may be revoked in accordance with its express terms, or, in the absence of such express terms, on reasonable notice. This notice must be properly and explicitly directed to the revocation of the licence and not, for example, propose terms for its continuance.[31] In circumstances where the licensor purports to revoke a revocable licence, but gives no or insufficient notice of such revocation, the licensee cannot ignore the revocation totally and treat the licence as if it was continuing to subsist. On the other hand, the licensee in such circumstances, cannot be treated as a wrongdoer or an infringer for continuing to do what the licence permitted him so to do until the expiry of the period which would have constituted a proper or a reasonable notice.[32]

The Copyright, Designs and Patents Act 1988 and licences granted for the use of computer programs[33]

Back-up copies

Prior to 1 January 1993[34] unless a computer software licence expressly granted the right to the end-user to make a back-up copy of the licensed software then the making of such copy could have been an infringement of copyright unless an argument, such as implied licence or an acquiescence could be raised. Of course, many software licences often did expressly permit the making of back-up copies.

However, section 50A of the Copyright, Designs and Patents Act 1988 provides that lawful users (in other words, licensees) of a copy of software are allowed to make back-up copies even if not expressly permitted by the contract if it is "necessary for him to have for the purposes of his lawful use". The owners of the copyright in computer software products may be able to argue that they have such good and immediate facilities for providing licensees with copies in the event of a disaster and that there is therefore no necessity for the licensee to be entitled to make a back-up copy. In those circumstances the right to make a back-up copy would not apply. But the

30 **Williams v Feldman** [1911–16] MacCC 98; **Hart v Hayman etc. Ltd** [1911–16] MacCC 301; **Hurst v Picture Theatres Ltd** [1915] 1 KB 1; **British Actors Film Co Ltd v Glover** [1918] 1 KB 299; **Chaplin v Leslie Frewin (Publishers) Ltd.**

31 **Redwood Music Ltd v Chappell & Co Ltd.**

32 **Martin-Baker Aircraft Co Ltd v Canadian Flight Equipment Ltd** [1955] 2 QB 556; **Dorling v Honnor Marine Ltd** at 567.

33 See Chap 2 with respect to the changes in the Copyright, Designs and Patents Act 1988 wrought by The Copyright (Computer Programs) Regulations 1992.

34 The commencement date for the Copyright (Computer Programs) Regulations 1992.

software community has always been at ease with the notion of reasonable numbers of back-up copies being made by a licensed end-user. There is nothing in the Copyright, Designs and Patents Act 1988 that restricts the right of a licensor to require contractually, for example, that the back-up copies should be kept in a safe or secure place and marked with the licensor's proprietary notices. Indeed, many software houses who produce complex applications which are used in "mission critical" areas of a business, seek to encourage their licensees to make back-ups since they will seek to avoid liability for the large damages and economic loss that may occur if data is lost due to errors in the licensor's computer programs. A lawful user is one that has the right to use the program. In addition, any condition in the licence which prohibits the making of a copy for back-up purposes will be void where it is necessary for the licensee to have such back-up copies.

Reverse engineering – decompilation

By section 50B of the Copyright, Designs and Patents Act 1988 it is not an infringement of copyright for a lawful user of a copy of a computer program, expressed in a low-level language, to convert it into a version expressed in a higher level language or, when so converting it, to copy it. This has always been problematic for the software industry, since the source code to computer programs reveals the methodologies adopted by the computer program developer. These methodologies themselves may constitute no more than mere ideas on how to address or solve a problem and will therefore be unprotected by the law of copyright – only the manner in which an idea or approach is expressed will be protected. Nevertheless the software house may have invested considerable sums of money in inventing or evaluating the best approach to employ which, when discovered by its competitors, will be devalued and the competitive edge thus developed may be lost. There can seem little argument that this is not a valid concern. It is important to note that it is only lawful users of a computer program who can undertake this decompiling; in other words one must be a licensed user beforehand. The second point is that there are strict conditions which must be met. These are as follows:

(i) It must be necessary to decompile the program to obtain the information necessary to create an independent program which can be operated with the program decompiled or with another program. This is known as the "permitted objective". Therefore there is no right to decompile simply to create an independent program. That

program must be one which operates with the decompiled program or another program.

(ii) The information obtained from the decompiling should be used for no purpose other than the permitted objective.

There will be no right to decompile where any of the following four conditions apply:

(i) Where the user has readily available to him the information necessary to achieve the permitted objective. It is submitted that there is much scope for argument over what the expression "readily available" means. It may mean that the user must have the information to hand or from public sources or it may be sufficient that the licensor could supply the information. What time-scale would ensure ready availability and whether a fee can be charged is utterly unclear and this is a most unsatisfactory situation since it is decompiled code, usually source code therefore, which reveals the innermost secrets of a computer program's functionality and decompilation is therefore the very last activity that a software house would wish end-users to be able to undertake lawfully and is a direct attack on the software house's investment in the product.

(ii) The user can only decompile where he confines his acts to those which are necessary to achieve the permitted objective. If he goes further in decompiling, whether out of intellectual curiosity or for the purposes of developing a separate program for his own business uses, then there will be no right to decompile.

(iii) Where the information which is obtained is given to a third party where that is not necessary to achieve the permitted objective.

(iv) The user should not use the information to create a program which is substantially similar in its expression to the program decompiled. This would appear to be the case even if that substantially similar program is to be operated with the program decompiled. It is contended that it should be noted that it should not be substantially similar in its "expression" and this is consistent with copyright protecting the expression of ideas rather than the ideas themselves. Nor must the information be used to do any act restricted by copyright. For example, the information could not be used to import infringing copies.

Any condition in the contract which prohibits any of the activities of decompilation which are allowed will be void. There can be no doubt that the law has been changed to give greater rights to decompilers, but, on the other hand, there is no licence generally to decompile. Decompilation is only allowed, *prima facie*, in the very restrictive circumstances set out for the permitted objective.

It is argued that policing this provision will be extremely difficult and that infringers could easily raise a decompilation defence, arguing that they were pursuing the permitted objective at the relevant time; nor is the question really answered as to why the licensee should have the right to decompile in the first place. If a software house is prepared to develop a proprietary method for its computer software products to achieve a high degree of interoperability, the question is begged as to why a mere licensee should have the right to unravel the fabric of the copyright work so that he can interface a program of his own design with the software house's products. This seems to be another example where the law perceives a lack of value in the literary worth of computer programs; for such provisions are entirely unique to computer programs and go far beyond, say, the common law right to repair.

Adaptation

Under the provisions of section 50C of the Copyright, Designs and Patents Act 1988 it is not an infringement of copyright for a lawful user to copy or adapt the program where that is necessary for his lawful use and also it is not prohibited under any term of his licence agreement. Therefore, it is submitted that subject to the decompilation right and the right to make back-up copies, a licence agreement can prohibit copying and adaptation.

Error correction

In particular it is specified in section 50C(2) of the Copyright, Designs and Patents Act 1988 that it may be necessary for the lawful use of a program for the licensee to copy or adapt it for the purpose of correcting errors. Many licensors will not permit error correction by licensees and licensors can continue to prohibit that; and the right to copy and adapt where necessary for lawful use, in the absence of prohibition, does not apply to the right to make a back-up copy and to decompile.

Devices or means to observe functionality

There is also provision in section 296A of the Copyright, Designs and Patents Act 1988 that conditions in a licence will be void when they prohibit or restrict the making of back-up copies and decompilation as discussed above, but also where they restrict the use of any device or means to observe, study or test the functioning of the program in order to understand the ideas and principles which underlie any element of the program. This right is far too wide, for it negatives to some degree the copyright owner's right to keep his novel and, perhaps, unique ideas a secret since they are the source of his competitive advantage. Of course it can be said that it is not possible to stop an end-user watching a computer program work and gain some insight into it or derive ideas from it. But it seems inconsistent with the general tenets of copyright that a licensee, without the express authorisation of the copyright owner, is permitted to apply a device or some other means (which would include a software tool) to the computer program in order to study the principles underlying it. It is certainly entirely unclear whether copying the computer program code is to be permitted when studying the principles embodied in or underlying it. There seems a very fine line indeed between observing the principles underlying a computer program and observing the secret methodologies expressed within it so as to produce a competitive product. These provisions therefore seem open to considerable abuse.

Exclusive licences

The expression "exclusive licence" is defined by section 92(1) of the Copyright, Designs and Patents Act 1988 as a licence made in writing, signed by or on behalf of the copyright owner authorising the licensee to the exclusion of all others[35] to exercise a right which otherwise would be excisable exclusively by the copyright owner. The licensee under an exclusive licence has the same rights as against a successor in title, who is bound by the licence as he has against the person granting the licence itself.[36] The main operative part of section 101(1) of the Copyright, Designs and Patents Act 1988 provides that the exclusive licensee has, except against the copyright owner, the same rights and remedies in respect of matters occurring after the grant of the licence as if the licence had been an assignment. Such rights and remedies are concurrent with the rights and remedies of the copyright owner, and references to the copyright owner are to be construed accordingly.[37] The rights of the exclusive licensee against the owner of the copyright in the licensed work lie in contract only and may, of course, be defeated by a purchaser for value of the copyright without actual or constructive notice.[38] It is further provided in the Copyright, Designs and Patents Act 1988 specifically with respect to exclusive licences that, where an action for

35 Which, for the avoidance of doubt, includes the copyright owner.
36 Copyright, Designs and Patents Act 1988, s 92(2).
37 *Ibid*, s 101(2).
38 *Ibid*, s 90(4).

infringement of copyright brought by the copyright owner or an exclusive licensee relates to an infringement in respect of which they may have concurrent rights of action, the copyright owner or, as the case may be, the exclusive licensee may not, without the leave of the court, proceed with the action unless the other is joined as a plaintiff or added as a defendant.[39] The importance of this particular provision lies in the fact that, unlike a non-exclusive licensee, the exclusive licensee may proceed on a matter of infringement in the absence of the owner of the copyright with the leave of the court. The Copyright, Designs and Patents Act 1988 further provides in this respect that, the copyright owner or exclusive licensee who is added as a defendant, is not liable for any costs in the action, unless he takes part in the proceedings;[40] and it is further provided that these provisions do not affect the granting of interlocutory relief on an application by a copyright owner or exclusive licensee alone.[41]

The principle of non-derogation from grant

It will be recalled that in the case of the licensees of computer programs, section 50C(2) of the Copyright, Designs and Patents Act 1988 provides that it may be necessary for lawful use of a program for a licensee to copy or adapt it for the purpose of correcting errors. Many licensors will not permit error correction by licensees as they often derive revenue from supplying error correction and support services; and licensors can continue to prohibit that; and the right to copy and adapt where necessary for lawful use, in the absence of prohibition, does not apply to the right to make a back-up copy and to decompile. But this does not seem to address a licensee's common law right to repair that was argued to exist before the decision of the House of Lords in *British Leyland Motor Corp Ltd v Armstrong Patents Company Ltd*.[42] Before *British Leyland Motor Corp Ltd v Armstrong Patents Co Ltd* there were a number of decisions to the effect that a purchaser of an article was entitled, by virtue of an implied licence from the vendor, to reproduce a copyright work if this was done in the course of the repair of the article. Such decisions were reached by analogy with patent cases where the form of the letters patent[43] forced the courts to imply some licence to enable the purchaser of a patented article to use and repair it. The licence in such cases extends no

39 *Ibid*, s 102(1).
40 *Ibid*, s 102(2).
41 *Ibid*, s 102(3).
42 [1986] AC 577.
43 "To make, use, exercise and vend" the invention.

further than enabling the purchaser to prolong the life of the article by repair but not to make a new article under the cover of repair;[44] and as such it could be argued that these situations are distinguishable because computer programs when executing do not, as a general rule, suffer from "wear and tear" and thereby need "repairing". They, in fact, contain design defects (bugs) which end-users would prefer not to be there. The cases with respect to the "right to repair" in relation to copyright established that such an implied licence extended to enable the purchaser to make spare parts himself and to have such parts made for him[45], and probably to have two or more made at the same time against future breakdowns of the article.[46] As indicated above, the applicability of these cases to computer program technology is not obvious, but nevertheless it is asserted that they form an important body of copyright law which ought not to be ignored since, it is contended, it is in the nature of computer programming technology that, as it continues to advance, more areas of copyright law which seem only to apply to out-dated species of copyright works eventually seem perfectly able to apply properly to computer program technology.

The use by the courts of an implied licence theory became seen to be increasingly artificial and gave rise to a number of technical difficulties, especially where there was no direct contract between the manufacturer of the original article and its owner of the spare-part manufacturer. The principle was largely abandoned by the House of Lords in *British Leyland Motor Corp Ltd v Armstrong Patents Co Ltd*, where the question arose whether an independent manufacturer of replacement car exhausts could be stopped by the owner of the copyright in the manufacturing drawings of such systems. Starting from the premise that the purchaser of an article such as a car has an inherent right to repair it, it was held, by an extension of the principle of non-derogation from grant, that the common law would not allow a copyright owner to assert a monopoly right to detract from the rights of ownership, thereby affecting the value and utility of the article sold. The principle applied was that a grantor would not be allowed to derogate from his grant by using intellectual property retained in such a way as to render property granted by him unfit or materially unfit for the purpose for which the grant was made.[47] If one accepts that it is possible in theory for a computer

44 **Dunlop Pneumatic Tyre Co v Neal** [1899] 1 Ch 807; **Sirdar Rubber Co Ltd v Wallington Weston and Co** (1907) 24 RPC 539.

45 **Solar Thompson Engineering Co Ltd v Barton** [1977] RPC 537; **Gardner and Sons Ltd v Paul Sykes Organisation Ltd** [1981] FSR 281; **Weir Pumps Ltd v CML Pumps Ltd** [1984] FSR 33.

46 **Hoover plc v George Hulme Ltd** [1982] FSR 565; **British Leyland Motor Corp Ltd v Armstrong Patents Co Ltd.**

47 At 641, relying on **Browne v Flower** [1911] 1 Ch 219.

program to suffer faults through use akin to "wear and tear"[48] then the decision in this case is relevant. The House of Lords recognised that it was employing a novel application of the principle of non-derogation from grant to prevent a party exercising a statutory right[49] but it is contended that there is nothing in the Copyright, Designs and Patents Act 1988 which affects its general application to computer programs. Following this case, certain principles may be hesitantly stated:

(i) In a case where a question of patent protection simultaneously arises, the principles relating to implied licences in such cases will still apply and the principle of non-derogation from grant need not, and perhaps should not, be invoked.[50]

(ii) None of the "repair" cases[51] decided under the implied licence principle were disapproved on their facts and the result in each case would, it is argued, be the same today.

(iii) The newly applied principle enables the owner of an article to have a replacement part made either by himself or another, as before, but also enables a supplier to manufacture such stock in advance of anticipated orders.[52]

(iv) The principle appears to go further than the implied licence principle when applied in relation to patent cases in that the copyright owner is not entitled to complain of the manufacturing of an entirely new part as opposed to simply the repair of the existing one.

(v) The distinction between the two principles is further emphasised by the fact that the right to repair and thus reproduce copyright works cannot, it is submitted, be withheld even by the express terms of the contract of purchase.[53]

(vi) A subcontractor who designs a part for manufacture, knowing the

---

48 *e.g.* it may be possible that an error introduced into a computer program during its development causes it, when run hundreds of times, to accumulate unnecessary variables or other types of data which it fails to delete; thus after extended use the computer program might crash and cease to be usable until the accumulated data has been excised or the error corrected. Although it is accepted that the foregoing may not be, arguably, a very compelling scenario, it is strongly contended that computer programming technology advances at such a pace that no eventuality may be ruled out utterly.

49 At 627.

50 **British Leyland Motor Corp Ltd v Armstrong Patents Co Ltd** [1986] AC 577 at 625 *per* Lord Bridge.

51 **Dunlop Pneumatic Tyre Co v Neal; Sirdar Rubber Co Ltd v Wallington Weston and Co.**

52 **British Leyland Motor Corp Ltd v Armstrong Patents Co Ltd** at 625 *per* Lord Bridge.

53 *Ibid* at 643.

purpose for which it is to be used, cannot assert his copyright against the purchaser (end-user).[54]

(vii) The right does not permit a defendant to take copies of the plaintiff's copyright works directly.[55]

54 *Ibid.*

55 **Warman International Ltd v Envirotech Australia Pty Ltd** (1986) 67 ALR 253 (Federal Court of Australia).

Chapter 8

Primary Infringement of Copyright in Computer Programs

Introduction

This chapter will address the infringement of copyright that subsists within computer programs. In doing so, attention will be directed in this chapter to primary infringement solely; and how the courts may deal with the primary infringement of the different species of copyright work which subsist within computer programs. Regard will also be had to how, in practice, the courts actually assess the presence of primary infringement (in the sense of copying) in this type of literary work which is not quite like any other.

Infringements of copyright are divided into primary, or direct infringements, which consist of the unauthorised exercise by persons (not being the copyright owners) of rights restricted by the Copyright, Designs and Patents Act 1988; and secondary, or indirect infringements, which consist for the most part of unauthorised dealings with articles which were made in infringement of copyright. The fundamental distinction between primary and secondary infringement is that secondary infringement requires the infringer to have some degree of knowledge that what is being done is an infringement of copyright, whereas in the case of primary infringement any such knowledge is not an ingredient which needs to be proved at all in a successful action. Further, it ought always to be borne in mind that the Copyright, Designs and Patents Act 1988 applies to acts of infringement which occur after 1 August 1989.[1]

1 Copyright, Designs and Patents Act 1988, Sch 1 para 14(1).

Primary Infringement

Definition

The Copyright, Designs and Patents Act 1988 provides that copyright in a work is infringed by a person who, without the licence[2] of the copyright owner, does, or authorises another to do[3], any of the acts which are designated as being "acts restricted by the copyright".[4] This class of acts, which are expressed in the Copyright, Designs and Patents Act 1988 as being the acts which the copyright owner has the exclusive right to do in the United Kingdom[5], can be summarised as follows:

(i) In relation to all species of copyright work, to copy the work;[6]

(ii) In relation to all species of copyright work, to issue copies of the work to the public;[7]

(iii) In relation to literary, dramatic and musical works, to perform the work in public, and, in relation to sound recordings, films, broadcasts and cable programmes, to play or show the work in public;[8]

(iv) In relation to literary, dramatic, musical and artistic works, sound recordings, films, broadcasts and cable programmes, to broadcast the work or include it in a cable programme service;[9]

(v) In relation to literary, dramatic and musical works, to make an adaptation of the work, or to do any of the acts set out in the previous sub-paragraphs *(i)* to *(iv)* in relation to an adaptation of the work.[10]

In addition to the foregoing, the Copyright, Designs and Patents Act 1988 specifically provides that the doing of any of the acts set out above is a restricted act whether done in relation to the work as a whole or a substantial part of it.[11] It is further immaterial as to whether such copying is effected directly or indirectly;[12] and in relation to copying which is effected indirectly, it is also immaterial whether any of the intervening steps between the original and the final copy are themselves infringements of copyright.[13]

2 Meaning permission, whether express or implied.
3 Copyright, Designs and Patents Act 1988, s 16(2).
4 *Ibid.*
5 *Ibid*, s 16(1).
6 *Ibid*, ss 16(1)(a) and 17.
7 *Ibid*, ss 16(1)(b) and 18.
8 *Ibid*, ss 16(1)(c) and 19.
9 *Ibid*, ss 16(1)(d) and 20.
10 *Ibid*, ss 16(1)(e) and 21.
11 *Ibid*, s 16(3)(a).
12 *Ibid*, s 16(3)(b).
13 *Ibid*, s 16(3).

General principles relating to the copying of all species of copyright works

In considering the general principles which relate to the primary infringement by copying of all species of literary works (which is germane since computer programs and their preparatory design material[14] can contain a large number of different species of copyright work existing contemporaneously, each with the other[15]); consideration will need to be given to case law which predates the Copyright Act 1911 and precedents which arise under that Act. While the basic nature of infringement has not changed since then, a brief understanding of the pertinent mechanisms within the Copyright Act 1911 would be of assistance and permit one to place the case cited in the context of the Act extant at that time so its proper application to the modern law can be divined. The Copyright Act 1911 provided that the copyright in a work would be infringed if a person, without the consent of the owner of the copyright in the work, did a thing which was the sole right to do of the owner of the copyright.[16] The fundamental right conferred by the Copyright Act 1911 on the copyright owner was "the sole right to produce or reproduce the work or any substantial part thereof in any material form whatsoever".[17] It is submitted that it should further always be borne in mind that when considering the nature of the law with respect to infringement, one must always consider the nature of the thing which is protected by the law of copyright. It is in this area that the disciplines concerned with infringement and the doctrines concerned with the subsistence of copyright in the first instance overlap and merge. One must first of all decide whether copyright subsists in that which has been copied; and then look to see whether infringement has taken place. For the purposes of this chapter, it will be assumed that copyright exists in a work (or the part of it which has been copied) in accordance with the tenets set out in Chapters 3 and 5 above.

Definition of copying

It is not possible for an infringement of copyright to occur without use having been made, whether directly or indirectly, of the plaintiff's copyright work.[18]

14 As defined in Chap 3 pp 35–36.

15 See Chaps 3 and 4 above.

16 Copyright Act 1911, s 2(1).

17 Copyright Act 1922, s 1(2).

18 **Wesman v McNamarar** [1923–28] MacCC 121; **Thomas Forman & Sons Ltd v Balding & Mansell** [1928–35] MacCC 501. In particular **Francis Day & Hunter Ltd v Bron; LB (Plastics) Ltd v Swish Products Ltd** [1979] RPC 611 (HL). See also **Catnic Components Ltd v Hill & Smith Ltd** [1979] FSR 619 at 625 (CA).

Under the Copyright, Designs and Patents Act 1988, it is a restricted act "to copy" a copyright work; and in relation to literary, dramatic, musical or artistic works, "copying" is further defined to mean "reproducing the work in any material form".[19] The term "reproduce" rather than the term "copy" was also used in the Copyright Act 1911 and Copyright Act 1956 in this context; and thus it is submitted to reproduce a work a work means to copy or represent it.[20] For there to be an infringement of copyright there must be a causal connection between the copyright work and the infringing work.[21] Thus two photographs made independently of each other may be almost identical, but no copying would have taken place, thus a separate and independent original copyright would subsist in each of them.

A computer programming illustration

Similarly, if two computer programmers were set a short programming task, that might very well produce a short piece of computer code, having identical functionality, and where each line of code is identical between the two sets of code. Assuming that sufficient literary knowledge, skill and taste has been exercised by both programmers (even though they may have drawn upon the common stock of computer programming)[22] then these identical computer programs would both be a copyright work – a separate copyright subsisting in each of them. Accordingly these works may be similar, or even identical, but in the circumstances previously described, neither work would be an infringement of the other.[23] However, if there was a common source of computer programming routines available in the public domain, which one computer programmer used and included in his computer program (and the whole work was of sufficient complexity to warrant copyright protection (in so far as it had passed the usual tests of originality)) and another programmer used the first computer programmer's computer program, it is likely that this would be an infringement.[24]

19 Copyright, Designs and Patents Act 1988, s 17(1).

20 **Ladbroke (Football) Ltd v William Hill (Football) Ltd** at 276.

21 **Francis Day & Hunter Ltd v Bron; Brigid Foley Ltd v Ellott** [1982] RPC 433; **British Leyland Motor Corp Ltd v Armstrong Patents Co Ltd** per Lord Griffiths.

22 See Chap 3 p 35 above.

23 **Toole v Young** [1873] 9 QB 523; **Schlesinger v Bedford** [1890] 63 LT 762; **Robl v Palace Theatre Ltd** [1911] 28 TLR 69; **Corelli v Gray**; **Harman Pictures NV v Osbourne** [1967] 1 WLR 723; **Krisarts SA v Briar Fine Ltd** [1977] FSR 557.

24 **Elanco Products Ltd v Mandops (Agrochemicals Specialists) Ltd** [1979] FSR 557.

Reproduction as an infringement

The concept of reproduction in the sense of infringement of copyright therefore consists of two elements; neither element alone being sufficient to prove infringement.

- *First element* There must be sufficient resemblance between the copyright work and the reproduction (being the alleged infringement).
- *Second element* There must have been a causal connection between the two.[25]

In any case of infringement of copyright therefore, the plaintiff has to establish (evidential burdens apart) that the work in respect of which complaint is made in fact so resembles the "original" work as to be capable of being an infringement; but also that the "infringing" work has in fact been produced by the use of those features of the "original" work which, by reason of the knowledge, skill, taste and labour employed in its reduction to material form, constitutes it an original copyright work.

Proof of copying

In most cases of copyright infringement copying can only by proven through the drawing of inferences from all of the surrounding circumstances[26] since normally there would be no evidence capable of being evinced of a witness "being present and looking over the defendants' shoulder"[27] at the time the infringement occurred. In most cases of allegations of infringement of a literary work, the courts have generally taken the occurrence of identical errors in both the plaintiff's and defendants works[28], or concurrences in stylistic idiosyncrasies[29], or the occurrences of identical redundancies[30] to indicate copying.

The indicia of copying and computer programs

When considering the copying of literal elements of computer programs, the courts have tended to increase this general focus and concentrate specifically

25 **Billhöfer Maschinenfabrik GmbH v Dixon & Co Ltd** [1990] FSR 105.

26 **Antocks Lairn Ltd v I Bloohn Ltd.**

27 **Sifam Electrical Instrument Co Ltd v Sangamo Weston Ltd** [1973] RPC 899. See also **LB (Plastics) Ltd v Swish Products Ltd.**

28 **Deeks v Wells** [1928–35] MacCC 353.

29 **Ravenscroft v Herbert & Anor** [1980] RPC 193.

30 **Billhöffer Maschinenfabrik GmbH v Dixon and Co Ltd.**

on issues of concurrences of style, idiosyncrasies, errors and redundancies. For example, in *IBCOS Computers Ltd v Barclays Mercantile Highland Finance Ltd* Jacob J considered coincidences in idiosyncrasies, errors and redundancies very carefully and gave great weight to them. The learned judge considered issues of the coincidence of program and file headings[31] in the following manner:

> "Then there are the identical comment headings. A document called X11 conveniently shows a series of headings in comments which are the same in an important program of ADS (SKPER, for manufacturers' prices of spare parts) and the corresponding program in Unicorn (PAMUPP). For instance the word FORD is presented in a comment in both programs with 23 hyphens to the left and 30 to the right."[32]

Jacob J also specifically sought redundancies which he saw as important indicia of copying:

> "It is not only comments, labels and names which are involved in identity. There are bits of ADS[33] and Unicorn[34] in the program code which were also identical. These too would be copied by a disk to disk copying.[35] It would technically not matter if they were redundant code[36] or if they had a purpose in ADS and were redundant in Unicorn. But their presence would betray copying. The difficulty from Mr. Poole's[37] point of view is that those portions of code are in Unicorn at all. For if he was genuinely writing it from scratch one would not expect redundant code at all. That is the sort of thing that arises when a program is first written and then modified as time goes on. One would certainly not at all expect identical pieces of redundant code in Unicorn and ADS or bits of redundant code in Unicorn which had a function in ADS. Yet that is what we find here."[38]

The learned judge has here lighted upon a very important (and unique) matter with respect to the identification of the indicia of copying of computer program products. As described in Chapter 3 above, the computer software producer often makes modifications to a computer software product. It is common in most sectors of the software industry (if not all) for the manufacturers of commercial computer software products to continually

31 Sometimes referred to as "headers" in the software industry.

32 At 298.

33 The original computer program.

34 The infringing computer program.

35 The learned judge is propounding the view that copying has taken place by the program files of the original program being copied from one diskette to another so as to facilitate the making of a fresh copy. Work would then be carried out on the "fresh copy" so produced to alter the program code but take advantage of the original literary work and effort done in producing ADS' functionality.

36 The term "redundant code" in this sense being used to describe computer program code which does not function but is, in a sense, inert.

37 The gentleman responsible for the infringement and one of the defendants.

38 At 299.

evolve the functionality of their products to meet changing market demands. As new functionality and therefore new computer programs or routines are added to the product (bearing in mind that the computer software product might be made up of a large number of discrete computer programs) the software manufacturer has the choice of excising from the body of the code as a whole, those old parts of computer code which have become redundant.

Now in an ideal world, every manufacturer of commercial software products would wish to have clean and contiguous computer code which is all directed to the functionality of the product and to have no extraneous or redundant code, offering no functionality, but making the computer software product larger than it needs to be and possibly slower than it would ordinarily be without the redundant code.[39] However, in the real commercial world, software houses (the producers of commercial computer software products) often feel themselves unable, as a matter of cost, to go back and remove areas of computer program code which have become redundant. Rather, they assess, as a commercial matter, whether the cost of leaving redundant or disabled code in a product outweighs the cost of its removal. In most cases, software houses merely disable certain areas of code as they add functionality to their products; it being left inert in the computer software product. Only with major new releases of a computer software product will software houses take the opportunity of "cleaning up" the code and removing redundant programming code.

Bearing this in mind; and taking into account that infringers of copyright usually wish to appropriate the labour and effort of another rather than exercise that expertise, labour and effort themselves; it is highly likely that a putative infringer will not go to the trouble of removing inert or redundant code. Thus this indicia of copying becomes very important and of high probative value in cases of literal copying.[40]

---

39 Since the computer upon which the computer software product will execute will read all of a computer program into memory and "read" every line when executing it, time is taken in reading the redundant code and this can adversely affect the performance of the computer software product in question. Performance is often a critical issue to computer software product manufacturers and redundant code, in so far as it unnecessarily enlarges the size of the computer software product, can also cause performance degradation since not all of the product may be able to be stored in RAM; and therefore more disk-reading activities will be generated. Reading computer memory is always much, much faster than reading a disk and thus the execution of the computer software product would slow in this fashion also.

40 Due to the importance of this particular species of indicia of copying, it is submitted that the software programming security practice of "watermarking" has become of greater use and importance. "Watermarking" is a computer programming practice whereby a

General test for primary infringement

In the case of all species of copyright work, the appropriate test for primary infringement of copyright in the sense of reproduction within the meaning of the Copyright, Designs and Patents Act 1988 has the following parts:

(i) there must be a sufficient degree of objective similarity between the two works;[41]

(ii) there must be a causal connection between the two works;[42]

(iii) it is irrelevant to inquire whether the defendant was or was not consciously aware of such a causal connection;

(iv) where there is a substantial degree of objective similarity between the two works, this will, of itself, be prima facie evidence to show that a causal connection exists and is an inference that can be justifiably drawn;[43]

(v) the denial by the defendant that the infringing work was consciously copied from the "original" work affords some evidence to rebut the inference of a causal connection arising from the objective similarities between the two works, but is in no way conclusive.[44]

Thus it can be summarised that if there is sufficient objective similarity between the plaintiff's work and the defendant's; and the defendant has had an opportunity to copy the plaintiff's work, whether directly or indirectly, this will establish a *prima facie* case of copying which the defendant has to answer. The defendant may do this by bringing forth some alternative

40 *(cont.)*
redundant set of irrelevant computer program routines (which may not be inert and might be quite complex in their action, *e.g.*: generating a number of random numbers, performing calculations upon them and the generating further numbers) are deliberately inserted into a computer program of high functional value. The precept being that an infringer would be likely to "take" the valuable computer program (valuable in the sense that it contains difficult, well de-bugged code which provides important or key functionality) and would not wish to invest the time and effort of removing the redundant sub-routines even if the infringer had identified that such active routines were, in fact, functionally redundant. The resultant infringing program would contain the watermark and thus it could be easily and successfully argued that it was not possible statistically for another independent and original work to contain such a complex and highly identifiably obscure piece of redundant programming.

41 **Billhöfer Maschinenfabrik GmbH v Dixon & Co Ltd** at 107.

42 *Ibid.*

43 *Ibid.*

44 This test was considered to be correct by Wilmer LJ in **Francis Day & Hunter Ltd v Bron** at 611 and was found to be "helpful" by Whitford J in **LB (Plastics) Ltd v Swish.**

explanation of the similarities;[45] and the judge's task will then be, on the evidence presented to him as a whole, to decide whether there has been copying or not. The fact that the judge disbelieves a witness who denies copying does not necessarily prove that copying did, in fact, take place.[46] In this way, objective similarities coupled with proof of access to the plaintiff's copyright work gives rise to an inference of copying that leads to a shift in the evidential burden from the plaintiff to the defendant; placing an obligation on the defendant to prove on the balance of probability that copying did not occur.[47]

Indirect copying

Generally

Copyright may be infringed by the unauthorised copying of something which itself is a copy of the "original" work and the Copyright, Designs and Patents Act 1988 expressly provides that references to the doing of an act restricted by the copyright in a work are to the doing of it either directly or indirectly.[48] The position was the same under the Copyright Act 1911 and the Copyright Act 1956.[49] It is submitted that in most cases of alleged infringement outside of the infringement of computer programs, the copying complained of has been effected indirectly. For example, the plagiarist may never have seen the original manuscript, the engineering drawing, dress designer's sketch; but has only seen the published work which was derived from the original work.[50]

45 *e.g.* in the case of primary infringement of a computer program; the defendant might argue that identical CASE tools were used and applied to similar or identical processes. The defendant may also argue, as in the case of **IBCOS Computers Ltd v Barclay Mercantile Highland Finance Ltd** [1994] FSR 275that the similarities arose because of the use of software tools and routines which were available in the public domain (often referred to as "Shareware"). It may also be argued that identical programming protocols were applied to discrete and identifiable programming problems where there was only one, best solution.

46 **Johnstone Safety Ltd v Peter Cook (International) Plc** [1990] FSR 161 at 175.

47 **Sifam Electrical Instrument Co Ltd v Sangamo Western Ltd; LB (Plastics) Ltd v Swish Products Ltd; Oscar Trade Mark** [1980] FSR 429

48 S 16(3)(b).

49 It is suggested that the Court of Appeal produced an appropriate review of the law arising therefrom in **British Leyland Motor Corp Ltd v Armstrong Patents Co Ltd.**

50 **Dorling v Honnor Marine Ltd; Merchant Adventurers Ltd v M Grew and Co Ltd** [1971] FSR 233; **Sifam Electrical Instrument Co Ltd v Samgamo Western Ltd** [1971] FSR 337; **Antocks Lairn Ltd v I Bloohn Ltd** [1971] FSR 490; **Temple Instruments Ltd v Hollis Heels Ltd** [1971] FSR 634; **Lerose Ltd v Harwick Jersey Int Ltd** [1973] FSR 15; **British Northrop Ltd v Texteam Blackburn Ltd** [1973] FSR 241; **Catnic Components Ltd v Hill and Smith Ltd** [1975] FSR 529.

If however, notwithstanding that there is a chain of copying from the defendant's work indirectly back to the plaintiff's, it should always be borne in mind that if its is the "idea" which has been copied and not its expression, then there will be no infringement of copyright.[51]

On the other hand, if the "original"[52] has been reproduced within the meaning of the Copyright, Designs and Patents Act 1988, it is no answer nor a defence to say that it has been copied from a work which is itself, whether licensed or unlicensed, a copy of the "original".[53] Thus, for example, where a plaintiff's plans are reproduced in three dimensions, and the results photographed without permission, the taking of the photograph will infringe any copyright in the plans if a substantial part of the plans has been thereby reproduced.[54]

Indirect copying and computer programs

Although no case exists on the following hypothesis, it is suggested that it would therefore follow that where preparatory design materials[55] are reproduced in the form of a computer program; the taking of a photograph of the computer program in operation (such photographs commonly being referred to in the computer industry as "screenshots") will infringe any copyright in the preparatory design material if a substantial part of the preparatory design material has been thereby reproduced.[56] This will be so, even if the intervening work is of a nature not capable of being an

51 **Gleeson v HR Denne Ltd** [1975] RPC 471.

52 When the word original is being used in a sense other than that usually associated with a copyright work – i.e. not in the sense of being an original work in which sufficient originality subsists within it to render it susceptible to copyright, then the word original will be encompassed by inverted commas. "Original", in the sense of infringement, is used in this work to denote the work which is alleged to be the subject of infringement, the original thus being the precursor of the infringements which came later.

53 Copyright, Designs and Patents Act 1988, section 16(3)(b); **Murray v Bogue** [1853] 1 Drew. 353; **Reade v Lacy** [1861] 1 J & H 524; **Fairlie v Boosey** [1878] 4 App Cas 711; **Hanfstaengl v Empire Palace** [1984] 3 Ch 109 [1895] AC 20; **King Features Syndicate v O & M Kleeman Ltd** [1941] AC 417.

54 **Dorling v Honnor Marine Ltd** [1965] Ch 1; **Merchant Adventurers Ltd v M Grew and Co Ltd** [1971] FSR 233; **Sifam Electrical Instrument Co Ltd v Samgamo Western Ltd** [1971] FSR 337; **Antocks Lairn Ltd v I Bloohn Ltd** [1971] FSR 490; **Temple Instruments Ltd v Hollis Heels Ltd** [1971] FSR 634; **Lerose Ltd v Harwick Jersey International Ltd** [1973] FSR 15; **British Northrop Ltd v Texteam Blackburn Ltd** [1973] FSR 241; **Catnic Components Ltd v Hill and Smith Ltd.**

55 See Chap 3.

56 It will be recalled from Chap 2 that the definition of "literary work" in the Copyright, Designs and Patents Act 1988 was extended by the Copyright (Computer Programs) Regulations 1992 whereby a new s 3(1)(c) was added in which "preparatory design material for a computer program" was expressly protected as a literary work. It is

infringement of copyright nor capable of having copyright subsist within it[57], or even if there is no intervening work in the sense of a work existing in a material form, the link being an aural description.[58] The latter point underlines the risk that, even if an independent designer is employed to avoid infringement in circumstances where he does not have any access to the "original" copyright work, it may be necessary to give him so much information concerning the "original" work that the work he, in fact, produces will still be an infringement.[59] This is a very important lesson for software developers. Software houses typically pay a very great deal of attention to the functionality of their competitors' products and the computer software industry is one in which there is great movement of personnel between competing organisations.

Consequently, with issues of confidentiality and possible breaches of contracts of employment aside; circumstances where an employee of a competing software producer joins the employ of another software house; descriptions of functionality, design structure and user interface look and feel which result in being included in the new employer's computer software product, may very well result in infringement. Indeed, it may not be possible for a defendant to escape a charge of infringement by giving the designer very loose instructions and then prompting him to produce, for example, a result derived through a process of trial and error which resembles or reproduces the "original" copyright work.[60] Where there are intermediate stages in the chain of copying, it is suggested that each intermediate stage must, in some real and intelligible sense, be a copy or representation of the "original" work in which copyright subsists. In *Purefoy Engineering Co Ltd v Sykes Boxall Co Ltd*[61] the defendant compiled a catalogue from the plaintiff's machinery parts, thereby bringing into being a catalogue similar to the plaintiff's. It was

56 *(cont.)*
submitted that not every piece of preparatory design material will be automatically protected, but will have to satisfy the ordinary tests for the subsistence of copyright as set out in this chapter and Chap 2. However, it is submitted that the documentation produced in describing and refining the concept meets the criteria for the subsistence of copyright. It is submitted that it should therefore be possible to extract from the dicta set out in Chap 2 what the elements of originality that need to be present before copyright in preparatory design material arises and, furthermore, in what degree those elements need to be present.

57 Copyright, Designs and Patents Act 1988, s 16(3)(b); **Murray v Bogue** [1853] 1 Drew 353; **Reade v Lacy** [1861] 1 J & H 524; **Fairlie v Boosey** [1878] 4 AppCas 711; **Hanfstaengl v Empire Palace; King Features Syndicate v O & M Kleeman Ltd.**

58 **Gleeson v HR Denne Ltd** [1975] RPC 471; **Solar Thomson Engineering Co Ltd v Barton; Plix Products Ltd v Frank M Winstone (Merchants) Ltd.**

59 **Solar Thomson Engineering Co Ltd v Barton.**

60 **House of Spring Gardens Ltd v Point Blank Ltd** [1983] FSR 213.

61 [1954] 71 RPC 227; [1955] 72 RPC 89.

held that the copyright in the plaintiff's catalogue was not infringed since the machinery parts offered by the plaintiff did not represent in any physical form the descriptions of those parts in the catalogue. Accordingly, a book describing the functionality of a computer software product to aid and assist the users of such a computer software product, could not be said to be an infringement of the computer software product itself since there were no intermediate stages, for the purposes of copyright infringement, between the computer software product or its preparatory design material and the instructive book.

Ignorance is no excuse

If the defendant, as a matter of fact, has derived his work, either directly or indirectly, from the plaintiff's, the fact that the defendant was unaware that the work he had copied existed (*e.g.* where what he had copied, such as a dress, was made from a sketch of which he had no knowledge), or was the plaintiff's, or was the subject of copyright, does not negative the actuality of infringement nor afford the defendant with a defence against an allegation of infringement of copyright. Copyright being a proprietary right, ignorance is no excuse for infringement.[62] Similarly, it is no defence to infringement that the defendant had erroneously relied on a licence or an assign which did not in fact or in law occur, even though he believed, and had reasonable grounds to believe, that he had the legal capacity to do the act complained of.

Accordingly, in a situation where a computer programmer has copied a third party's computer program into his own (assuming the third party's computer program is susceptible to copyright), believing it to be in the public domain when it was not, then this would constitute an infringement. Further, if, in the situation just described, the computer programmer thought that he had a valid licence to so use the third party's computer program but did not, honestly believed that he owned the copyright in the second computer program but did not, or honestly believed that copyright did not subsist in the third party's computer program that he copied; his actions would still constitute an infringement of copyright. Nor is it a defence to an allegation of infringement that the infringement has caused no damage to the copyright owner. The right of the owner of copyright is not determined or measured by the amount of actual damage suffered by him by reason of the infringement. Copyright is a right in property, and the copyright owner is entitled to come

62 **Lee v Simpson** (1847) 3 CB 871; **Wittman v Oppenheim** (1884) 27 ChD 260; **Mansell v Valley Printing Co** [1908] 2 Ch 441; **Byrne v Statist Co.**

to court to protect that property, even though he does not prove or show any actual damage flowing from the infringement or at all.[63]

Unconscious copying

It is undecided whether there can be "unconscious copying", that is, whether there can be infringement where the defendant honestly states that he was unaware that his work was a copy of the plaintiff's; even if the court is satisfied that the defendant must have made some unconscious use of it from memory, rather than conscious use by deliberate copying. Such a possibility has been judicially discussed, particularly in relation to the infringement of musical works;[64] and there is some judicial support for the view that if the work has been copied as a matter of fact, it is irrelevant whether the defendant copied the work consciously or unconsciously so long as there was a causal connection between the plaintiff's "original" work and his own.[65] A particularly difficult situation may arise where the defendant is accused of copying an earlier work of his own which he no longer has the right to reproduce, since it may be very hard for him to put his earlier work, or substantial parts of it, completely out of his mind.[66] It may be very difficult, if not in fact impossible, for a computer programmer specialising in one type of programming or specialising in programming a particular type of computer application program not to reproduce large sections of computer code with which he is intimately familiar; even though he may no longer have any rights to such code. The court touched on just this matter in *John Richardson Computers Limited v Flanders and Chemtec Ltd* where Ferris J commented:

63 Per Parkes J in **Weatherby & Sons v International Horse Agency and Exchange Ltd** [1910] 2 Ch 297, which was approved in **Hawkes & Son (London) Ltd v Paramount Film Service Ltd** [1934] Ch 593.

64 **Rees v Melville; Sinanide v La Maison Kosmeo** (1927) 44 TLR 371; **Ricordi (G) & Co Ltd v Clayton & Waller Ltd** [1928-35] MacCC 154; **Francis Day & Hunter Ltd v Bron; Seager v Copydex Ltd.**

65 **Francis Day & Hunter Ltd v Bron**, per Wilmer LJ at 614. Upjohn LJ declined to express a view on the matter stating that it was not necessary for the court to consider the issue on the evidence laid before it, whilst Diplock LJ felt unable to address the matter as no evidence of the mental processes involved had been adduced.

66 **Galago Publishers (Pty) Ltd v Erasmus** [1989] 1 SA 276 at 293; **Industrial Furnaces Ltd v Reaves** at 623. Bearing in mind that computer programs may be or may "contain" artistic works, the Copyright, Designs and Patents Act 1988, s 64 provides that where the author of an artistic work is not the copyright owner, he does not infringe the copyright in his earlier work in making another artistic work provided he does not repeat or imitate the main design of the earlier work. In the context of computer programs, it cannot be argued on any satisfactory or empirical basis as to what would constitute the main design of an artistic work within a computer program.

> "I do not accept the evidence .... as establishing deliberate copying of the BBC program[67] by Mr. Flanders. But the fact remains that he had, as I have said, an intimate knowledge of the BBC program at all levels of abstraction (to use the term employed in *Nichols v Universal Pictures Corporation* and other United States authorities that I have mentioned) and it is possible that he has, unconsciously or unintentionally or in some other way that he did not consider to be objectionable, made use of that knowledge in a way that amounts to copying in the context of breach of copyright."[68]

Significance to the structure of the software industry

This matter, although seemingly an obscure one, is in fact of significant importance to consulting (freelance) computer programmers and software houses generally. As averred to above[69], a great deal of "cross-fertilisation" is carried on amongst the employees at all levels of commercial software producers. By this it is meant that computer programmers producing computer software products often produce them for specific "vertical markets".[70] The computer programmers become experienced in areas other than the programming language or environment in which they hold themselves out to be expert. For example, a programmer may become very experienced in producing computer software products to be used in banks. Other computer programmers may become experienced in producing computer software products for estate agents, dentists or pharmacists. As a computer programmer's experience in a particular vertical market grows, he becomes acquainted with the modus operandi of that particular industry; becomes used to the types of people who work within the sector he services and therefore the computer programmer is perceived as becoming more valuable by software houses who compete in that vertical market since he will bring not only computer programming skills, but an ability to apply them in the context of what may be a very specific vertical market if he was employed by them. Assuming then that the copyright works he produces for his employer software house A are owned by this software house; if he moves to software house B, who is active in the same vertical market as software

67 The "original" copyright work.

68 At p 548.

69 See pp 154 above.

70 A "vertical market" is a market defined by a particular industry or sector. *e.g.* computer software produced specifically for the needs of pharmacists, would, in the software industry, be described as being vertical market specific. However, and conversely, a computer software product which dealt generally with sales order management would not be defined as being a vertical market application, since it could be used across a number of market sectors.

house A; he may very well be called upon to produce computer programs which address scenarios or problems which he has personally addressed before. Now we know that there is nothing to impede the computer programmer in question from drawing on the common stock of knowledge of computer programmers generally;[71] but, on the precedents examined above, if he unconsciously reproduces significant sections of computer code from his time of employment at software house A, the computer programs he writes may be capable of being infringing copies of software house B's copyright. It is suggested that this was never the intent of the Copyright, Designs and Patents Act 1988 and that copyright should not be used as a method for restraining individuals from earning their living in a legitimate, but albeit specialised, fashion. It would not, under the forcgoing circumstances, matter that software house B and the computer programmer had been collectively assiduous in ensuring that he had no access to his previous work and therefore worked in what has become known in the computer software industry as a "clean room" environment.

If believing that he was writing brand new code from scratch, yet addressing a problem that he may have addressed many times before, the computer programmer might be unconsciously recalling his previous work and reproducing it thinking the new work is new. However, it might very well be an infringement and raises the question that, without the exemption applicable to artistic works applied to this area, a creative but specialised computer programmer may find it almost impossible not to infringe the copyright in his previous works which he no longer owns. This problem will also apply in equal part to the freelance computer programmers who are very prevalent in the software industry. As a freelance computer programmer moves from client to client, assigning the copyright in the works he has produced to each client, a new copyright may not be arising in later works since they may be unconscious reproductions of original works fashioned much earlier, the copyright in which might have been assigned to such earlier client. On the other hand, if the computer programmer is, consciously or unconsciously, infringing his previous copyrights or, for that matter, the copyrights of others, as he produces new works; if he adds a significant amount of labour, skill and judgement to his subsequent works, a new copyright may arise in them even though they infringe the copyright of others.[72]

---

71 See Chap 3.

72 **Redwood Music Ltd v Chappell and Co Ltd; ZYX Music GmbH v Chris King.**

Reproductions and copies

Any material form

In the case of literary, dramatic, musical and artistic works the Copyright, Designs and Patents Act 1988 provides[73], that it is an infringement of copyright to reproduce the work "in any material form". In general, therefore, a change of medium will not prevent there being an infringement. The Copyright Act 1956 provided that "reproduction" in the case of a literary, dramatic or musical work included the reproduction of the work in the form of a record[74] or a cinematograph film[75], but the word "reproduce" is not further defined in the Copyright, Designs and Patents Act 1988. It is submitted that the general position on this point has not altered between the Copyright Act 1956 and the Copyright, Designs and Patents Act 1988.[76]

Colourable imitation

It is contended that it is, however, generally unusual for an infringement to consist of an exact copy or use of the whole of the plaintiffs work. In some cases, the defendant's work may to a greater or lesser degree resemble the whole of the plaintiff's work, in which case the question is whether the defendant's work is a colourable imitation.[77] Alternatively, the defendant's work may have been taken from only part of the plaintiff's work. Here, the defendant's work may be an exact reproduction of that part of the plaintiff's work or it may only to a greater or lesser degree resemble that part.

In this alternative class of case, it is suggested that the first step is to identify the part of the plaintiff's work which is alleged to have been reproduced and then decide whether it constitutes a substantial part of the plaintiff's work. If it does, but it is not an exact copy of that part, it must then be decided whether it is a reproduction or colourable imitation of that part of the plaintiff's work.[78]

Where the alleged infringement resembles either the whole or a substantial part of the plaintiff's work to a lesser or greater degree, and assuming that

73 S 17(2). This position is unaltered from the Copyright Act 1956 ss 2(5)(a) and 3(5)(a).

74 S 48(1). **Compo Co Ltd v Blue Crest Music Inc** (1980) 105 DLR (3rd) 249.

75 S 48(1). This sub-section also defined "record" to mean any disc, tape, perforated roll or other device in which sounds are embodied so as to be capable (with or without the aid of some other instrument) of being automatically reproduced therefrom. "Cinematograph film" was defined in s 13(10) of the Copyright Act 1956.

76 See the general interpretation provisions set out in s 172 of the Copyright, Designs and Patents Act 1988.

77 **Sillitoe v McGraw-Hill Book Co (UK) Ltd** [1983] FSR 545.

78 **Spectravest Inc v Aperknit Ltd** [1988] FSR 161.

the defendant's work has, as a matter of fact, been taken from the plaintiff's; the courts have never allowed a defendant to evade the provisions of the Copyright Acts by merely altering the form of the "original" work. But the Copyright, Designs and Patents Act 1988, as was the case in the Copyright Act 1956, does not contain any direct statement that an imitation is to be treated as a reproduction. The term "adaptation" in section 2(5)(f) of the Copyright Act 1956 had a special and restricted meaning, as it does in section 16(1)(e) of the Copyright, Designs and Patents Act 1988; but, it is submitted, this did not limit the generality of the word "reproduction" under the Copyright Act 1956[79] and it is submitted that the position is the same under the Copyright, Designs and Patents Act 1988. The expression "colourable imitation" was used in the Copyright Act 1911 in defining the word "infringing" when used in relation to a copy[80], but this expression does not appear in either the Copyright Act 1956 nor the Copyright, Designs and Patents Act 1988. However, in *Sillitoe v McGraw-Hill Book Co (UK) Ltd*, the Court of Appeal accepted that the term "reproduction" embraced a colourable imitation. The question therefore appears to turn solely on the interpretation of the expression "reproduction" and the further definition of this word in section 17 of the Copyright, Designs and Patents Act 1988 is of limited assistance as this definition merely includes special forms of reproduction. Accordingly, the expression "reproduction" in the Copyright, Designs and Patents Act 1988 has the same meaning that the word "copy" has acquired in copyright law generally. Various definitions of the expression "copy" have been suggested[81], but it is submitted that the correct view is that where the court is satisfied that the defendant has, in producing the alleged infringement, made a substantial use of those features of the plaintiff's work in which copyright subsists[82], an infringement will have been committed. If the defendant has made such use in an unauthorised fashion, then he has unlawfully exercised the sole right which is conferred upon the copyright owner[83] by the Copyright, Designs and Patents Act 1988.

---

79 **Francis Day & Hunter Ltd v Bron.**

80 S 35(1).

81 **West v Francis** (1822) 5 B & Ald 737 at 743; **Hanfstaengl v WH Smith & Sons** at 524; **McCrum v Eisner** (1918) 87 LJ Ch 99 at 102; **King Features Syndicate v O & M Kleeman Ltd.**

82 Which, it is submitted, in the context of computer programs could be a wide portfolio of literary, artistic and musical works including films and photographs.

83 **Krisarts SA v Briarfine Ltd** [1977] FSR 557; **LB (Plastics) Ltd v Swish Products Ltd.**

Partial copy made

Where only part of the plaintiff's work has been taken, it is submitted that difficult questions arise as to the amount of copying or use necessary to pass the threshold beyond which infringement occurs. It should be borne in mind that the Copyright, Designs and Patents Act 1988 provides that references to the doing of an act in relation to a copyright work include the doing of that act in relation to either the whole of the copyright work or any substantial part of it.[84] The question, therefore, of the nature and ambit of a "substantial part" is of significant relevance in relation to all acts of infringement and all categories of work that might subsist in or be recorded in the medium of the computer program; but will most often arise in relation to the issue of reproduction.

Substantial part

It has repeatedly been held that the expression "substantial" in this connection relates much more to the quality of what has been taken rather than the quantity.[85] The quality, or importance[86], of the part taken is frequently more significant than the proportion which the appropriated part bears to the whole work. Thus if so much is appropriated that the value of the original is sensibly diminished, or that the labours of the author of the "original" work are substantially, and to an injurious extent, appropriated by another, that is sufficient in law, it is contended, to constitute infringement *pro tanto*. There is in existence a line of older (or ageing) decisions which support the view that in deciding questions on this issue, regard must be had to the nature and objects of the selection made by the alleged infringer, the quantity and value of the materials used, and the degree to which the unlawful use may prejudice the sale, or diminish the profits (whether direct or indirect) or supersedes the objectives of the "original" work.[87] It is submitted that this line of cases should now not be followed since, as set out above, copyright is a right in property and is actionable *per se*. The court should not, therefore, inquire as to the damage suffered by the plaintiff with respect the value of that appropriated to test whether his proprietary rights have been infringed.

84 S 16(3)(a).

85 *e.g.* Lord Reid in **Ladbroke (Football) Ltd v William Hill (Football) Ltd** at 276. See also: **Industrial Furnaces Ltd v Reaves** at 623; **Antocks Lairn Ltd v I Bloohn Ltd; George Hensher Ltd v Restawile (Upholstery) Lancashire Ltd** [1975] RPC 31.

86 **Catnic Components Ltd v Hill and Smith Ltd** at 223.

87 **Bramwell v Halcomb** (1836) 3 My & Cr 737; **Saunders v Smith** (1838) 3 My & Cr 711; **Neale v Harmer** (1897) 13 TLR 209; **Campbell v Scott** (1842) 11 Sim 31; **Chatterton v Cave** (1878) 3 App Cas 483.

More modern decisions are based on a purely qualitative test of that which has been appropriated[88] and that is how the position ought to be assessed. The essence of the matter is that the question of substantiality is very much a matter of degree in each case and ought to be considered having regard to all of the circumstances.[89]

If it can be so that even a few bars of music may be a substantial part of a musical work if they constitute a recognisable reproduction of an essential part of the melody;[90] then the appropriation of a relatively small amount (quantitively) of computer program code could constitute the appropriation of a substantial amount of the computer program if it could be shown that the appropriated code was, from a qualitative perspective, sufficiently important to the work as a whole. It could not be safely argued that any amount of code, no matter how small, would satisfy the test because its absence would cause the computer program to crash[91], but rather regard would be made to the functional importance of the appropriated code to the computer program overall and even relatively small pieces of computer code may be of critical importance since they may represent many hundreds of man hours in programming and de-bugging to produce short (and therefore high-performing) code which achieves its objectives in an elegant and efficacious manner. It is often said that "what is worth copying is prima facie worth protecting";[92] but the plaintiff must be able to identify for the court the substantial part which he alleges has been copied.[93] Further, where the plaintiff has himself copied from another's work, then if what has been copied has been taken without alteration, it may be disregarded by the court in deciding whether what the defendant has copied is a substantial part of the plaintiff's work, on the basis that, on its own, that part lacks originality.[94] Thus it may prove easier, in an infringement action concerning a computer program, to defend such an action on the basis that what has been appropriated was not original, rather than seeking or attempting to establish

---

88 Neither of the learned judges in the decisions in **John Richardson Computers Ltd v Flanders and Chemtec Ltd** and **IBCOS Computers Ltd v Barclays Finance Ltd** made any such consideration, but concentrated solely on a qualitative evaluation of that which was alleged to be appropriated to measure how substantial it was.

89 **Ravenscroft v Herbert.**

90 *e.g.*: **Hawkes & Son (London) Ltd v Paramount Film Service Ltd; Ricordi (G) and Co Ltd v Clayton & Waller Ltd** (in which the court indicated that even eight bars of an air might constitute a substantial part of the air).

91 Stop executing or running by reason of a fault.

92 Per Petersen J in **University of London Press Ltd v University Tutorial Press Ltd** at 610 and approved by both Lord Reid and Lord Pearce in **Ladbroke (Football) Ltd v William Hill (Football) Ltd** at 279 and 293 respectively. See also Chap 2, pp 29, 30.

93 **Gomme Ltd v Relaxateze Upholstery Ltd** [1976] RPC 377.

94 **Warwick Film Productions Ltd v Eisinger** [1969] Ch 508.

that the plaintiff's copyright work as a whole lacks originality, and is thus not entitled to copyright.

Copying in relation to literary works

The general principles in relation to literary works have already been considered above. Due to the usual depth of original literary work in commercial computer software products which represent the most common form of computer program compilations; the type of problems that the law of copyright has experienced with respect to compilations as a species of literary work will not, it is suggested, be broadly or regularly experienced with respect to computer software products. The law of copyright with respect to the primary infringement of compilations has, it is submitted, centred on compilations such as dictionaries, gazetteers, grammars, maps, arithmetical tables, almanacs, encyclopaedias and guide-books. The new publications dealing with a similar subject-matter must, of necessity, resemble existing publications, and the defence of "common source" is frequently made where the new publication is alleged to constitute an infringement of copyright of an earlier one. When considering a set of computer programs working together as a compilation, it seems that the law has little to offer since the possibility of collections of computer programs acting together offer little capacity for infringement in the usual or traditional sense. However, compilations in this technology area occur in the following example classes:

- A disk or CD-ROM could be produced which contained a compilation of computer code routines or computer programs (some routines being useful to a computer programmer but too small to be susceptible to copyright in themselves);
- Computer software products often contain what is known as "look-up" tables. These will be data (either held within the body of a computer program itself or in separate files), being information which the computer program "looks up" as one would a reference book before conducting a calculation. This might be better explained by the giving of examples. A computer software product concerned with the calculation of certain taxation regimes across different jurisdictions might use a look-up table to acquire the data for it to perform its calculations with respect to the end-users' commands. A computer software product that calculates the tidal ranges or times of slack tide at locations entered or chosen by the end-user might use a look-up

table in order to acquire the basic data on which to make its calculations. The use of look-up tables in such circumstances is favoured by the software industry since it represents a more structured method of programming which is easier to de-bug and, secondly, where the data is likely to change from time to time or need updating (such as might be the case in a tax calculating computer software product) the files containing the look-up tables can be easily updated without reissuing complete computer program files.

- Multimedia programs are compilations for the purposes of the Copyright, Designs and Patents Act 1988.[95] It is submitted that as the technology of the multimedia program has produced a new form of encyclopaedia; the cases concerning encyclopaedias and other types of similar compilation are likely to be on point and of great significance.

Defence of common source

The defence of "common source" may merely consist of pointing out that the defendant's work might have been taken from earlier matter, and that its similarity to the plaintiff's does not create any necessary inference that it has been copied from the plaintiff's, rather than from other similar works. But a bare assertion that the plaintiff's work was not copied, without any explanation from the defendant as to how or when he worked or how long it took him, may not be sufficient in itself to rebut the inference of copying.[96] Whereas, with a strictly original work, any identity of phrase or programming is sufficient evidence of copying, the usual indicia of copying with respect to computer programs will be absent, and thus it is submitted that with many compilations it is only from external evidence, or from the most minute examination of textual errors, that infringement can be established.[97]

Defence of no copyright in plaintiff's work

Alternatively, the defence may be that the plaintiff has no copyright in his work of compilation, because it is not original but is a mere reproduction of earlier matter. But it is submitted that it should always be borne in mind that though the individual constituent parts of a compilation may not, in

95 See Chap 4 for a discussion of the technical aspects of multimedia programs.

96 **Harman Pictures NV v Osbourne** [1967] 1 WLR 723.

97 **Murray v Bogue; Kelly v Morris** (1866) LR 1 Eq 697; **Cox v Land & Water Journal Co** (1869) LR 9 Eq 324; **Pike v Nicholas** (1870) LR 5 Ch 251; **Jarrold v Heywood** (1870) 18 WR 279; **Cadieux v Beauchimin** [1901–04] MacCC 4; **Mathieson v Universal Stock Exchange** [1901–04] MacCC 80; **Emmett v Meigs** [1921] 56 DLR 63; **Deeks v Wells.**

themselves, be susceptible to copyright, copyright may arise in the arrangement of the component parts as a compilation.[98] Thus, for example, the work involved in the arrangement of a list of football fixtures in chronological order may be sufficient to make the work original, so that the systematic copying of a chronological list constitutes an infringement[99] – and there is no reason, hypothetically, why such a list should not exist as a look-up table in a computer program directed to football fixtures.[1] The position where the compilation has been scrambled by the defendant is uncertain.[2] This issue will depend upon whether the assembly of the compilation in the first instance itself involved sufficient effort, skill and labour to justify copyright protection.[3] Although there is no monopoly in a copyright work, yet, with strictly original copyright works, any use of an earlier work in an unauthorised fashion to produce a new work will result in an infringement. Published compilations, in the ordinary sense[4], are intended not merely to be read, but to be used, and the question therefore arises as to how far they may be used in the preparation of a subsequent compilation by a person other than the copyright owner. The publication of certain books of this character imply a licence to reproduce their contents; thus, a book of legal precedents is intended to be used by practitioners, unless otherwise stated; and a writer is entitled to use prior compilations on a similar subject in order to ascertain where he may go to research his material. However, the limits upon this implied licence from publication are reasonably clear, and in no circumstance authorise the use of the copyright material in the first work for the purpose of producing a second work of a similar nature.[5] Accordingly the author of a book of legal precedents authorises the use of his forms for use in practice, unless otherwise stated, but not in a competing book of precedents; and the

---

98 **Ladbroke (Football) Ltd v William Hill (Football) Ltd; Coral Index Ltd v Regent Index Ltd** [1970] RPC 147.

99 **Football League Ltd v Littlewoods Pools Ltd** [1959] Ch 637

1 This statement assumes that sufficient literary taste and effort has gone into the compilation for, with respect to **Football League Ltd v Littlewoods Pools Ltd**, the work involved in setting out lists of data in a chronological order would, nowadays, be carried out very swiftly by computer. Nevertheless, it is contended that the principles set forth therein are still valid today and directly applicable to the sometimes very complex sets and tables of information contained in look-up tables.

2 This question was left unanswered in **Football League Ltd v Littlewoods Pools Ltd**, but in **Demerara Turf Club v Phang** (1963) WIR 177, it was held that the publication in the defendant's coupon of a list of names of all horses in a race, taken from the plaintiff's programme and coupon, but in a scrambled format, was an infringement.

3 **Independent Television Publications Ltd v Time Out Ltd** [1984] FSR 64; **British Columbia Jockey Club v Standen** 22 DLR (4th) 467.

4 Such as dictionaries, gazetteers, grammars, maps, arithmetical tables, almanacs, encyclopaedias and guide-books.

5 **Waterlow Publishers Ltd v Rose**.

compiler of a directory may use a prior directory in the same way as any other purchaser of the directory as a guide, say, to what streets he must go to for his information, but he may not copy the information from the prior guide into his competing publication. This is comparable to the scenario suggested above where a disk or CD-ROM could be produced which contained a compilation of computer code routines or computer programs (some routines being useful to a computer programmer but too small to be susceptible to copyright in themselves) for other computer programmers to use.

The author of a publication of computer program routines authorises the use of his computer program code for use in practice (and thus to be included in computer programs being written by other computer programmers), unless otherwise stated, but not in a competing book, disk or CD-ROM of computer program routines.

Look-up tables and compilations

As look-up tables may often contain statistical data or the type of information which would ordinarily be found in directories or street maps[6], it is therefore suggested that a consideration of the case law with respect to these species of compilations would assist in an understanding of how the modern law of copyright would or ought to be applied to these species of works; a series of nineteenth-century cases go to show that where a plaintiff has assembled a set of statistical data and publishes it, and the defendant copies the whole of the plaintiff's work which then comprises a substantial proportion of the new work, the court will have regard to the quantity and nature of the information which is appropriated without the exercise of any independent thought or labour and in doing so may find that such an appropriation amounts to infringement.[7] If the defendant, after collecting the information himself, had checked his results by a comparison with the plaintiff's tables, that would have been a very different matter and not an infringement; since it would not be a wholesale extraction of the vital part of the plaintiff's work.

6 For example, the hypothetical computer program which calculated the tidal movement of the sea at different points on a coast may contain a look- up table which itself contains data as to tidal streams, phases of the Moon and other types of statistical data ordinarily found in an almanac. A computer program product which calculates the optimum road routes for vehicles may contain look-up tables which, in turn, contain information representing maps, one-way systems etc.

7 **Scott v Stanford** (1867) LR 3 Eq 718; **Morris v Ashbee** (1868) LR 7 Eq 34; **Mawman v Tegg** (1826) 2 Russ 385; **Jarrold v Houlston** (1857) 3 K & J 708; **Cox v Land & Water Journal Co; Trade Auxiliary Co v Middlesborough etc Assoc** (1889) 40 ChD 425; **Cate v Devon etc Newspaper Co** (1889) 40 ChD 500.

No person is entitled under the law of copyright to avail himself of the previous labours of another for the purpose of conveying to the public the same information, even though he adds additional and novel information to that already published. It is suggested that this statement is consistent with the rule laid down in the case of *Kelly v Morris* which was expressed by the court as follows:

> "In the case of a dictionary, map, guidebook, or directory, where there are certain common objects of information which must, if described correctly, be described in the same words, a subsequent compiler is bound to set about doing for himself that which the first compiler has done. In the case of a road-book, he must count the milestones for himself, ... and the only use that he can legitimately make of a previous publication is to verify his own calculations and results when obtained."[8]

It is not to be inferred from the foregoing that in compiling a directory the compiler may not look into the previous directory of another for the purpose of ascertaining where a particular person lives and whether or not it is appropriate to call upon that person. Nothing further is implied than that he may not take a passage or section from a directory, ascertain whether the directory is accurate on that point, and, if it is found to be accurate, copy the data into his own directory.[9] In the same way where a defendant copied the entries from the plaintiff's directory and then sent out canvassers to private residences to validate the information, subsequently reprinting the information bodily into his own work (even where he had been unable to obtain confirmation that it was correct) the plaintiff's copyright was held to have been infringed.[10] The position is no different if each entry is verified and permission is received from the person canvassed for the insertion of the entry relating to him[11], or if a defendant sends blank enquiry forms to persons, having found their names and addresses from the plaintiff's directory.[12] The rule is therefore that it is perfectly legitimate for a defendant to refer to the plaintiff's work as a guide, leading him to various authorities and sources, and then to compile his own copyright work from these authorities or sources.[13] The principle to hand is that the defendant is not at liberty to use or avail himself of the **labour** which the plaintiff has been to for the purpose of producing his work; for that is merely to take away

8 (1866) LR 1 Eq 697 at 700.

9 **Morris v Wright** (1870) LR 5 Ch 279; **Scott v Stanford** (1867) LR 3 Eq 718; **Cox v Land and Water Journal Co**; **Pike v Nicholas**; **Hogg v Scott** (1874) LR 18 Eq 444; **Lamb v Evans** [1893] 1 Ch 218; **Kelly's Directories Ltd v Gavin** [1902] 1 Ch 631.

10 **Kelly v Morris.**

11 **Morris v Ashbee**; **Waterlow Publishers Ltd v Rose.**

12 **Waterlow Directories Ltd v Reed Information Services Ltd,** *The Times,* 11 Oct 1990.

13 **Morris v Wright**; **Pike v Nicholas.**

the result of another man's labour, or in other words, his intellectual property.[14]

The extent to which earlier/other compilations may be used

While, as has been described immediately above, the compiler of certain types of compilation may lawfully use prior compilations for the purpose of ascertaining the sources available, the position is not the same in regard to those compilations in which part of the merit lies in the selection of what has been compiled. Thus, for example, in cases involving a selection or compilation of quotations, a defendant is not at liberty to use another's anthology of quotations in the sense of going to the sources to see if they are correctly quoted and, if so, introducing them into his own work. This is because the whole merit in such a compilation is the appropriateness of the quotation, its adaptability to a particular end or its illustration of a particular characteristic. The choice of one quotation over another is one which may involve the exercise of knowledge, intelligence and intellectual labour. Its aptness does not depend on the particular place where it may be found. One person may not imitate or adopt the quotations selected and arranged by another.[15]

Computerised anthologies and multimedia encyclopaedias

A computerised anthology of quotations in a multimedia format will have two principal constituent parts. The first will be a computer program engine which handles the display of the selected quotations on the computer monitor and their printing through a computer printer. This computer software (which may be made up of a number of modules each responsible for a different task; thus making the computer software product a compilation in its own right) will also be used to search the anthology itself. This is often seen to be one of the principal advantages of having anthologies, encyclopaedias or dictionaries[16] in a computerised format since the user can perform searches upon the work in different formats. Thus searches for criteria #1 AND criteria #2 OR criteria #3 can be performed at high speed. An anthology of quotations in CD-ROM format would therefore not only contain the computer software product thus described; but contain the quotations

14 **Hogg v Scott.**

15 **Moffatt & Paige Ltd v Gill (G) and Sons Ltd** (1902) 86 LT 465 at 471; **Harman Pictures NV v Osbourne; Ravenscroft v Herbert & Anor; Fernald v Jay Lewis Productions Ltd** [1975] FSR 499.

16 *e.g. The Oxford English Dictionary* is available in CD-ROM format.

themselves in a machine-readable format. Since it is immaterial, for the purposes of copyright, in which material form the work subsists; it is contended that the cases described above with respect to anthologies are directly applicable to such works which are published in computerised formats. It should be borne in mind that the Copyright, Designs and Patents Act 1988 broadened the previous definitions of material form by providing that in relation to literary, dramatic or musical works, copying includes storing the work in any medium by electronic means.[17] This very wide definition makes it clear that virtually any form of storage by modern technological means will amount to copying. The Copyright, Designs and Patents Act 1988 goes further in that it provides that in relation to all categories of copyright work the making of copies which are transient or incidental to some other use of the copyright work will also amount to copying.[18] Thus the transient reproduction of a work, including the computerised access of computerised anthologies and multimedia encyclopaedias which are copied, in part, from the storage medium to the computer's primary memory, will amount to copying. It follows that in relation to these species of computerised works, as their use will at some stage inevitably involve their being copied in this sense, unless licensed (whether expressly or impliedly), such use will constitute an infringement of copyright.

Copying in relation to dramatic works

It will be recalled from Chapter 4 that a plot, similar to that which would subsist in a dramatic work, can subsist in a computer program – especially modern games programs.[19] Consequently a short discussion of the law of copyright with respect to the primary infringement of dramatic works is appropriate. Where the language of a dramatic work has been copied, no special considerations apply and the general principles set out above will apply. However, a basic distinction between literary works and dramatic works is that, in the case of the latter, the choice of dramatic incident and the arrangement of situation may constitute, to a far greater extent, the real value of the work.

---

17 S 17(2). The expression "electronic" is defined to mean actuated by electric, magnetic, electro-magnetic, electro-chemical or electro-mechanical energy (s 178).

18 S 17(6).

19 The Japanese games producer Nintendo, has licensed the characterisations, incidents and plots subsisting in their computer games programs "Super Mario Brothers" and "Street Fighter" to be used in films, cartoons and a wide range of merchandising material.

This section of this chapter will accordingly concern itself with whether infringement of a dramatic work can occur where only situations and plots, but not language, have been reproduced.

Since the passing of the Copyright Act 1911, it has been established that a dramatic work may be infringed by a second dramatisation which reproduces dramatic incidents without using or imitating language. It is not necessary that the words in the dialogue should be the same, for the situations and incidents, and the mode in which the ideas are worked out and presented, may constitute a material portion of the whole work. The court will have regard to the dramatic value and importance of what has been taken, even though the portion may in fact be small and the actual language not copied. On the other hand, the fundamental idea of the dramatic plot of two separate computer games programs might be the same, but if worked out separately and on independent lines, they may be so different as to bear no resemblance to one another.[20] In the same way, the incidents in common between the two works may be drawn from common stock and common knowledge.[21] This may explain the similarities between the two works, so that a defence that there was no copying succeeds, or, even if there was copying, there may be no infringement since there was no originality in the part copied.[22] On the other hand, the fact that a dramatic work prepared for performance in one medium is performed in another should make no difference to the issue of infringement. The question remains whether a substantial use has been made of the series of dramatic incidents in which copyright subsists.

Copying in relation to musical works

As averred to in Chapter 4, computer programs can be the medium in which a musical work is recorded and the means (the instrument) through which it is played or performed. The principal question in cases involving the copying of musical works remains whether the alleged infringement has made use of

20 **Rees v Melville; Sutton Vane v Famous Players Film Co Ltd; Bolton v British International Pictures Ltd; Poznanski v London Film Production Ltd; Ashmore v Douglas-Home.**

21 It is suggested that certain " genres" have now become established in computer games programming. *e.g.* two well-known genres are "Shoot'em Up" and "Beat'em Up". In Shoot'em Up computer games, the main focus of the game is centred on controlling a space ship which shoots other oncoming enemy space ships. Beat'em Up computer games are centred upon a heroic character fighting wicked characters. It is suggested that there is now emerging an allegory in computer game programming of what would ordinarily be known as common stock.

22 **Robl v Palace Theatre** (1911) 28 TLR 69; **Bagge v Millar** [1917–23] MacCC 179; **Dagnall v British & Dominion Film Corp Ltd.**

a substantial part of the skill and labour or the original composer.[23] Whether this has been done or not does not depend upon a note for note comparison but falls to be determined by the use of the ear as well as the eye.[24]

Thus the courts take the view that it is possible for the most uneducated in music to recognise that an altered work of music is, in fact, the same as the "original" work.[25] Nevertheless, the courts almost invariably permit the calling of expert witness evidence to assist the court in recognising the similarities or differences which may exist between two musical works. The courts have accepted that a musical work can be copied without taking a single note from the original;[26] but where only a small part of the plaintiff's work has been taken, it is appropriate to inquire whether, even from a qualitative view-point, the amount taken is so small that it would be impossible to recognise it in isolation. However, in *Hawkes & Son (London) Ltd v Paramount Film Service Ltd* the court held that the 28 bars taken from the march "Colonel Bogey" was such that it "would be recognised by any person" and upon that basis the court held that the 28 bars in question constituted a substantial part of the "original" work. Difficult cases have arisen where the work alleged to have been infringed consisted of an arrangement of tunes too short or basic to be susceptible to copyright;[27] or where the infringing work was produced by using an intervening work. In all such cases it is submitted that the question of infringement is one of fact; as to whether the plaintiff's skill and labour has been appropriated, and similar musical errors may be evidence of such appropriation.

Copying in relation to artistic works

The general principles set out above are equally applicable to the primary infringement of the copyright in artistic works and it will be recalled from Chapters 3 and 4 that some preparatory design material for computer software may qualify as artistic works and the characterisations of characters in games programs also qualify as artistic works within the meaning of the

23 **Hawkes & Son (London) Ltd v Paramount Film Service Ltd; Ricordi (G) and Co Ltd v Clayton & Waller Ltd** (in which the court indicated that even eight bars of an air might constitute a substantial part of the air); **Francis Day & Hunter Ltd v Bron.**

24 **Austin v Columbia Gramophone Co Ltd; Francis Day & Hunter Ltd v Bron.**

25 **D'Almaine v Boosey** [1835] Y & C Ex 288; **Francis Day and Hunter Ltd v Bron.**

26 **Austin v Columbia Gramophone Co Ltd.**

27 As may be the case where the computer program in question (*e.g.* a games program) will play a number of very short discrete melodies or tunes which, in themselves, would be too short or lack sufficient musical input and labour (as in a scale of ascending notes) to attract copyright protection.

Copyright, Designs and Patents Act 1988.[28] Thus, as has been examined in detail above, there is no copyright in an idea as such; so that if all the defendant has copied is the plaintiff's idea, and he has not appropriated the plaintiff's labour in putting the idea into practice, there will be no infringement.[29] In the same way, the fact that the plaintiff's work may have been the inspiration for the defendant's will not of itself make the defendant's work an infringement[30], although if the "feeling and character" of the plaintiff's work has been taken this will be relevant; but will not constitute a conclusive consideration.[31] In accordance with general principles, it has to be determined whether the defendant has used a substantial part of those features of the plaintiff's work upon the preparation of which skill and labour has been employed.

Once it has been established that there has been such a use of the plaintiff's work, there will be an infringement, whether or not the defendant has used a different medium, and whether or not the infringing work has been derived directly from the plaintiff's. It is suggested that in the computer technology field, this general point is of significant importance with respect to the primary infringement of computer programs. Although these principles have an obvious application to the artistic characterisations contained in games programs such as "Sonic the Hedgehog" or "Mega Bomberman";[32] the issue becomes a more subtle one when considering the artistic works which go to make up preparatory design material in the production of commercial computer software products. The Copyright, Designs and Patents Act 1988 is not directed, with respect to this matter, to the means of production but only to the result. Thus, if a manufactured article in fact reproduces the details which go to make up the copyright in the artistic work, the method of reproduction is immaterial. Similarly, the fact that the defendant's work is reproduced in a different form from the plaintiff's will not prevent it from being an infringement since, under the Copyright, Designs and Patents Act 1988, it is an infringement to reproduce an artistic work "in any material form"[33] It is therefore suggested that the flow-charts which are produced in the design of computer programs[34], because they are artistic works within the meaning of the Copyright, Designs and Patents Act 1988, are protected

28 For examples of the identification of artistic works related to computer programs see Chaps 3 and 4.

29 **LB (Plastics) Ltd v Swish Products Ltd; Kleeneze Ltd v DRG (UK) Ltd** [1984] FSR 399; **George Ward (Moxley) Ltd v Richard Sankey Ltd** [1988] FSR 66.

30 **Baumann v Fussell.**

31 **Baumann v Fussell; Brooks v Religious Tract Society.**

32 See Chap 4.

33 S 17(2).

34 See Chap 3.

by copyright in the manner explained directly above. Thus, if a defendant appropriated the plaintiff's labour in flow-charts by inputting them into a CASE tool[35] and thereby produced computer programs (whether that be computer executable code or pseudo-code) then the computer programs so produced would be infringing copies of the "original" flow-charts; even though the code so produced bore no resemblance at all to the computer program code the plaintiff may have produced from the same flow-charts.

Flow-charts – substantial part

In the case of artistic works, the issues surrounding or going to the matter of whether a substantial part of the original work has been appropriated are a little more problematic as identified in the exposition of general principles set out above. Thus, in the case of an artistic work, whether the part reproduced is substantial may depend on how important that part is to the recognition and appreciation of the plaintiff's work.[36] Where the purpose of the artistic work is to convey information (as in the case of a flow-chart or some other species of programming/design diagram) the importance of the part reproduced may fall to be judged by how far it contributes to the conveying of that information (but not, on the other hand, how important that information is *per se*)[37], for the essence of an artistic work is that which is visually significant.[38]

Visual significance generally

In this context, the expression "visually significant" means visually significant to the person to whom the information conveyed would normally be addressed, for example, in the case of an engineering drawing, an engineer and not an ordinary member of the public;[39] and thus, it is submitted, in the case of computer program design flow-charts, a computer programmer and not an ordinary member of the public.

35 For an explanation of Computer Aided Systems Engineering see Chap 3.

36 **Catnic Components Ltd v Hill & Smith Ltd** at 233; approved in **Interlego Industries AG v Tyco Industries Inc** [1989] AC 217.

37 *Ibid.* See also **Johnstone Safety Ltd v Peter Cook (International) plc.**

38 **Rose Plastics GmbH v William Beckett & Co (Plastics) Ltd** [1989] FSR 141; approved in **Interlego Industries AG v Tyco Industries Inc.**

39 **Billhöfer Maschinenfabrik GmbH v TH Dixon & Co Ltd.**

Copying in relation to photographs

The purpose of the Copyright, Designs and Patents Act 1988 is to protect the photographer's work and, as has been mentioned above, multimedia programs often contain photographs either embedded in the program itself or, more usually, as digitised and computerised files. Where a photographer takes a photograph of some scene, a defendant who uses the photograph to obtain an accurate impression of the relative positions of the individuals or objects in the scene, but otherwise recreates the scene in his own style, may well not infringe. This is because the relative positions of the individuals or objects are not the work of the photographer.[40] This may even be the case where the scene photographed is not a commonplace one and the plaintiff's photograph may have been the inspiration for the defendant's work.[41] But where the defendant has in addition recreated the feeling and artistic character of the plaintiff's work this may be sufficient to amount to an infringement if a substantial portion of the plaintiff's work has thereby been appropriated.[42] The position may also be different if the photographer had arranged the subject-matter of the photograph to create some harmonious design[43] or has composed his photograph to include a particular selection of features which the defendant copies.[44]

Copying in relation to sound recordings

The purpose of the Copyright, Designs and Patents Act 1988 is to protect the sound recordist's work and, as has been mentioned above with respect to photographs, multimedia programs often contain sound recordings either embedded in the program itself or, more usually, as digitised and computerised files. There is no further definition in the Copyright, Designs and Patents Act 1988 of "to copy" in relation to sound recordings. It is an infringement of the copyright in a sound recording to copy it[45], or a substantial part of it[46], whether directly or indirectly.[47]

---

40 **Baumann v Fussell.**
41 *Ibid.*
42 *Ibid*; **Brooks v Religious Tract Society.**
43 **Baumann v Fussell.**
44 **Krisarts SA v Briarfine Ltd.**
45 Ss 16(1)(a) and 17(1).
46 S 16(3)(a).
47 S 16(3)(b).

Copying in relation to films

The purpose of the Copyright, Designs and Patents Act 1988 is to protect the film-maker's work and, as has been mentioned above with respect to photographs and sound recordings, multimedia programs often contain short exerts of video footage (films) either embedded in the program itself or, more usually, as digitised and computerised files. Under the Copyright, Designs and Patents Act 1988 it is an infringement of the copyright in a film to make a copy of it[48], or a substantial part of it[49], whether directly or indirectly.[50] This includes making a photograph of the whole or any substantial part of any image forming part of the film.[51]

Copying in relation to broadcasts

Due to the susceptibility of computer programs to be digitised, they are also susceptible to being broadcast. The Copyright, Designs and Patents Act 1988 give no further definition of "copying" in relation to a broadcast other than that it includes making a photograph of the whole or any substantial part of any image forming part of the broadcast.[52] In the usual way, it will also be an infringement to copy the whole or any substantial part of a broadcast[53], whether directly or indirectly.[54]

Copyright infringement by the issue of copies to the public

One of the acts restricted by the Copyright, Designs and Patents Act 1988 in all species of copyright works is the issuing of copies of the work to the public without the authorisation of the copyright owner or some other person with the legal capacity to do so.[55] With certain exceptions, the expression "the issue to the public of copies of a work" in this context, means the act of putting into circulation copies not previously put into circulation, whether in the United Kingdom or elsewhere.[56] It is further provided in the Copyright,

48 Ss 16(1)(a) and 17(1).
49 S 16(3)(a).
50 S 16(3)(b).
51 S 17(4).
52 *Ibid.*
53 S 16(3)(a).
54 S 16(3)(b).
55 Ss 16(1)(b) and 18(1).
56 S 18(2).

Designs and Patents Act 1988 that any subsequent distribution, sale, hire or loan of those copies, or any subsequent importation of those copies into the United Kingdom, will not amount to an infringement under this class of restricted act.[57] Exceptions to this last provision are made in the case of sound recordings, films and computer programs, where any rental of copies to the public will amount to an infringement for this purpose.[58] For this purpose, the expression "Rental" means any arrangement under which a copy of the work is made available:

(i) for payment (in money or money's worth); or

(ii) in the course of a business, as part of services or amenities for which payment is made; and

in either the case in *(i)* or *(ii)* above, on terms that the copy will or may be returned.[59]

Copyright infringement by the showing or playing of the work to the public

Under the Copyright, Designs and Patents Act 1988 it is an act restricted by the copyright in a literary, dramatic or musical work to perform the work in public.[60] In this context, the expression "performance" is defined to include delivery in the form of lectures, addresses, speeches and sermons[61] and, in general, includes any mode of visual or acoustic presentation, including presentation by means of a sound recording, film, broadcast or cable programme of the work.[62] These latter expressions are all further defined in section 19(2)(b) of the Copyright, Designs and Patents Act 1988. Thus, in addition to the obvious ways in which such works may be performed, a musical work embodied or recorded in the medium of a computer program may be performed by it being "played" on a computer in public. In relation to a dramatic work subsisting within a computer program, it is contended that if the incidents of the plot are visually presented through the use of computer technology, this will amount to an infringement of copyright, it not being necessary that the same language is employed.

57 Ss 18(2)(a) and 18(2)(b).
58 S 18(2).
59 S 178.
60 S 19(1).
61 S 19(2)(a).
62 S 19(2)(b).

Copyright infringement by the making of an adaptation

In general

It will be recalled from Chapter 2 that subsequent to the implementation of the Copyright (Computer Programs) Regulations 1992, section 21(4) of the Copyright, Designs and Patents Act 1988 changed the law with respect to the making of adaptations in the following manner (set out afresh for convenience), whereby computer programs are completely excluded from the previous action of section 21(3) and the transformations occurring during the running of a computer program are now included in section 21(5):

> "**21.** – (1) The making of an adaptation of the work is an act restricted by the copyright in a literary, dramatic or musical work.
> For this purpose an adaptation is made when it is recorded, in writing, or otherwise.
> (2) The doing of any of the acts specified in sections 17 to 20, or subsection (1) above, in relation to an adaptation of the work is also an act restricted by the copyright in a literary, dramatic or musical work.
> For this purpose it is immaterial; whether the adaptation has been recorded, in writing or otherwise, at the time the act was done.
> (3) In this Part "adaptation" –
> (a) in relation to a literary work, other than a computer program, or dramatic work, means –
> (i) a translation of the work;
> (ii) a version of a dramatic work in which it is converted into a non-dramatic work or, as the case may be, of a non-dramatic work in which it is converted into a dramatic work;
> (ii) a version of the work in which the story or action is conveyed wholly or mainly be means of pictures in a form suitable for reproduction in a book, or in a newspaper, magazine or similar periodical;
> (ab) in relation to a computer program, means an arrangement or altered version of the program or a translation of it;
> (b) in relation to a musical work, means an arrangement or transcription of the work.
> (4) In relation to a computer program, a "translation" includes a version of the program in which it is converted into or out of a computer language or code or into a different computer language or code.
> (5) No inference shall be drawn from this section as to what does or does not amount to copying a work."

It can therefore be seen that these new amendments to the Copyright, Designs and Patents Act 1988 tend not to take into account the possibility of artistic or dramatic works, films, musical works or sound recordings being recorded in the medium of a computer program and it is submitted that a proper interpretation of the new law is that it has not altered the position with respect to all of these classes of work and the making of an adaptation of any of these classes is still a primary infringement of copyright as it was in the Copyright, Designs and Patents Act 1988 before the implementation of the Copyright (Computer Programs) Regulations 1992. It is suggested that when interpreting the provisions of sections 21(1) to 21(5) of the Copyright, Designs and Patents Act 1988, reference to computer programs should be construed narrowly, so that one is directing oneself to the fundamental computer program code as would be found in the simpler computer software application product.

Adaptation is not conversion into a (non) dramatic work

The Copyright, Designs and Patents Act 1988 therefore tells us that with respect to fundamental computer program code, it is not susceptible, as an adaptation, of being made into a non-dramatic work or, as the case may be, into a dramatic work. Nor can fundamental computer program code be converted into a version of the work in which the story or action is conveyed wholly or mainly by means of pictures in a form suitable for reproduction in a book, or in a newspaper, magazine or similar periodical. This is a pity, for it is argued that in the Copyright (Computer Programs) Regulations 1992, Parliament had the opportunity of matching the new emergent computer programming technologies but, as seems always to be the case, the law is lagging significantly behind computer technology, and imaginative interpretation of the new form of Copyright, Designs and Patents Act 1988 will be required of the courts to ensure that the labour, skill and expertise embodied and reflected in modern computer program technology is adequately protected by the area of law which, ostensibly, is designed to protect it.

Adaptation and arrangement

As can be seen in section 21(3)(ab) of the Copyright, Designs and Patents Act 1988 the expression "adaptation" in relation to a computer program, means:

- *(i)* an arrangement; or
- *(ii)* an altered version; or
- *(iii)* a translation of it and the expression "translation" includes a version of the program in which it is converted into or out of a computer language or code or into a different computer language or code.[63]

63 S 21(4).

No definition of the expression "arrangement" is given in the Copyright, Designs and Patents Act 1988, but it seems that a computer program can be "arranged" in the same manner as a musical work.[64] An "arrangement" of a musical work would include, for example, arranging the score for an opera so that it can be played on the piano[65] or arranging an old air with an accompaniment.[66] It seems, it is suggested, highly problematic as to how this concept can be applied directly and sensibly to computer programming technology and this change to the Copyright, Designs and Patents Act 1988 has produced an unnecessary complication. One could speculate that the arranging of a computer program written for a mainframe computer so that the principal areas of functionality were reproduced so it would execute on a personal computer would constitute an "arrangement" within the meaning of the Copyright, Designs and Patents Act 1988; but the application of this area of the law should be direct, obvious, useful and thoughtful and speculation should not be a requirement in the interpretation of this important part of the Copyright, Designs and Patents Act 1988. Then what is meant by the expression "altered version" and how is this to be matched to the expression "translation"?

In so far as a computer program may subsist in many forms; for example, in different computer languages, different types of computer code[67] and as preparatory design material and flow-charts;[68] these forms would all qualify as translations of the computer program. It is consequently suggested that the construction of an "altered version" of a computer program would not involve the process of translation but some other process which altered the original program. It is suggested that such a process might include the process known as "porting"[69] where changes might be made in the substitution of a certain area of computer code so that the code would execute on one type of computer rather than another. The ambit of the expression "altered version" is a very wide one and may encompass any change to a computer program which was not a translation and fell short of producing a new copyright work.

64 It is an adaptation to make an arrangement of a musical work under s 21(3)(b) of the Copyright, Designs and Patents Act 1988.

65 **Wood v Boosey.**

66 **Lover v Davidson** (1856) 1 CBNS 182.

67 *e.g.* unexecutable source code and executable object code.

68 Since s 21(4) of the Copyright, Designs and Patents Act 1988 tells us that a computer program can exist in a form outside of computer code or language.

69 See Chap 3.

Primary infringement and the future of computer programming technology

As made out above in this chapter, a great deal of attention is made by the courts to certain indicia of copying when evaluating instances of primary infringement of copyright by copying with respect to computer programs. However, computer programming technology is rapidly moving away from the notion that computer programmers write computer programs line by line and thus, when one programmer appropriates the labour of another by copying, areas of redundant code will be transferred from the original to the copy, thus allowing the court to see direct and powerful evidence of copying. Rather, with the advent of CASE technology and Object Oriented Programming, computer programmers use sophisticated programming tools which often produce the line by line code themselves. Indeed, since computer programmers are writing products to work within industry standard environments[70], the programmer's discretion has become curtailed since there may be only one preferred way of making a system call to a peripheral, or only one way of drawing a sculptured "yes" or "no" box to the screen. It is suggested that more emphasis, therefore, will need to be directed to the processes of a computer program and to its preparatory design material, since programming discretion and idiosyncrasies will become almost impossible as the current trends continue. The programmer will be expert in mapping a business process into a computer program process and using software tools and will be less expert in line by line programming. This is not to say that no programming will go on as it has been previously known – there will always be code cut from scratch in small bespoke programming consultancies and the giant software houses developing software tools and operating systems. It is contended though, that the greater majority of computer programming will not involve line by line programming and thus the small number of opportunities the courts of law have had to inspect this type of related copying will be even less frequent in the near future. In fact, that time may already be upon us.

70 In other words, industry standard operating systems such as the Microsoft Corps "Windows" operating system used on the vast majority of personal computers around the world.

Chapter 9

Secondary Infringement of Copyright in Computer Programs

Introduction

The Copyright, Designs and Patents Act 1988 provides for secondary or indirect classes of copyright infringement. The principal characteristic which differentiates this species of tort from that of primary infringement is that the defendant in a successful action must possess the requisite degree of "guilty knowledge". The Copyright, Designs and Patents Act 1988 provides for three broad classes of secondary infringement. The first consists of various types of dealings with infringing copies, the second consists of the provision of the means for the manufacture of infringing copies, and the third provides the sanctions for the permitting or providing of the means for infringing performances of a copyright work to take place. This chapter will examine these species of secondary infringement and also consider a more modern species of secondary infringement, being concerned with the use of devices designed to circumvent copy protection.

Secondary Infringement

Definition

The Copyright, Designs and Patents Act 1988 with respect to secondary infringement applies essentially to acts done in relation to infringing copies. An article is an infringing copy if its making constituted an infringement of the copyright in the work in question.[1] An article is also an infringing copy if:

1 S 23.

(i) it has been or is proposed to be imported into the United Kingdom; and

(ii) its making in the United Kingdom would have constituted an infringement of the copyright in the work in question, or a breach of an exclusive licence agreement relating to that work.[2]

Where in proceedings it is proved that an article is a copy of a work, and that copyright subsists or has at any time subsisted in the work, then for the purposes of deciding whether the article is an infringing copy it is to be presumed until the contrary is proved that the article was made at a time when copyright subsisted in the work.[3] This broad definition of infringing copy is, it is submitted, important with respect to computer programs, computer software products and their preparatory design material. Since a significant number of different species of copyright work can subsist contemporaneously within a computer program, it is argued that all may be the subject of secondary infringement. Under section 23 of the Copyright, Designs and Patents Act 1988, the copyright in a work is infringed by any person who, without the licence of the copyright owner:

(i) possesses in the course of a business,

(ii) sells or lets for hire, or offers or exposes for sale or hire,

(iii) in the course of a business exhibits in public or distributes, or

(iv) distributes otherwise than in the course of a business to such an extent as to affect prejudicially the owner of the copyright,

an article which is, and which he knows or has reason to believe is, an infringing copy of the work. The copyright in a work is also infringed by any person who, without the licence of the copyright owner, imports into the United Kingdom, otherwise than for his private and domestic use, an article which is, and which he knows or has reason to believe is, an infringing copy of the work.[4]

Importing

Consequently, in the case of an article which has been imported or which is proposed to be imported into the United Kingdom, the article in question would qualify as an infringing copy if the making of it in the United Kingdom would have constituted an infringement of copyright or a breach of an

2 S 27(3). The expression "exclusive licence" is defined in s 92(1).
3 S 28(4).
4 S 22.

exclusive licence agreement relating to that work of which the article constitutes a copy. Thus the owner of the United Kingdom copyright or the exclusive licensee for the United Kingdom can object to the importation of and subsequent dealings in copies made outside of the United Kingdom without authority or licence.[5] This is so even though the articles made outside of the United Kingdom were legitimately purchased there on the open market, for the sale of articles in the ordinary course of business in one territory without restriction on resale does not carry with it any implied licence to import and sell those articles in another territory. The definition of an infringing copy in the case of an imported article involves making an assumption as to the circumstances in which the article was made. It was established under the equivalent provisions of the Copyright Act 1956 that the only assumption which had to be made for this purpose was that the article was made in the United Kingdom by the actual person who made it outside of the United Kingdom.[6] The provision of the Copyright, Designs and Patents Act 1988 relating to exclusive licence agreements means that a person who is a licensee under such an arrangement covering the United Kingdom may object to the importation of and dealings in articles even in circumstances where they were made outside of the United Kingdom by the owner of the United Kingdom copyright.

5 However, it should be borne in mind that s 27(5) of the Copyright, Designs and Patents Act 1988 expressly provides that nothing in these provisions under examination here may be construed as applying to an article which may be lawfully imported into the UK by virtue of any enforceable EU right within the meaning of s 2(1) of the European Communities Act 1972. Therefore, if an article is in free circulation within the EU it will not constitute an infringing copy for any of these purposes. On this point, it should be borne in mind that the Copyright (EC Measures Relating to Pirated Goods and Abolition of Restrictions on the Import of Goods) Regulations 1995 (SI. 1995/1445) which commenced on 1 July 1995 amend s 111 of the Copyright, Designs and Patents Act, which entitles a copyright owner to give notice to the Commissioners of Customs and Excise of infringing material, requesting that they are treated as prohibited. These Regulations add new provisions requiring that such requests are limited to goods which arrive in the UK from outside the European Economic Area (EEA) or from within the EEA but which have not been entered for free circulation. However, this restriction does not apply to goods entered, or expected to be entered, for free circulation, export, re-export or for a suspensive procedure in respect of which an application may be made under EC Council Regulation 3295/94 Art 3(1) laying down measures to prohibit the release for free circulation, export, re-export or entry for a suspensive procedure of counterfeit or pirated goods.

6 **Barson Computers (NZ) Ltd v John Gilbert & Co Ltd** [1985] FSR 489; **Polydor Ltd v Harlequin Record Shop** [1980] FSR 194 and 362 (CA); **The Who Group v Stage One (Records) Ltd** [1980] FSR 268; **CBS Ltd v Charmdale Record Distributors Ltd** [1981] Ch 91.

Territorial extent

The interesting difficulties that may arise with respect to these particular provisions of the Copyright, Designs and Patents Act 1988 is that, unlike cases of primary infringement[7], acts of secondary infringement, apart from importation, are not restricted expressly by the Copyright, Designs and Patents Act 1988 to acts done solely within the territory of the United Kingdom. However, it is suggested that as this part of the Copyright, Designs and Patents Act 1988 is extended by section 157(1) to England, Wales, Scotland and Northern Ireland, and the general principle of statutory construction with respect to territoriality is that unless the contrary is expressly enacted, English Acts of Parliament and subordinate legislation do not extend to acts of foreigners who have never come into the jurisdiction[8], then if an article whose making in the United Kingdom constituted an infringement of copyright (and which was thereby an infringing copy) came into the hands of a person in a foreign jurisdiction, those persons would not be liable under the Copyright, Designs and Patents Act 1988 for selling the article in the foreign jurisdiction even in circumstances where they had the necessary knowledge. It should be acknowledged that the provision that an "infringing copy" may also include one which is "proposed" to be imported into the United Kingdom indicates a contrary position to the one enunciated, and that the Copyright, Designs and Patents Act 1988 is intended to extend beyond the territory of the United Kingdom. Thus it might be argued that the Copyright, Designs and Patents Act 1988 expressly contemplates a situation in which the infringing article is not yet in the United Kingdom, and since possession of the infringing copy, its exposure for sale, exhibition in public and distribution[9] are all acts of infringement, the Copyright, Designs and Patents Act 1988 also contemplates that acts done outside of the United Kingdom may be infringements.

However a true and proper construction of the Copyright, Designs and Patents Act 1988 can be given whereby the Copyright, Designs and Patents Act 1988 applies to the United Kingdom only. For the purposes of these specific provisions, an act can be done in the United Kingdom in relation to an article even though the article in question has not been imported into the United Kingdom. Thus, although the expression "import" is not defined in the Copyright, Designs and Patents Act 1988 it is submitted that it means the bringing of an article from outside of the United Kingdom into a port of the

7 See s 16(1).

8 *ex p Blain* (1879) 12 ChD 522; **Clark v Oceanic Contractors Inc** [1983] 2 AC 130.

9 (With the requisite knowledge.)

United Kingdom, such that the carriage of the article involved is ended or its continuity is in some way broken.[10] Secondly, it should be borne in mind that acts done on a British ship, aircraft or hovercraft will be treated as if they had been done in the United Kingdom[11] and, in addition, the territorial waters of the United Kingdom are to be treated as part of the United Kingdom.[12]

It follows therefore, that acts can be done in what is the United Kingdom for the purposes of the Copyright, Designs and Patents Act 1988, for example on board a British ship, in relation to articles which are "proposed to be imported into the United Kingdom" without having reached a United Kingdom port. If this proposition is a correct interpretation of the Copyright, Designs and Patents Act 1988 then it would be an infringement of copyright to possess, with the required level of knowledge, an infringing copy on board a British ship if it was proposed to import it into the United Kingdom, but it would not be an infringement to possess such an article on board a British ship if the article was neither made in the United Kingdom nor had ever been imported into the United Kingdom and it was not proposed to import it.

In the course of business – defined and explained

As identified above, under the Copyright, Designs and Patents Act 1988, copyright in a work is infringed by any person who, without the licence of the copyright owner, and with the requisite knowledge, possesses an infringing copy in the course of business.[13] The expression "business" is defined as including a trade or profession;[14] and the "business" in question must be that of the party possessing the infringing work, and not that of some other person who sold it to him.[15] Due to the paucity of prominent precedent available with respect to the Copyright, Designs and Patents Act 1988 on these matters, it is argued that a short comparison between the 1988 Act on this subject and the Copyright Act 1956 as one proceeds through the remainder of these provisions, will be useful and apposite in assessing the weight that may be applied in using the precedents arising under the aegis of the Copyright Act 1956 so as to permit a proper interpretation of the Copyright, Designs and Patents Act 1988. Under the Copyright, Designs and

10 **Wilson v Chambers & Co Pty Ltd** (1926) 38 CLR 138; **Grammaphone Co of India Ltd v Pandey** [1985] FSR 136.

11 S 162.

12 S 161.

13 S 23(a).

14 S 178.

15 **Reid v Kennett** [1986] Crim LR 456 which was decided under the equivalent provision of the Copyright Act 1956 (s 21(4A)).

Patents Act 1988 the exhibition of an infringing article in public is only an infringement if done in the course of business, trade or profession. It is therefore not an infringement under these provisions to invite offers for sale, for example by sending out a price list.[16] Nor does a person infringe copyright who merely attempts to effect a sale but who does not in the course of doing so commit one of the specific acts of infringement.[17] Whether a sale has taken place will be judged on an objective basis, and the fact that one party had no subjective intention to enter into a contract or create a legal relationship will be irrelevant.[18] Where a defendant has delivered copies on a "sale or return basis" he is not liable for any subsequent sale because he cannot demand the return of the copies.[19] On the matter of secondary infringement by distribution, the provisions of the Copyright, Designs and Patents Act 1988 and the Copyright Act 1956 are identical in effect. To constitute an infringement the distribution must either be in the course of a business, profession or trade, or be carried on to such on an extent as to prejudicially affect the owner of the copyright. With respect to secondary infringement through importation, the onus is on the importer to show that the article was imported only for private or domestic use.

Requisite knowledge

As was indicated above, the Copyright, Designs and Patents Act 1988 provides with respect to secondary infringement that it is necessary in proving this tort, to prove that the defendant knew or had reason to believe he was dealing in an article which was an infringing copy of the work in question.[20] For the purposes of the Copyright Act 1956 the plaintiff was obliged to prove that the defendant knew that the making of the article constituted or (in the case of an imported article) would have constituted an infringement of copyright.[21] The introduction of the words "had reason to believe" in the Copyright, Designs and Patents Act 1988 might suggest, it is argued, that it is easier under the 1988 Act for a plaintiff to prove "knowledge" than under the Copyright Act 1956. In the light of the interpretation of the pertinent areas of the Copyright Act 1956, it is suggested that the Copyright, Designs and Patents Act 1988 has not made any material change to the law except to

16 **Norgren Co v Technomarking**, *The Times*, 3 March 1983.
17 **Wolff v Wood**, *The Times*, 31 Oct, 1903; **Britain v Kennedy** (1903) 19 TLR 122.
18 **Phillips v Holmes** [1988] RPC 613, decided under s 21(1) Copyright Act 1956.
19 **Schofield & Sims Ltd v Gibson (R) & Sons Ltd** [1928–35] MacCC 64.
20 Ss 22 and 23.
21 Copyright Act 1956, ss 5(2), 5(3), 16(2) and 16(3).

render liable a defendant who has negligently failed to make inquiry. The decisions under the Copyright Act 1956 established that knowledge in this sense means actual and not constructive knowledge.[22] In every case it will be a question of fact as to whether the defendant had this requisite knowledge. It has been said that in this context the knowledge involved means notice of facts such as would suggest to a reasonable man that a breach of copyright law was being committed, or which would at least put him on inquiry.[23] It is submitted that this means no more than that where it is necessary to draw inferences the court is entitled to infer knowledge on the part of a particular person on the assumption that that person had the ordinary understanding expected of persons in his line of business.[24] In the usual manner of proving knowledge, the defendant's statements and gestures will constitute evidence as to his state of knowledge. But a person who deliberately refrains from inquiry and is wilfully blind to the facts which would be apparent to him cannot successfully contend that he lacks the requisite knowledge.[25] The provisions in the Copyright, Designs and Patents Act 1988, however, contemplate specific knowledge about the circumstances in which a specific article was made and it may be that a defendant's general knowledge that an article may be an infringing copy would not be sufficient to fix him with the required level of knowledge.[26] However, if the defendant has knowledge of the relevant and required facts then that is all that is necessary.[27] Thus it is no defence for a defendant to say that although he knew the facts he nevertheless believed that as a matter of law no infringement had or would have been committed, even if this was on the basis of legal advice.[28]

Fixing the requisite knowledge in the defendant

Where it is thought possible that a person may not be aware that he is dealing in infringing goods, it is usually necessary to give him notice of the matter, commonly by letter, before it can safely be said that further dealing in the

22 RCA Corp v Custom Cleared Sales Pty Ltd [1978] FSR 576; Politechnika v Dallas Print Transfers Ltd [1982] FSR 529; Hoover plc v George Hulme Ltd; International Business Machines Corp v Computer Imports Ltd [1989] 2 NZLR 395.

23 Albert v Hoffnung & Co Ltd [1921] 22 SR(NSW) 75; Gramophone Company Ltd v Music Machine (Pty) Ltd [1973] 3 SALR 188; Infabrics Ltd v Jaytex Shirt Co Ltd [1978] FSR 451.

24 RCA Corp v Custom Cleared Sales Pty Ltd.

25 Columbia Picture Industries v Robinson [1987] Ch 38.

26 *Ibid.*

27 Sillitoe v McGraw-Hill Book Co; International Business Machines Corp v Computer Imports Ltd at 418.

28 *Ibid.*

goods by him will amount to infringement.[29] Questions then arise as to the type of information which must be given and the period of notice that is allowable and appropriate. On the foregoing principles, it is submitted that sufficient information must be given to suggest to the recipient that an infringement of copyright will be committed if he continues to deal in the articles in question. The information must not, it is contended, be of such a general nature that the recipient can form no proper view as to what is being alleged.[30] The requirement of knowledge is an important ingredient of secondary infringement under the Copyright, Designs and Patents Act 1988 and was well expressed by Morritt J in *LA Gear Incorporated v Hi-Tec Sports Plc*[31] where he said:

> "...it seems to me that 'reason to believe' must involve the concept of knowledge of facts from which a reasonable man would arrive at the relevant belief. Facts from which a reasonable man might suspect the relevant conclusion cannot be enough. Moreover, as it seems to me, the phrase does connote the allowance of a period of time to enable the reasonable man to evaluate those facts so as to convert the facts into a reasonable belief."[32]

This dicta was approved of in the recent case of *Hutchinson Personal Communications v Hook Advertising*[33] where it was held that the supply of complicated pleadings to the defendant was insufficient to fix the requisite degree of knowledge in him. Accordingly, in cases of an alleged secondary infringement concerning computer programs where the technology is positively not well understood generally, it is submitted that a very great level of care needs to be exercised in fixing the appropriate level of knowledge with the defendant. The copyright work in question ought to be identified with clarity and if a copy is not supplied to the defendant then, at least, facilities should be offered for its inspection. Thus it can be seen, it is argued, the importance of the computer software product producer identifying the species and nature of copyright works that exist within the product. At the time of infringement, there may be little opportunity to indulge in a rigorous review of the works subsisting in a product necessary to mount an appropriate action against the suspected infringer; especially in cases where only some of the technology has been appropriated. A person is not fixed with the requisite knowledge at the instant he receives notice of a claim;[34] and a period of time must be permitted which is sufficient to give him a

29 **Cooper v Whittingham** (1880) 15 ChD 501.
30 **Hoover plc v George Hulme Ltd.**
31 [1992] FSR 121.
32 At 129.
33 [1995] FSR 365 at 378.
34 **Van Dusen v Kritz** [1936] 2 KB 176.

reasonable opportunity to make inquiries, obtain legal advice and make up his mind.[35] A period of 14 days is often taken to be sufficient[36], but in each case it will be a matter of fact.[37]

Thus once again, due to the lack of precedent on this matter and the novelty of the technology involved together with the possible complexity of the subject-matter, great care ought to be exercised in determining the notice period in the case of the secondary infringement of a copyright subsisting in computer software.

The means for making infringing copies

The Copyright, Designs and Patents Act 1988 contains provisions making persons liable who knowingly possess or provide the means for making infringing copies. The Copyright, Designs and Patents Act 1988 specifically provides that the copyright in a work is infringed by a person who, without the licence of the copyright owner:

(i) makes,
(ii) imports into the United Kingdom,
(iii) possesses in the course of a business, or
(iv) sells or lets for hire, or offers or exposes for sale or hire,

an article specifically designed or adapted for making copies of that work, knowing or having reason to believe that it is to be used to make infringing copies.[38] Once again, the expression "business" is taken to include a trade or profession. The reference to an article "specifically designed or adapted for making copies of **that** work" means, it is submitted, that dealing in an article which is generally designed for making copies will not fall within this provision. The provision therefore appears to be directed to dealings in articles such as photographs, moulds, master recordings and the like. Thus an article specifically designed or adapted for making copies of a specific games cartridge would be covered by this provision. Indeed, it is submitted that the "article" could itself be a computer program or suite of computer programs specifically designed to copy another computer program in circumstances where there was no copy protection. However, a general operating system which had the facility, as they invariably do, to copy computer files would not fall under this provision.

35 **RCA Corp v Custom Cleared Sales Pty Ltd.**

36 **Infabrics Ltd v Jaytex Ltd.**

37 **Sillitoe v McGraw-Hill Book Co.** In **Rexnold Incorporated v Ancon Ltd** [1983] FSR 662, it was held that a notice period of nine days was insufficient where the defendant had to make inquiries of manufacturers and suppliers abroad.

38 S 24(1).

Transmission

The copyright in a work is also infringed by a person who, without the licence of the copyright owner, transmits the work by means of a telecommunications system (in circumstances not including broadcasting or inclusion in a cable programme service), knowing or having reason to believe that infringing copies of the work will be made by means of the reception of the transmission in the United Kingdom or elsewhere.[39] The expression "telecommunication system" is defined in section 178 Copyright, Designs and Patents Act 1988 as meaning a system for conveying visual images, sounds or other information by electronic means.[40] Thus the transmission of computer programs, preparatory designs materials or any other species of copyright work (whether subsisting in the computer program itself or independently) across computer networks, to or through computer bulletin boards or via electronic mail-providing services knowing that infringing copies will then be made will constitute secondary infringement. In such cases the person transmitting the work will often have committed a primary infringement, since copying the work is a necessary incident in transmitting such data.

Performance

The Copyright, Designs and Patents Act 1988 provides that where the copyright in a literary, dramatic or musical work is infringed by a performance at a place of public entertainment, any person who gave permission for that place to be used for the performance is also liable for the infringement, unless when he gave permission he believed on reasonable grounds that the performance would not be an infringement of copyright.[41] For this purpose, a "place of public entertainment" includes premises which are occupied mainly for other purposes but are from time to time made available for hire for the purposes of public entertainment.[42] One of the crucial issues therefore, is whether permission was given for the use of the premises in question for the performance. It is submitted that the giving of permission for the use of the premises generally is not sufficient since the permission must be for the premises to be used for the performance complained of. Under the equivalent provisions of the Copyright Act 1911, it was held that a person does not permit what he cannot control, and does not permit the use of a place for the

39 S 24(2).
40 The expression "electronic" is also defined in s 178 (see also Chap 2 p 22).
41 S 25(1).
42 S 25(2).

performance of a work if he does not know that the work is going to be performed.[43] Thus where a person permits premises to be used knowing which works will be performed, this will be sufficient to establish "permission", but not if the choice of works to be performed is solely a matter for the performers and the defendant has no knowledge of what, in fact, will be performed.[44] Permission may be inferred from acts which fall short of the giving of explicit, positive permission; and may be inferred from indifference, but permission will not be inferred from a mere general authority to use a theatre for the performance of musical or dramatic works.[45]

Provision of apparatus

The Copyright, Designs and Patents Act 1988 makes further provision for secondary infringement where the copyright in a work is infringed by the public performance of that work or by the playing or showing of it in public. Thus various classes of persons may also be liable where such infringement has occurred by means of apparatus for playing sound recordings, showing films or receiving visual images or sounds conveyed by electronic means.[46] Modern computer hardware technology, which therefore means the computer software running on it, can constitute such apparatus and, it is further argued, effect all of the foregoing classes of event. The Copyright, Designs and Patents Act 1988 makes it clear that a person can only be liable under these provisions where there is already some other person liable for the primary infringement of the work in question. Firstly, section 26(2) of the Copyright, Designs and Patents Act 1988 provides that a person who supplied the apparatus, or any substantial part of it, is liable for the infringement if, when he supplied the apparatus:

- (i) he knew or had reason to believe that the apparatus was likely to be so used as to infringe copyright, or
- (ii) in the case of apparatus whose normal use involves a public performance, playing or showing, he did not believe on reasonable grounds that it would not be so used as to infringe copyright.

In situation *(i)*, it is argued that an infringement would occur where a person supplied an oversize computer monitor equipment for use in public, such as in an exhibition, knowing that no sufficient licence had been obtained. In

43 **Performing Right Society Ltd v Ciryl Theatrical Syndicate Ltd** [1924] 1 KB 1.

44 **Monaghan v Taylor** 2 TLR 685, cited in **Performing Right Society Ltd v Ciryl Theatrical Syndicate Ltd.**

45 **Performing Right Society Ltd v Ciryl Theatrical Syndicate Ltd.**

46 S 26(1).

situation *(ii)*, it is argued an infringement would occur where, for example, specialised computer display projection equipment was supplied for use in public. Although the burden of proof as to the requisite degree of knowledge rests with the plaintiff, the intention of the Copyright, Designs and Patents Act 1988 with respect to situation *(ii)* appears to make that burden easier to discharge. Secondly, section 26(3) Copyright, Designs and Patents Act 1988 provides that an occupier of premises who gives permission for the apparatus to be brought onto the premises is also liable for the infringement if, when he gave the permission, he knew or had reason to believe that the apparatus was likely to be used to infringe copyright. Thirdly, section 26(4) Copyright, Designs and Patents Act 1988 provides that where a person who supplies a copy of the sound recording or film[47] used to infringe copyright is also liable for infringement, if when he supplied it, he knew or had reason to believe that what he supplied, or a copy made directly or indirectly from it, was likely to be used so as to infringe copyright.

Devices Designed to Circumvent Copy-Protection

The technology explained

For the first time in copyright law in the United Kingdom, a copyright act expressly contemplated the use of mechanisms which prevent the unauthorised copying of computer programs. There are two principal methods used in the computer software industry to inhibit the unauthorised copying of computer programs: one is oriented towards the provision of an additional piece of hardware directed towards the security of the software; the other methodology is purely software oriented. In the first method, the computer software product is supplied with a small piece of hardware commonly known as a "dongle". The dongle would usually be fitted to the computer hardware on which the software is to be run[48] and contains a small

47 Which might be recorded digitally as a computer file or actually recorded within the medium of a computer program.

48 Most computers, especially personal computers, have a number of "ports". These are connectors to which cables are connected to link the computer to peripherals such disk drives, printers and monitors. The dongle will often be a small grey box approximately 5 cm x 5 cm x 2 cm with a connector at either end. The connector at one end makes the attachment with the computer, the other connector mimics the original connector of the computer which the dongle is occupying so that the overall number of connectors (ports) on the computer is not reduced.

amount of software which will communicate with the main computer software product. Thus, when executing, the computer software product will make "calls" to the dongle. In a manner of speaking, the computer software product will check for the presence of the dongle, it might even interrogate (ask questions of) the dongle's software and then match the results derived from the dongle software with its "expectations". The presence of the dongle and the type and configuration of the dongle software will then permit the computer software product to continue operating. The dongle software might be configured to certain specific types of hardware or may be configured to permit a maximum number of users for the software.[49] In any event, the dongle will prevent unauthorised use, that is copying, of the computer software product.

The second methodology may be used as an alternative to the first but they are not mutually exclusive. In the wholly software oriented methodology, the software itself might be encoded so that it makes calls to the specific hardware environment in which it is to be used and will cease to operate if it finds itself copied to some other hardware. Other software copying protection systems involve the software counting the number of times it has been copied and writing special routines on to a disk to prevent its unauthorised copying. Copy protection, like other aspects of computer programming technology is constantly in motion and new and more complex systems are being developed all the time.

The provisions in the Copyright, Designs and Patents Act 1988

The pertinent part of Copyright, Designs and Patents Act 1988 dealing with devices designed to circumvent copy-protection is as follows:

> "**296.** – (1) This section applies where copies of a copyright work are issued to the public, by or with the licence of the copyright owner, in on an electronic form which is copy-protected.
> (2) The person issuing the copies to the public has the same rights against a person who, knowing or having reason to believe that it will be used to make infringing copies –
> (a) makes, imports, sells or lets for hire, offers or exposes for sale or hire, or

49 A great many computer software products are used over networks and the software houses often licence their products according to usage. Thus a licensee might purchase a licence for five users at a lower licence fee than a licensee purchasing a 100-user licence for a much higher fee. The software house will therefore not wish a customer who has paid for five users, putting the software up on a 100-user network.

advertises for sale or hire, any device or means specifically designed or adapted to circumvent the form of copy-protection employed, or

(b) publishes information intended to enable or assist persons to circumvent that form of copy-protection,

as a copyright owner has in respect of on an infringement of copyright.

(3) Further, he has the same rights under section 99 or 100 (delivery up or seizure of certain articles) in relation to any such device or means which a person has in his possession, custody or control with the intention that it should be used to make infringing copies of copyright works, as a copyright owner has in relation to on an infringing copy.

(4) References in this section to copy-protection include any device or means intended to prevent or restrict copying of a work or to impair the quality of copies made."

Thus one can see that offences under this section are committed by a person who, knowing or having reason to believe that it will be used to make infringing copies, either makes, imports, sells or lets for hire, offers or exposes for sale or hire, or advertises for sale or hire, any device or means specifically designed or adapted to circumvent the form of copy protection employed, or publishes information intended to enable or assist persons to circumvent that specific form of copy-protection. It is suggested that in practice no concern needs to be taken over the fact that section 296 applies to the circumvention of a specific form of copy protection or encryption, on the ground that this might be too narrow an approach to be effective.

Analysis

Although a security software house producing specialist dongles and copy-protection software routines may have thousands of different client software houses using its protection techniques (in other words although many software products may share a copy protection technique) a non-specific circumvention technique could not be possible, but would have to be a solution directed specifically at the copy-protection technology in question. It is also important to note that the requirement of knowledge or belief governs both the offence of making, importing, selling, letting for hire, and exposing for sale or hire a device and the offence of publishing information. Such knowledge or belief is that the device or information will be used to make infringing copies, presumably, it is argued, of a copyright work or works, but not necessarily infringing copies of the copyright work in question, but of any copyright work.[50] The use of the expression "means" would also

50 Comparing s 24 with s 296(1) and (3).

cover, it is suggested, the use of computer programs themselves which defeat copy protection.

Rights against the tortfeasor

If an offence under section 296 Copyright, Designs and Patents Act 1988 is committed, then the persons issuing the copies of the copyright work to the public are given the same rights against the offender as a copyright owner has in respect of an infringement of copyright. Issuing copies of a work to the public means the act of putting into circulation copies not previously put into circulation in the United Kingdom or elsewhere; and not to any subsequent distribution, sale, hiring or loan of those copies (or any subsequent importation of those copies into the United Kingdom).[51] It is clear from section 296(1) of the Copyright, Designs and Patents Act 1988, that the person having these rights will not necessarily by the copyright owner, although given the rights of the copyright owner. Importantly, section 296 Copyright, Designs and Patents Act 1988 only refers to such persons having the same "rights" as a copyright owner; they are not described as having the same "rights and remedies" as the copyright owner. It is still not clear how far proceedings under section 296 Copyright, Designs and Patents Act 1988 will be a true parallel to proceedings for infringement of copyright. Certainly this is an unsatisfactory situation for provisions which have specific and far-reaching application to the computer software industry.

51 S 18(2).

Chapter 10

THE EUROPEAN UNION

INTRODUCTION

In this chapter, the individual structures and mechanisms with respect to the law of copyright in each of the individual Member States of the European Union (together with some other relevant countries in Europe) will be examined with particular reference to the application of the local Law of Copyright to computer software. It is unavoidable that, in the context of this work, such an examination can only be a brief one and that it can merely be an attempt to highlight and point to the differing mechanisms of copyright application for computer programs that exist throughout the European Union. However, a short examination will be made of the manner in which the local law applies to other species of copyright works since computer software technology, as made out above, can contain, express and/or create many disparate classes of works. A brief history of the European Union's history of copyright law integration (or harmonisation as it is often referred to) is also given in this Introduction so as to build some contextual reference for the examination to follow.

COPYRIGHT AND EUROPEAN UNION LAW

Harmonising the treatment of copyright works

In compliance with the European Union Commission's Green Paper on Copyright in 1989[1] the European Union adopted and is continuing to introduce a number of measures which seek to harmonise specific aspects of the treatment of copyright works throughout the European Union. Despite the general and misplaced apprehension in the computer software industry that there is a "European" law applicable to their products, the European

1 COM (88) 172 final of 2 March 1989.

Union recognised that the manner in which "copyright" protection is extended to dramatic, literary and artistic works varies strikingly between legal jurisdictions throughout the union. Accordingly, the European Commission has had to adopt a piecemeal approach, consisting of a variety of parallel legislative proposals, in a response to the very complicated and fragmented nature of copyright throughout the jurisdictions constituting the European Union and the stark differences in the solutions followed by different Member States

From the 1970s onwards, the rapid and ever accelerating growth of the computer software industry has forced a number of Member States of the European Union to introduce various legislative solutions to produce an explicit protection of computer programs as copyright works. The solution of expressly adopting computer programs as a form of copyright work has gradually emerged as the preferred and most appropriate (or least controversial) form for the protection of computer programs. Copyright protection does not require any formalities that could stifle the rapid development of new software and, it is submitted, benefits from an existing, long established system for international protection based on multilateral agreements[2] which have been ratified by a very large number of countries throughout the world. Consequently, the European Union opted for copyright as the appropriate vehicle for the harmonisation of the legal protection of computer programs.

The EC protection of computer programs

This led to the adoption of the Council Directive of 14 May 1991 on the legal protection of computer programs.[3] This Directive required implementation by the Member States of the European Union before 1 January 1993, but most Member States failed to achieve this deadline. The Council Directive on the legal protection of computer programs[4] seeks to protect computer programs by copyright, as literary works within the meaning of the Berne Convention on Copyright.[5] It is submitted that this

2 The Berne Convention on Copyright and the Universal Convention on Copyright.

3 Council Dir 91/250 of 14 May 1991 on the legal protection of computer programs – 91/250/EEC; OJ 1991 L122/42.

4 *Ibid.*

5 Art 2(1) of the Berne Copyright Convention (Paris Revision, 1971) defines "literary and artistic works" as including "every production in the literary, scientific and artistic domain, whatever may be the mode or form of its expression, such as books, pamphlets and other writings; lectures, addresses, sermons and other works of the same nature; dramatic or dramatico-musical works, choreographic works and entertainments in dumb show; musical compositions with or without words; cinematographic works to which are assimilated

protection applies to the expression, in any form, of a computer program, including preparatory design material.[6]

Ideas and concepts

The ideas and principles which underlie any element of a computer program, including those which underlie its interfaces, are not protected by copyright under the Council Directive on the legal protection of computer programs.[7]

Interfaces and interoperability

The protection of interfaces became a subject of intense lobbying during the preparatory stages of this Directive and the computer software industry generally assumed that the degree to which copyright protection could also cover interfaces would define the leading industry players' power to dominate the hardware and software market in the years to come. The contrary position argued that an excessive protection of interfaces could extinguish further progress towards interoperability and lead to abuses of the leading manufacturer's dominant position. The solution provided in Council Directive 91/250's text is generally regarded as a compromise that may favour, to some extent, the proprietors of rights in standard software operating environments. However, this solution is easier to align with general copyright and intellectual property principles across Europe and, further more, extreme abuses of dominant position can, in any event, be limited through recourse to European Union's and national competition rules. However, it should be always borne in mind that copyright in each jurisdiction arises under the aegis and in the context of that jurisdiction's law of copyright and despite the movement towards harmonisation, the actual and real-life application of the law of copyright can be, in some cases, narrower or broader than the European Union directives concerned would lead one to believe.

---

5 *(cont.)*
works expressed by a process analogous to cinematography; works of drawing, painting, architecture, sculpture, engraving and lithography; photographic works to which are assimilated works expressed by a process analogous to photography; works of applied art; illustrations, maps, plans, sketches and three-dimensional works relative to geography, topography, architecture or science."

6 See Chap 3 above for an explanation of the nature of preparatory design material.

7 Council Dir 91/250 of 14 May 1991 on the legal protection of computer programs – 91/250/EEC; OJ 1991 L122/42.

Originality

The concept of originality was one of the key issues that had to be dealt with; in respect of the disparate tests applied to originality and the computer program throughout the Member States of the European Union. For example, earlier German decisions suggested that computer programs should have a particularly high level of originality in order to qualify for copyright protection. This principle was not followed in the Council Directive on the legal protection of computer programs and under Article 1(3), it is sufficient that the computer program be original in the sense that is the author's own intellectual creation.

Subsistence generally

The subsistence of copyright in computer programs under the Council Directive on the legal protection of computer programs is not subject to any formalities and the author of a computer program is defined as being the natural person or group of persons who has created it, or, where the legislation of a Member State permits, the legal person designated as the right holder by the legislation. Where a computer program is created by an employee in the execution of his duties or following the instructions given by his employer, the economic rights in the program are conferred on his employer, unless otherwise agreed.

Rights of the copyright owner

The exclusive rights which vest in the owner of the copyright in a computer program under the Council Directive on the legal protection of computer programs include the right to do or authorise the following:

- the permanent or temporary reproduction of a computer program by any means and in any form, in part or in whole;[8]
- the translation, adaptation, arrangement and any other alteration of a computer program and the reproduction of the results thereof, without prejudice to the rights of the person who alters the program; and

8 Authorisation by the copyright holder is also required for loading, displaying, running, transmission or storage of the computer program in so far as these acts necessitate reproduction.

- any form of distribution to the public, including the rental, of the original computer program or its copies.[9]

Term

Originally, the protection granted by the Council Directive on the legal protection of computer programs would expire 50 years after the death of the computer program's author, or after the death of the last surviving author. In cases of anonymous or pseudonymous works, computer programs or programs whose author is a legal person would enjoy a term of protection of 50 years from the date of its first publication. Member States already providing for longer terms of protection were allowed to maintain them. These provisions have now been deleted and replaced by the general provisions governing the duration of protection of literary works under the Council Directive of 29 October 1993 harmonising the term of protection of copyright and certain related rights.[10] Consequently, copyright in computer programs runs for the life of their authors and for 70 years after their death.[11]

Acts not requiring the copyright owner's permission

The Council Directive on the legal protection of computer programs further provides that the following acts do not require the copyright owner's authorisation:

- unless otherwise agreed, reproductions, translations, adaptation and arrangements by the lawful acquirer in accordance with the intended purpose of the computer program, including for example, error correction;
- the making of a back-up copies by a lawful user;[12]
- within certain specified limits, the observation, study or testing of the program by a lawful user; and

9 This right is subject to the "exhaustion of rights principle" (generally applying to all intellectual property rights) whereby the first sale of a licence to use in the European Union of a copy of a program by the copyright holder or with his consent exhausts the distribution right, within the European Union, on that copy, with the exception of the right to control further rental of the program or its copies.

10 Council Dir 93/98/EEC; OJ 1993 L 290/9.

11 See Chap 2 for the manner in which this Directive is to be implemented in the UK.

12 This provision is mandatory and may not be contracted out of by the parties to a licence agreement.

- the decompilation of the program, albeit subject to the detailed conditions specified in the Directive.[13]

Rental

The home rental of videos has been so successful that it is even threatening to eclipse the theatrical exploitation of films. At the same time, and for different reasons, rental of copyright-protected music works is also increasingly popular. Compact discs are much more resistant to use than the old and rapidly vanishing vinyl records and computer games programs in cartridge format are difficult to copy (perhaps impossible for the ordinary home user) and these advances in technology make them far easier to rent on a profitable basis. Until recently, the extent to which copyright owners could control these forms of exploitation was not always clear and remained legally fragmented along national lines. In the absence of any express rules, the "exhaustion of rights" principle could arguably threaten authors' right to control the rental and lending of their works once these had been put on the market with their consent. The need to address these problems led to the adoption of the Council Directive of 19 November 1992 on rental right and lending right and on certain rights related to copyright in the field of intellectual property.[14] This Directive required implementation by Member States before 1 July 1994. However, it gives Member States the option to implement certain provisions as late as 1 July 1997. This Directive's provisions on application in time are complicated, detailed and include an substantial number of possible deviations and options. This is a result of last-minute efforts to arrive at a political agreement on what had turned out to be a controversial proposal. Consequently, the practical implementation of the Directive is likely, it is submitted, to remain subject to a certain fragmentation in the applicable legal regimes across the borders of the European Union, at least in the near future.

This Directive provides a right to authorise or prohibit the rental and lending of:

- originals and copies of copyright works;
- the fixation of artists' performances;
- phonograms; and
- fixations of a film.

---

13 In principle, decompilation is allowed only for the purpose of achieving interoperability. between the program licensed to the lawful user and another computer program. Contractual provisions under which a licensor aims at imposing stricter restrictions on decompilation than those allowed under this directive are null and void *ab initio*.

14 Dir 92/100/EEC; OJ L346/61.

The expression "rental" in this Directive means making available for use, for a limited period of time, and for direct or indirect economic or commercial advantage. The expression "lending" in this Directive means making available for use, for a limited period of time and not for direct or indirect economic or commercial advantage, when it is made through establishments which are accessible to the public.

Legal protection of databases

At the time of the writing of this work, an amended proposal for a Directive on the legal protection of databases is advancing towards adoption by the EC Council. The proposal aims to harmonise copyright protection of databases and to introduce a parallel, *sui generis* form of protection that would be automatically available for all databases, but would be more limited than copyright protection. The proposed date of implementation was originally 1 January 1995, but the actual date of implementation has already been postponed a number of times and is likely to be postponed further. Under the proposal, electronic databases will be protected by copyright as "collections" within the meaning of the Berne Convention on copyright.[15] This is without prejudice to the protection, if any, of the works or materials contained therein and the computer program used in the making or operation of the database. These remain separate matters, not covered by the proposal. In order to be protected by copyright, a database must be original in the sense that it is a collection of works or materials which, by reason of their selection or their arrangement, constitutes the author's own intellectual creation. The author of a database protected under the proposal is the natural person or group of persons who created the database, or, where the legislation of the Member States permits, the legal person designated as the right holder. The economic rights in a database created by an employee in the course of his duties belong to his employer, unless otherwise provided by contract. In principle, beneficiaries of this Directive must be citizens or companies of a Member State; but the EU Council, acting on a proposal from the European Commission, may extend this right to citizens and companies of non-European Union countries.

15 Art 2(5) of the Berne Copyright Convention (Paris Revision, 1971) tells us that: "Collections of literary or artistic works such as encyclopaedias and anthologies which, by reason of the selection and arrangement of their contents, constitute intellectual creations shall be protected as such, without prejudice to the copyright in each of the works forming part of such collections." It is argued that this definition seems to be very similar in action to the concept of compilations under English law and may therefore not signal a significant change in the legal protection of databases from the existing position.

The owner of the copyright in a database under this proposed directive will have in respect of the selection or arrangement of the contents of the database, as well as its thesaurus, index or system for obtaining or presenting information, the following exclusive rights:

- the reproduction right;
- the right to translate, adapt, arrange or otherwise alter the database;
- the right to reproduce the results of any of the previous acts;
- the right of distribution to the public in any form, including rental;[16] and
- the right to communicate, display or perform the database to the public.

In addition to the copyright protection granted to those databases that fulfil the usual conditions of originality, the proposed directive also introduces a *sui generis* right. The scope of the *sui generis* right will be limited compared to copyright, but it will have the advantage that it will exist automatically, irrespective of the "originality" of the database which may be helpful in the protection of some computer software products "look-up tables"[17] which may not be sufficiently original for copyright itself to subsist within them. The *sui generis* right will consist of a right to prevent the unauthorised extraction or re-utilisation of the contents of a database, in whole or in substantial parts, for commercial purposes. This right will belong to the owner of the rights in the database, and will apply irrespective of the eligibility of a database for copyright protection. The duration of copyright protection of databases will be the same as that provided for literary works and it is submitted that in an analogous manner with respect to copyright, insubstantial changes to the selection or arrangement of the contents of the database will not extend its original period of protection. The *sui generis* right is expected to run from the date of the creation of the database and will expire at the end of a period of 15 years from the date when the database was first lawfully made available to the public. The lawful user of the database will have the right to perform any of the restricted acts described above in order to use the database in the manner determined by the contractual arrangement with the copyright owner or the authorised licensor, or in order to gain access to the contents of the database. In addition, it is expected that certain "fair use" restrictions of copyright will also apply,

16 In line with the "exhaustion of rights principle", the first sale of a licence in the European Union of a copy of a database by the copyright owner or his authorised licensee or with his consent will exhaust the distribution right on that copy, with the exception of the right to control further rental of the database or any copy thereof.

17 See Chap 8.

allowing, for example, brief quotations and illustrations for the purposes of teaching.

Anticipated changes to the term of copyright

At the time of writing[18], the draft statutory instrument for the Publication Right and the Duration of Copyright and Rights in Performances Regulations 1995 became available which, when coming into force[19], will radically alter some aspects of the nature of copyright subsisting in computer programs and the other species of copyright works which can subsist within or be recorded in computer programs.[20]

The Publication Right and the Duration of Copyright and Rights in Performances Regulations 1995 will implement the provisions of European Council Directive 93/98/EEC[21] and is intended to harmonise the term of protection of copyright and certain other related rights throughout the European Union. The Copyright, Designs and Patents Act 1988 already grants a number of the rights required by the European Council Directive 93/98/EEC (which, for the purposes of ease of reference, will be referred to in this part of Chapter 10 as the EC Directive) and the Publication Right and the Duration of Copyright and Rights in Performances Regulations 1995 will amend and extend the Copyright, Designs and Patents Act 1988 in so far as its provisions do not conform to or comply with the requirements of the EC Directive. The Publication Right and the Duration of Copyright and Rights in Performances Regulations 1995 will also implement in respect of the Copyright, Designs and Patents Act 1988, the obligation imposed by the European Economic Area Act 1993 in accordance with the United Kingdom's obligations under the European Economic Area Agreement, to substitute for any reference to a Member State of the European Community, a reference to an EEA State.

The EC Directive seeks to harmonise the duration of copyright and performer's rights; it provides for the principal director of a film to be treated as an author of the film; introduces a new publication right for works in which copyright has expired but which have never before been published; the right arising upon first publication or communication to the public and lasting for 25 years. The provisions harmonising the duration of copyright increase the existing period of copyright in literary, dramatic, musical and

18 July 1995.
19 Which is currently expected to be 1 Nov 1995.
20 For a full account of these issues, see Chap 5.
21 OJ 1993 L290/9.

artistic works and films in the United Kingdom from the life of the author plus 50 years to the life of the author plus 70 years. The manner in which the duration of copyright in films is calculated is modified by the Publication Right and the Duration of Copyright and Rights in Performances Regulations 1995 so as to be similar to that of literary, dramatic, musical and artistic works. The Directive also requires reciprocal duration of copyright and performer's rights in the case of works and performances connected with countries not members of the European Economic Area.[22]

Transitional provisions

The transitional provisions of the Publication Right and the Duration of Copyright and Rights in Performances Regulations 1995 will have the following effect: in relation to films, the right of a principal director to be treated as an author of a film will not apply to films made before 1 July 1994; in relation to duration of copyright, for those works in which copyright subsists on 1 November 1995 (the date upon which the Publication Right and the Duration of Copyright and Rights in Performances Regulations 1995 are expected to come into force) or where the duration of copyright has expired in the United Kingdom before 1 July 1995, but which are protected on that date under the copyright legislations of any other State in the European Economic Area, copyright will revive on the date the Publication Right and the Duration of Copyright and Rights in Performances Regulations 1995 come into force and will then expire on a date 70 years after the author's death.

Summary of the expected effect of individual parts of the Publication Right and the Duration of Copyright and Rights in Performances Regulations 1995

Part I of the Publication Right and the Duration of Copyright and Rights in Performances Regulations 1995:

Principal film director an author	• will make the principal director of a film an author of it for copyright purposes in addition to the producer as at present;[23]

22 As defined by the European Economic Area Act 1993.

23 Publication Right and the Duration of Copyright and Rights in Performances Regulations 1995, reg 4.

Employed principal film director	• provides that where the principal director of a film is an employee, then his employer is to be the first owner of copyright as is already the case for any other employed author;[24]
Reciprocal term of copyright	• will make provisions for reciprocal duration of copyright in literary, dramatic, musical and artistic works, films, sound recordings and broadcasts connected with countries other than European Economic Area States, such that the period of protection granted in the United Kingdom to those works is that granted under the legislation of the country in which the work was first published or (in the case of sound recordings and broadcasts) of which the author is a national or subject. However, the application of this provision ought not to be at variance with any existing obligation of the United Kingdom under any international convention to which it became a party prior to 29 October 1993;[25]
Increase in copyright term	• will increase the duration of copyright in literary, dramatic, musical and artistic works of known authorship to life of the author plus 70 years and will, it is submitted, make new provisions for the duration of copyright in films to be linked to the lives of persons connected

24 *Ibid*, reg 5.
25 *Ibid*, reg 6 and 10.

with a film and to last until 70 years after the death of the last of those persons to die. It will also increase the duration of copyright in respect of works of unknown authorship to 70 years after the date upon which the work is either made, or if made available to the public during that period, from the date upon which it is first made so available;[26]

Modification of expression "released"

- will modify the meaning of the expression "released" in connection with the calculation of the duration of copyright in sound recordings so as to include the expression "playing in public";[27]

Changes in term calculation method

- since the period of copyright in a copyright work is to run from the same date throughout the European Economic Area, the Publication Right and the Duration of Copyright and Rights in Performances Regulations 1995 will make changes to those provisions which determine the commencement of that period other than by reference to the death of an author or to the date on which a work is made, so as to take account of events anywhere in the European Economic Area which cause the period to commence to run;[28]

26 *Ibid*, reg 7.
27 *Ibid*, reg 8.
28 *Ibid*, regs 7, 8 and 9.

Act permitted on expiry of term

- will make consequential amendments to the existing provisions of the Copyright, Designs and Patents Act 1988 relating to acts permitted on assumptions as to the expiry of copyright on the death of the author;[29]

New publication right

- will introduce a new "publication right" arising in respect of copyright works in which the copyright has expired and which have never been published during the period of copyright protection. The duration of the right is expected to be 25 years from the date of first publication or communication to the public of the copyright work; and the right will entitle the owner of it to the same exclusive rights as granted by copyright itself.[30] Other regulations make consequential changes to the jurisdiction of the Copyright Tribunal[31] and the index of defined expressions in the Copyright, Designs and Patents Act 1988;[32]

Duration of rights in performances

- will modify the existing provisions relating to the duration of rights in a performance such that these rights will be protected for 50 years from when the performance first takes place, or if a recording of the performance

29 *Ibid*, reg 11.
30 *Ibid*, reg 14.
31 *Ibid*, reg 12.
32 *Ibid*, reg 13.

is released within that period, for 50 years from when the recording is first released. In addition to this, where the performer of the work in making that first performance is not a national of an European Economic Area State, the duration of rights in the performance will be that accorded to the country of which the performer is a national in a similar manner to the provision on reciprocal duration of copyright;[33]

Part II of the Publication Right and the Duration of Copyright and Rights in Performances Regulations 1995 contains the heart of the transitional provisions and, in brief summary, provides as follows:

Application of the Regulations

- that the Publication Right and the Duration of Copyright and Rights in Performances Regulations 1995 will apply not only to works created after 1 November 1995 (the expected date upon which the Publication Right and the Duration of Copyright and Rights in Performances Regulations 1995 will come into force) but will also apply to copyright works created before that date;[34]

Retroactivity

- that no act done before the date on which the Publication Right and the Duration of Copyright and Rights in Performances Regulations 1995 come into effect will constitute an

33 *Ibid*, reg 15.
34 *Ibid*, reg 16(1).

infringement of any right coming into existence in pursuance of the Publication Right and the Duration of Copyright and Rights in Performances Regulations 1995;[35]

Longer term

- that where, under the Copyright, Designs and Patents Act 1988, the period of copyright protection for a copyright work would be longer than that provided for by the Publication Right and the Duration of Copyright and Rights in Performances Regulations 1995, the longer period would prevail;[36]

Director of a film = author

- the provisions of regulation 4 of the Publication Right and the Duration of Copyright and Rights in Performances Regulations 1995 where the principal director of a film can be treated, for the purposes of the Copyright, Designs and Patents Act 1988, as the author of the film, will not apply in respect of films made before 30 June 1994;[37]

Reciprocal term of copyright and performance rights

- the new provisions as to the reciprocal duration of copyright and performer's rights set out in regulations 6, 10 and 15 of the Publication Right and the Duration of Copyright and Rights in Performances Regulations 1995 will not apply to

35 *Ibid*, reg 16(2).
36 *Ibid*, reg 16(3).
37 *Ibid*, reg 17.

copyright works and performances which qualified for protection under the Copyright, Designs and Patents Act 1988 before the Publication Right and the Duration of Copyright and Rights in Performances Regulations 1995 come into force;[38]

Part II – Retroactivity

- the parts of the Publication Right and the Duration of Copyright and Rights in Performances Regulations 1995 which increase the duration of copyright in the United Kingdom to the life of the author plus 70 years will apply not only to copyright works created after the date on which the Publication Right and the Duration of Copyright and Rights in Performances Regulations 1995 come into force; but will also apply to copyright works created before that date in which copyright continues to subsist on that date, and further, to works in which copyright in the United Kingdom has expired before that date but which are protected on 1 July 1995 under legislation relating to copyright in any other European Economic State;[39]

Determination of copyright

- provides for the determination of ownership of both extended and revived copyright[40], in so far as the person who is the owner of

38 *Ibid*, reg 18.
39 *Ibid*, regs 19 and 20.
40 *Ibid*, regs 21 and 22.

an existing copyright work on the commencement of the Publication Right and the Duration of Copyright and Rights in Performances Regulations 1995 will be deemed to be the first owner of the extended copyright in it[41] and in relation to a copyright work out of copyright in which its copyright has been revived, where immediately preceding the expiry of the copyright in that work, the copyright was subject to an exclusive licence, ownership of the revived copyright in it vests in the exclusive licensee; but in any other case, the revived copyright vests in the person who owned the copyright on its expiry.[42] The Publication Right and the Duration of Copyright and Rights in Performances Regulations 1995 also make express provisions for agreements which take account of extended or revived copyright and permits them so long as the relevant party to the agreement is authorised to deal with the copyright in the work;[43]

Exercise of moral rights in revised works

- who is to exercise moral rights in respect of a revived copyright and provides that a waiver of moral rights will be effective with respect to revived works;[44]

41 *Ibid*, reg 21(1)(a).
42 *Ibid*, reg 21(1)(b).
43 *Ibid*, reg 21(3).
44 *Ibid*, reg 23.

Revived copyright works and acts done pursuant to an agreement

- the provision for acts done in relation to a revived copyright work on or after the commencement of the Publication Right and the Duration of Copyright and Rights in Performances Regulations 1995 in pursuance of any provision of an agreement entered into before 1 January 1995 will not constitute an infringement of the revived copyright in that work;[45]

Issuing to the public

- this provision produces a saving (making an act which would be an infringement of copyright not an infringement) in respect of the issue to the public after the date on which the Publication Right and the Duration of Copyright and Rights in Performances Regulations 1995 commence of copies of a revived copyright work made before 1 July 1995 and at a time when copyright in the revived work had expired;[46]

Owner of revived work cannot be found

- Regulation 25 further produces a saving for acts done in respect of revived copyright works after the date on which the Publication Right and the Duration of Copyright and Rights in Performances Regulations 1995 commence, where the owner of the right cannot be found by reasonable inquiry;

Restricted acts

- that a licence or right to do any of the acts restricted by copyright

45 *Ibid*, reg 24.
46 *Ibid*, reg 25.

in respect of a revived copyright works subject only to the payment of royalties or other payments as may be agreed or, in default of agreement, at a rate fixed by the Copyright Tribunal, except where a licence could be granted by a licensing body;[47]

Adaptation of revised work in a new original work

- where an original work is or contains an adaptation of a revived work and was made before 1 July 1995, and at a time when copyright did not subsist in the revived work, it will not be an infringement of copyright in a revived work for any person to do any restricted act in relation to the original work;[48]

Agreements and the extended copyright term

- that in relation to an extended copyright work, that any agreement effective throughout the duration of the original period of copyright continues throughout the extended copyright period;[49]

Acts done in the extended copyright term

- that in relation to an extended copyright work, that any act done during the period of extended copyright in pursuance of an agreement entered into before 1 January 1995, will be treated as licensed by the copyright owner subject to the payment of royalties or to other payment as may be agreed or, in default of agreement, be fixed by the Copyright Tribunal.[50]

---

47 *Ibid*, reg 26.
48 *Ibid*, reg 27.
49 *Ibid*, reg 28.
50 *Ibid*, reg 29.

The Law of Copyright in the Member States of the European Union

The law of copyright of Austria

In general

The Austrian Copyright Act dates from 1936 and provides a comprehensive protection of the "works" of authors as "copyright as such". It also contains complex and detailed provisions on "neighbouring rights" which grant less extensive protection to recitations and performances, photographic works (motion pictures and simple photographs), phonograms and radio broadcasts. In recent years, Austrian copyright law development has been substantially in line with the requirements of European Union law and the requirements of the Software Directive (Dir 91/250/EEC) and the Rental and Lending Right Directive (Dir 92/100/EEC) were implemented in 1993 by an amendment to the Copyright Act 1936. Further amendments to the Copyright Act 1936 are being considered which will bring Austrian copyright law into step with the Directive relating to satellite broadcasts and transmission by cable and the Directive on the term of copyright protection. Further amendments of Austrian copyright law (*e.g.* an obligation to pay remuneration for reprography) could be included in this amendment.

Computer programs

Original intellectual creations in the fields of literature, music, the fine arts and cinematography enjoy copyright protection as "works". Although recent Supreme Court rulings have, in particular with respect to works of fine art, abandoned the principle of "elevated level of originality", the "individual originality" of the work must still be examined in each particular case. The original character of the work stemming from the author's personality is determinative; and for this purpose it is not sufficient, however, that the work be statistically unique. The individual original achievement must stand out against the ordinary, common and usual and it presupposes that personal features of the creator of a work are expressed, in particular through the visual design and the intellectual structure of the work. Following a recent amendment of the Copyright Act 1936, computer programs are subject to special rules, generally reflecting the provisions of the Software Directive. Computer programs are thus deemed works within the meaning of the

Copyright Act 1936 if they are the result of the own intellectual creation of their author. The Austrian Supreme Court has not, so far, rendered any judgments relating to the copyright protection of computer programs, on the basis of these new provisions.

Copyright protection in Austria commences with the creation of the work and does not require any fixation in material form. The author of a work is the natural person that created it. Legal entities cannot be original copyright owners; but this rule is subject to some exceptions in favour of film producers, commercial photographers, phonogram producers and broadcasters. If a work is created by an employee in the course of his employment, copyright will vest in the employees subject to any contractual exploitation rights he may have granted to his employer. Specific statutory provisions governing works created by employees exist only for computer programs and where computer programs are created by an employee in fulfilment of his employment duties, the employer is entitled to an unrestricted exploitation right of this program, unless otherwise agreed with the author. Special provisions exist for professionally made cinematographic works and the exploitation rights are generally vested in the owner of the company (often the film producer). Exceptions also apply with respect to neighbouring rights. Thus, the exclusive rights in professionally produced photographic works are vested in the owner of the company employing the photographer and similar provisions apply in favour of phonogram producers and broadcasters. All of these categories of rights owners may, however, transfer their original rights to third parties.

Author's rights

Under Austrian copyright law, the author of a copyright work has a number of exclusive exploitation rights designed to protect his economic interests. The public communication of the content of a literary or cinematographic work is reserved to the author, provided the work itself, or a substantial part of its contents have not already been published with the author's consent.[51] The author of a translation or another adaption may use it in the manner reserved to him only to the extent permitted by the author of the adapted work.[52] Furthermore the author has the exclusive right to reproduce the work, regardless of the quantity and method used.[53] The author has the exclusive right to disseminate copies of the work[54] and without the author's

51 This is referred to in Austrian law as the right of first statement of content.
52 This is known as the right of adaption and translation.
53 This is known as the right of reproduction.
54 This is known as the right of dissemination.

consent, copies of the work may neither be offered nor otherwise brought into circulation in a manner making them accessible to the public. As long as a work has not been published, the author has the exclusive right to make the work accessible to the public by publicly posting, displaying, hanging it, exhibiting it or otherwise making use of the work. In general therefore, copies of a work put into circulation through a transfer of ownership with the consent of the original owner of the rights, cease to be subject to the original owner's right of dissemination. The right owner may, however, restrict the territory in which copies of his work may be disseminated. However, this does not apply to copies of the work which have been put into circulation with the consent of the right owner in a Member State of the European Union or EFTA. The author has the exclusive right to broadcast or otherwise transmit the work[55] and the author has the exclusive right to communicate the work in a non-material form.[56] In addition to these exclusive rights of economic exploitation, the author's moral rights are also protected under Austrian law. In particular, he has the exclusive right to decide whether, by whom and how his work will be made accessible to the public (right of publication). He has the unwaivable right to claim authorship if such authorship is challenged or if the work is attributed to another person. It is also up to him to decide whether an author's designation is to be affixed to the work, and if so which. Where a work is used in a way which makes it accessible to the public or is reproduced for the purpose of distributing it, the person who has been granted the relevant exploitation right by the author is also prohibited from altering the work, its title or the author's designation, unless either the author has given his consent, or this is permitted by law. The owner of a work must make it available to the author upon the latter's request, in so far as this is necessary to reproduce the work.

Copyright term

The copyright for literary, musical and artistic works generally lapses 70 years after the end of the year of the author's death. Where a work has been created by several authors jointly, copyright lapses 70 years after the end of the year of death of the last co-author. In the case of cinematographic works, the corresponding duration is 50 years after the end of the year these works were made; and if cinematographic works are published prior to the expiration of this deadline, the duration of protection is 50 years after the

55 This is known as the broadcasting right.
56 This is known as the right of recitation, public performance and display.

end of the year of publication. Neighbouring rights enjoy a more limited protection. In particular, the protection periods are shorter, for example:

- for recitations and performances the protection period is 50 years after the end of the year in which the work was first performed or recited;
- for photographic works the protection period is 30 years after the end of the year in which they were taken; and if published before this deadline, photographic works are protected for 30 years following the year of first publication;
- for phonograms the period of protection is 50 years after the end of the year in which they were recorded or, respectively, published.

Copyright in Austria is capable of being inherited; otherwise it cannot be transferred in the sense of a full assignment under English law. The author may, however, grant an exploitation permit (analogous to a non-exclusive licence under English law) or an exploitation right (analogous to an exclusive licence under English law) authorising others to use the work in a specific manner. There are no special formalities required.

The law of copyright of Belgium

In general

The law applying to copyright in Belgium arises by virtue of the Copyright Act 1994[57] which came into force on 1 August 1994, replacing the Copyright Act of 1886 and computer programs are subject to the provisions of a separate Act, also of 1994, which implements Council Directive 91/250/EEC.[58] The Copyright Act 1994 does not include a definition of the term "work". In addition, it does not detail the requisite conditions for entitlement to copyright protection. The intention of such an omission is to enable the courts to apply the provisions of the Copyright Act 1994 to a wide variety of works, including new types of works, unknown at present (*e.g.* works relating to new technology). A copyright work need not be novel, nor does it need to have artistic or aesthetic merit. It must, however, be original. This requirement means that the work must bear the "personal mark" of the author in so far as it must be the expression of the personal, individual intellectual effort of the author. Hence it is not sufficient that the author has

57 *Loi relative au droit d'auteur et aux droits voisins.*

58 *Loi transposant en droit belge la directive européenne du 14 mai 1991 concernant la protection juridique des programs d'ordinateur.*

invested substantial time and effort in, for instance, research. He must also have added his personal mark to the work. For example, a particular street map was considered capable of copyright protection, not because it resulted from intensive topographical and historical research, but owing to the personal choice of colours, letter-types and lay-out by the author. The requirements for a computer program to qualify for protection are, it is submitted, the same as other types of copyright work; however, there has not been any significant case law in this respect since the Act implementing Council Directive 91/250/ EEC came into force.

Qualifying aspects and authors

There are no formalities laid down by Belgian copyright law in respect of the subsistence of copyright in new works, such as registration or payment of fees. It is the creation of the work alone which gives the right to protection. However, in order to acquire protection, a work must be constituted in a explicit form. This does not mean that the work must be embodied in a material form (oral works or improvisations are equally protected) but merely that copyright protection only extends to the form of the work. Ideas, principles, theories, or a particular style cannot be protected by copyright. The copyright to a work vests in the individual who has created it. The person whose name or distinctive sign (whatever this may be) appears on the work will be deemed to be the author unless otherwise evidenced. Legal entities such as companies and corporations can never be the original owners of the copyright to a work. In respect of anonymous works, or of works under a pseudonym, the "editor" (*i.e.* the person who discloses the work to the public) will be considered to be the author in all relations with third parties. The copyright to works created by several authors vests in all of them jointly. In the absence of any contractual arrangement, the exploitation of the copyright to a work in which the individual author's contributions cannot easily be identified (*e.g.* a text written by several authors) can only be made jointly by the co-authors. Each co-author may, nevertheless, individually sue infringers. If each author's contribution can be identified (*e.g.* a music composer or lyricist), each author may exploit his individual contribution in the work (*e.g.* the melody or the lyrics) separately, without prejudicing the work as a whole. The rights to the latter remain common and must be exploited jointly. The economic rights to a work created by an employee in the framework of the performance of his duties under an employment contract vest with the employee, unless otherwise expressly provided in writing, either in the employment contract or by separate agreement. A similar rule under Belgian law applies to works resulting from the execution of a works under contract in the advertisement sector or, alternatively, in a non-cultural industry. In such a case, the economic rights can be assigned to the person who ordered the work, on condition that this assignment is explicit and relates to the exploitation of the work for advertisement or non-cultural purposes. Such provisions have an obvious and direct application to the commissioning of computer programs from contractors.

The Copyright Act 1994 provides that copyright to an audio-visual work[59] vests in all physical persons who have contributed a creative effort to the work. The following persons are, unless otherwise evidenced, deemed to have contributed a creative effort to the audio-visual work: the director, the author of the script, the person responsible for adaptation, the author of the texts, the composer of music especially composed for the audio-visual work, the author of the graphics[60], and the author of the original work which inspired the audio-visual work.[61] Unless otherwise agreed, and except for the composer of the music, the joint authors of an audio-visual work are presumed to have assigned their rights of audio-visual exploitation of the work (including dubbing and subtitling) to the producer.

Under Belgian law the copyright owner holds the exclusive right to reproduce the work, or to authorise its reproduction in any form whatsoever including the exclusive right to authorise the adaptation or translation of the work; and the exclusive right to authorise the rental and lending of the work. The copyright holder further has the exclusive right to communicate the work to the public by any means whatsoever. Under the Copyright Act 1994 the copyright holder exclusively holds moral rights including: the right to disclose the work; the right to be named as the author of the work (*i.e.* "right to paternity"); and the right to the integrity of the work *i.e.* the right to oppose any modification of the work (*e.g.* material modifications such as the use of the work in a context it was not intended for).

---

59 Which might very well be recorded in the medium of a computer program or be represented in the form of computer programming code.

60 This would normally be thought to include the artist responsible for the drawing in a cartoon, but could now, it is submitted, also include the computer graphics artist or the computer programmer who produced computer graphics directly by writing computer programming code.

61 *e.g.* the novel which inspired a film or, it is contended, the novel or cartoon which inspired the computer games program.

The law of copyright of Denmark

In general

The original provisions of the Danish Copyright Act were introduced in 1961. A number of amendments have been adopted since that date. The present Danish Copyright Act was enacted in 1989 as Act 453 of 23 June 1989. A few minor amendments were added in 1992. On 9 February 1994, a proposal introducing major amendments to the Copyright Act 1989 was presented in the Danish Parliament. The main objective of the proposal was to modernise the Copyright Act 1989 in line with technological developments, and to implement Council Directives 92/100/EEC (on rental and lending rights) and 93/83/EEC (on satellite broadcasting and cable retransmissions). It is important to note that the Fair Trade Practices Act[62] may also be invoked in intellectual property cases. In the field of copyright, this Act is particularly important with regard to, amongst others, software programs and minor literary works, for example simple drawings and specifications that may not fulfil the criteria for copyright protection, and in particular, the required degree of individuality. Protection on the basis of the Fair Trade Practices Act may be sufficient to ensure some protection in these cases.

Works of "literature" and "art"

Under the Copyright Act 1989, copyright protection is granted to anyone who produces a work of literature or art. Copyright can protect a work presented in writing or orally, in a literary or descriptive form, as a musical, theatrical, film or pictorial work, as a work of architecture or applied art, or as a work executed in other way. Also maps, drawings and other works of a purely descriptive nature are considered as works of literature. Computer programs are specifically mentioned in the Copyright Act 1989 as literary works. Due to its importance with respect to the structure and construction of computer software products, it is contended that regard should also be made to the so-called "catalogue rule" of the Copyright Act 1989 which grants *sui generis* protection to catalogues, tables, directories and other species of tabulation containing large amounts of information. This protection is granted to categories of works which would not be original enough to qualify for copyright protection, but which represent a considerable economic investment and interests deserving some form of

62 *Markedsforingsloven.*

protection. In practice the separation of the catalogue rule from the indicative list of works of literature and art enjoying copyright protection seems to be of minor importance. The same fundamental criteria for protection are still applied to both categories, but the scope of the *sui generis* protection granted under the catalogue rule is more limited than the one under copyright.

"Intellectual and creative production"

In order to qualify for copyright protection, the work of literature or art must be the result of an individual creative and intellectual production within the respective fields. In this context, literature and art are to be understood in the widest sense. The level of individuality required varies depending on the field of intellectual creation in question. Typically, this leads to higher requirements for applied arts than for "pure" or traditional fields of art. There are no novelty requirements in the patent sense: a work is protected by copyright, as long as it constitutes an individual (but not necessary novel) creation. There are no leading court cases so far offering an adequate definition of the level of individuality and originality computer programs must have in order to qualify for copyright protection. In legal theory in Denmark, it is assumed that these requirements must follow the indications given in the Software Directive (Dir 91/250/EEC) which was implemented in Denmark by the Copyright Act adopted in August 1993. It follows that protection can only be granted to a software program in its material form and not to the fundamental principles, concepts, ideas or structures it embodies. There are no formal requirements for copyright protection. Fixation is not necessary. Improvisations are therefore, in principle, also protected. The obligatory use of the copyright symbol "©" according to the Universal Copyright Convention, has no legal significance in Denmark. Consequently, a work of literature originating from a party to the Universal Copyright Convention is not required to carry a copyright mark in order to obtain protection in Denmark.

Authors and ownership

As a fundamental principle of the Copyright Act 1989, the copyright owner is the author or the artist who created the work. Therefore, in the vast majority of cases and areas, the original copyright holder can only be a natural person. In cases where several authors or artists have produced or performed a work jointly, they hold a joint copyright, unless the different parts of the work can be separated and attributed to each of the individual authors or artists. Where this is not possible, copyright must be exercised jointly, but the individual author or artist may act on his own against infringements. In general terms a legal entity such as a company or corporation cannot be an original copyright holder, except in the situations described below. However, a case dealt with expressly in the Copyright Act 1989 concerns computer software developed during employment. A provision is now included in the Copyright Act 1989 under which, in the absence of any agreement to the contrary, the copyright on software created by the employees is transferred to the employer. Unfortunately however, very little guidance can be found in the rest of the Copyright Act 1989 for the definition of authorship in the framework of other types of employment situations. However, legal theory and a few leading court cases seem to accept that original authorship, as such, may well remain with the individual or individuals who have produced the work of literature or art, but the employer should be deemed to acquire a right to exercise the employee's copyright to the extent normally required and justified under the employment contract. This rule only applies in the absence of agreement to the contrary. There are no special rules on authorship of films or related works. Neither is there a presumption in favour of the film producer. Under the current legal regime, which may well have to change shortly in view of the need to implement recent EC Directives, film authorship must be defined on the basis of a case-by-case interpretation of the contractual arrangements, if any, involved and application of the general principles of the Copyright Act 1989.

Term of copyright

The duration of copyright protection in Denmark is 50 years from the year in which the author or the artist died. In cases of joint copyright, the duration is calculated from the year in which the last surviving joint author or artist died. Where a work of literature has been published anonymously, the 50 year copyright protection is calculated from the year of publication. Copyright protection for performing artists is 50 years from the end of the year in which the performance took place. Similarly, copyright protection for phonographic recordings as well as radio and television recordings is 50 years from the end of the year of recording. The copyright protection in connection with the works covered by the previously mentioned "catalogue rule" is ten years from the end of the year in which this particular species of work was published.

The law of copyright of Finland

In general

The Finnish Copyright Act 404/61 enacted on 8 July 1961, replaced the Act of 3 June 1927 on Copyright in Products of Intellectual Activity. Neighbouring rights, such as the rights of performing artists, producers of records as well as radio and television organisations, are also protected by the Copyright Act 1961. Photographic pictures are still protected under a separate Act on Rights in Photographic Pictures (405/61). It has been put forward, in a Government proposal, that the protection of photographic pictures should be included in the Copyright Act 1961 and the consequent amendment is expected to enter into force during the second half of 1995. Since coming into force, the Copyright Act 1961 has frequently been subject to partial reforms in order to fulfil the requirements of rapidly changing environments, especially in respect of the technical developments regarding creation and reproduction of an original work. Copyright can subsist in a wide variety of works, whether literary or artistic, fictional or descriptive representations in writing or in speech, or whether they be musical, dramatic or cinematographic works, works of fine art, architecture, artistic handicraft, industrial art or works expressed in some other manner. Maps and other descriptive drawings, three-dimensional or graphically executed works, as well as computer software, are considered literary works.

Originality

Copyright arises automatically through the performance of the author. If the product of the author's creativity fulfils a certain level of originality the work is protected automatically without any registration. It is, nevertheless, usual and recommendable to emphasise the subsistence of copyright in a work by placing an appropriate copyright notice on it. The author of a work is always one or several physical persons. According to the Finnish copyright system, a legal entity such as a company or corporation, a computer or an animal cannot be considered authors. Thus, the copyright of a legal entity is always derived from a physical person. If a work is created by two or more authors whose contributions do not constitute independent works, the copyright belongs to the authors jointly. However, each of them may individually initiate an infringement action. The Copyright Act 1961 does not contain any specific provisions concerning the copyright of works created by employed authors. The employer and the employee may freely agree upon such transfer.

Computer programs

Computer programs and associated works (including what would be described under English law as preparatory design material) which have been created within the scope of ordinary duties of employment are expressly covered by the Copyright Act 1961 which expressly provides that the copyright automatically passes to the employer. This provision, however, does not apply to programs and works created by authors engaged in teaching or research in a university-level institution. There are no special provisions concerning authorship in audio visual works in the Copyright Act 1961 and consequently, the definition of the author of an audio-visual work is based on the general definition described above. Due to the often relatively large amount of contributors in the creation of audio-visual work, the lack of special provisions may sometimes cause problems when deciding who should be considered the author. According to a statement of the Finnish Copyright Council, which is responsible for giving non-binding advisory statements on the interpretation of the Copyright Act 1961, the copyright of an audio-visual work should belong to the persons who have participated in the creation of the work with sufficient effort. Such persons include at least the author of the script (providing that the audio-visual work is produced on the basis of the script) and the director (provided that his creative activity has influenced the final result of the work). Contributors such as cameramen, composers, wardrobe designers and the like may be regarded as co-authors if they contributed to the work in an independent and creative way.

Author's exclusive rights

In the Copyright Act 1961 the rights of an author have been divided into pecuniary and moral rights. An author of a work afforded protection under this Act has, in principle, an exclusive right to dispose of the work. The copyright holder may, for example, reproduce copies of his work and make it available to the public in an altered or unaltered form, or in the form of a translation or modification, or by using another production method. Moral rights encompass the right to be named as author (to the extent and in the manner required by proper usage) and the right to protect the integrity of the copyright work. A work may not be changed in a manner which is prejudicial to the author's literary or artistic reputation or to his individuality, nor may it be made available to the public in such form or context as to prejudice the author in the manner stated. The author may only waive his moral rights in regard to clearly specified uses of the work. Pecuniary rights may freely be assigned or licensed to a third party. The Copyright Act 1961 includes provisions governing the transfer of copyright but these provisions are applicable only in cases where the parties concerned have not agreed otherwise. There are, consequently, no formal or registration requirements with regard to copyright transfers. It should, however, be observed that, unless the transfer of copyright is duly made in writing, the transferee carries the burden of proving that a specific right has been transferred to him. Consequently, the transfer or licence of rights on unknown uses of a work is difficult to implement in practice, even though there is no explicit provision prohibiting such a transfer.

The law of copyright of France

In general

France has consistently pursued a policy of providing authors, artists, and inventors with a particularly high level of protection. French intellectual property legislation can be traced back to the law of 1791, one of the oldest measures ever adopted for the protection of inventions. The right to use a mark as a distinctive sign on products was granted by a law of 1857 which revived, to some extent, a similar right recognised in the Middle Ages for guilds and craftsmen. The law on designs was adopted on 14 July 1909. Until recently, intellectual property was protected by various legislative texts, each one dealing with a different type of right. However, a new code governing intellectual property has recently been introduced in France pursuant to a law of 1 July 1992. This code consolidates, with some abridgments, the pre-existing texts and is made up of seven books. The first part of the code is devoted to the protection of literary and artistic subject-matter. It deals with copyright, neighbouring rights and the general provisions governing their protection. The second part is sub-divided into four books. It governs the relevant administrative and professional organisations, *i.e.* mainly the National Institute of Industrial Protection, and sets out the rules for the protection of designs, patents, trade marks and other distinctive signs. France has further taken measures to enhance the protection afforded to the holders of such rights by adopting a new law dealing with these issues, on 5 February 1994. This new law sets out very severe civil penalties for counterfeiters and allows France to contribute significantly to the international fight against infringements of intellectual property rights. Most importantly in the context of this work, a law was passed on 10 May 1994, implementing the Software Directive of 14 May 1991 (Dir 91/250/EEC) into French law.

"Works of human intellect"

Copyright is governed by Law 54.298 of 11 March 1957, and is complemented by case law. Important amendments to this law were introduced by Law 85.660 of 3 July 1985. Among other changes, this law introduced express provisions for the protection of computer programs. French law grants the author of a work of the human intellect, by the mere fact of its creation, an exclusive, incorporeal and enforceable right in that work. The protection is granted to any work of the intellect, irrespective of type, form of expression, merit or purpose, under the sole condition that the work be original. The need for originality does not imply a requirement for innovation, or the creation of something which did not exist beforehand, as French law protects the creator, rather than his creation. The author is granted a specific form of protection for all his intellectual work, irrespective of the genre, the expressive form, the merit, or the destination. The originality is the mark of the author's personality and does not require an aesthetic character. It must be emphasised however, that only the form and expression of the creative personal effort are protected. French copyright law does not protect ideas.

Neighbouring rights

Finally, French law recognises and protects certain neighbouring rights of performing artists, and producers of records and videos. These rights cannot interfere with copyright, including, in particular, the authors' moral rights. Neighbouring rights are governed by specific provisions whose objectives are similar to those governing copyright, although the protection they afford is generally less comprehensive than the one granted by copyright.

Formalities and authors

Copyright protection is not subject to any formalities. Generally, the mere expression of the author's creative effort is sufficient; although the position is different with regard to pantomimes, choreographic works, and circus acts and routines. Here fixation is required, if not necessarily as a condition for protection, at least as a condition for proving infringement. Authorship belongs, in the absence of proof to the contrary, to the person or persons under whose name the work is disclosed. However, in some cases, French law provides that a legal entity might be invested with the quality of author. This can be the case, *inter alia*, with collective works. In collective works, the personal contributions of the various authors participating in its development are merged in the totality arising out of its original conception. It is therefore impossible to attribute to each of these authors a separate right in the total work thus produced. In the absence of proof to the contrary, the author's rights vest in the person or legal entity who edited, published and disclosed the work under his direction and name. It is not yet fully clarified by French courts whether audio-visual works can also qualify as collective works. This would have the effect of making the producer the copyright owner of the work. Normally however, audio-visual works are deemed to have been made in collaboration, that is by the joint efforts of several natural persons. French law provides for audio-visual works created in collaboration, a presumption of co-authorship in favour of the scriptwriters, the authors of the adaptation, dialogues, and musical compositions with or without words; and the directors. Where such a work is based on a pre-existing work or screenplay which is still protected, the authors of the original work are assimilated with those of the new work. Importantly, all the rights relating to computer software created by an employee in the course of his employment devolve to the employer, who can be a legal entity, unless the parties have entered into different contractual arrangements. Where the author is an agent of the state, or of a local authority, or of an administrative public entity, the latter are assimilated to an employer and are thus entitled to acquire by devolution of the relevant intellectual property rights.

Moral and pecuniary rights

Copyright is made up of two specific rights: the moral right (which has an extreme importance under French copyright law) and the pecuniary right. The moral right of copyright confers on the copyright owner or author the right to respect of his name, quality and work. This right is personal, perpetual, inalienable, imprescriptible and non-transferable. It appears that, at least in some extreme cases, choice-of-jurisdiction clauses cannot be relied upon to break this rule. Based on his moral rights an author may decide not to divulge his work. Divulgence is thus an essential and fundamental element of the author's moral rights. The other element is the right to respect for his name, his authorship and his work. The right to respect for his name entitles the author to be named as such. It also entitles him to use a pseudonym or to opt for anonymity. The indication of an author's name is thus not a legal requirement. The right to respect for his authorship entitles the author to have his authorship stated on each of his works, notably where the work in question is a collaborative one. The right to respect for the work finds its principal application where the exploitation rights have been transferred. The transferee is required to respect the integrity of the work. He may neither cut anything out of the work, nor add anything to it which might alter the work, whether in form or in spirit. Specific legislation applies to audio-visual works. An audio-visual work is deemed to be completed when its definitive version has been established by the common accord of the director, the co-authors, if any, and the producer. Furthermore, the destruction of the matrix of this version is forbidden except with the unanimous agreement of these persons. Nevertheless, where one of the (potential) co-authors refuses, or hinders, the termination of his contribution, he cannot oppose the completion of the work, and use the benefit of his legal protection to that effect.

Finally, pursuant to his moral right, the author may correct and retract his work if he is not satisfied with it. The author must thereby compensate the transferee for any prejudice resulting from the exercise of this right. The pecuniary right, which comes into existence with the divulgation of the work, is divided into three principal elements, the right of reproduction (*reproduction*); the right of performance (*representation*); and the *droit de suite*. A reproduction consists of a material fixation of a work by any method which allows it to be communicated to the public in an indirect fashion. Reproduction can be accomplished, for example by printing, drawing, photographing, cinematography or magnetic recording. The law does not define these means exhaustively. A performance consists in the communication to the public of works by any means. Such communication can be either direct, as in the case of a public recitation, or indirect, where, for instance, it is televised or broadcast by satellite. Once a work has been divulged, the author or the owner of neighbouring rights may not prohibit any private and free performances produced exclusively within the family circle.

The law of copyright of Germany

In general

On 3 October 1990, the German Democratic Republic (GDR) and the Federal Republic of Germany (FRG) were unified. As a consequence, the industrial and intellectual property laws of the FRG apply also in the territory of the former GDR. This implies that registrations of intellectual property rights, including European Patent and Patent Co-operation Treaty applications and registrations, as well as international trade mark registrations under the Madrid Agreement applied for on or after 3 October 1990, extend also to the territory of the former GDR. Furthermore, under the Law on the Extension of Industrial Property Rights, as from 1 May 1992, the industrial property rights valid on that date and applied for before 3 October 1990, in either the unenlarged FRG, or the former GDR, were automatically extended and in force in the entire territory of unified Germany, while retaining their priority date. Possible conflicts of rights due to this extension are dealt with comprehensively by the Law on the Extension of Industrial Property Rights. Under German law the traditional fields of copyright are literature and art. Examples of protected works, such as works of writing, music, art, architecture, photography, films and scientific pictorial representations are given in an indicative list contained in the German Copyright Act. Only human, personal creations which were not copied from someone else by the author are susceptible to copyright. Individuality of the work and a creative level are required, sufficient to enable the observer to distinguish the work from other ordinary objects. However, not only works of increased literary, or artistic value may be protected, and only relatively minor requirements have to be met in order to achieve the necessary level of creativity. Even the title of, for instance, a computer program, – be afforded copyright protection. However, more important in this respect is Article 16 of the Act Against Unfair Competition which provides sanctions against third parties who, in the course of business, make use of a special designation of a printed work-or, according to case law, the title of a computer program in a way which may cause confusion with a designation rightfully used to identify another work. Although protection for works of applied art is generally applied for under the Design Act, copyright protection has also been granted for works of applied art, such as furniture. The amendment of the Copyright Act 1985 introduced computer programs into the list of protected works, classifying them specifically as "literary works". More comprehensive protection is provided by the amendment of 1993, enacted to bring German copyright law into compliance with the EC Software Directive (Dir 91/250/EEC). This amendment incorporated language taken from the Directive in an undeviating fashion.

The basis of copyright

Copyright in Germany originates with the act of creation, in so far as this act is perceivable in the external world. No formalities must be met and fixation or registration of works are not prerequisites for copyright protection. The author is the creator of the work and special legal status, such as legal capacity, is not a precondition. Therefore, even a child or a legally incapacitated person may qualify as an author. It follows from the nature of a work as a personal intellectual creation that copyright can only originate from a natural person and not a legal person. Consequently, the concept of corporate or government works does not exist. The latter may nevertheless acquire derivative exploitation rights through employment or individual contracts. If a work is the collective creation of several persons in a way which does not allow the separation of their individual contributions and separate exploitation, these persons become joint authors and joint owners of the rights to publication and exploitation.

German copyright law protects the author in his rights to exploit the work. These rights include the right of an author to exploit his work in material form, comprising, in particular: the right of reproduction, the right of distribution, and the right of exhibition; as well as the exclusive right to communicate his work to the public in non-material form, comprising: the right of performance and presentation; the right to broadcast; the right of communicating the work by means of sound or visual recordings; and the right of communicating broadcasts. It ought to be noted that distribution rights are exhausted by the first sale made by or with the consent of the domestic copyright holder. However, even after exhaustion of his distribution rights, the author retains a claim to royalties, if copies of the work, such as books or records, are rented or lent commercially or in public institutions.

Moral and neighbouring rights

German copyright law also contains a special sub-section on the moral rights of authors, encompassing, in particular: the right of publication, the right to recognition of authorship; and the right for respect to be applied to the integrity of the author's work. Co-authors enjoy the right of public dissemination and exploitation jointly. Under the title "neighbouring rights", the Copyright Act affords a reduced level of protection to certain accomplishments which approach the creation of a work or which are closely related to the performance of a work. These neighbouring rights protect the artistic performance of the work, or an organisation's technical accomplishment embodied in a media production or computer program. In particular, the categories of individuals and legal entities entitled to neighbouring rights include, for example, performing artists, producers of sound recordings, broadcasting organisations, film producers and photographers (the latter in respect of photographs that are not sufficiently original to qualify for copyright protection).

Term of copyright

Copyright is a right limited in time, expiring 70 years after the end of the calender year in which the author died. The duration of protection for neighbouring rights is generally shorter and depends on the category of copyright owner or author and/or achievement protected. In Germany copyright as such is only transferable upon the death of the author. A transfer of copyright, including the author's moral rights, as a whole or in part, is excluded between living persons. However, during his lifetime the author may grant exclusive or non-exclusive rights of use. Furthermore, the author may, in favour of a third party, waive moral rights such as the right to be named as an author. Although a transfer of copyright is impossible, the grant of exclusive worldwide rights for all kinds of uses and for the whole period of protection comes very close to an assignment as it would be understood under English law. No special rules with regard to copyright contracts exist in German copyright law, and no registration of licences or related contracts is required or possible. The written form is required only for agreements to grant rights of use in the future works which are not yet specified in detail. However, it is not possible to license the rights on forms of exploitation of the work which are not yet known.

The law of copyright of Greece

In general

The Law of Copyright in Greece is governed by Law 2121/1993 enacted in 1993. Its provisions have introduced a modern legal framework for copyright protection, and have implemented the Software Directive (Dir 91/250/EEC), as well as the Rental and Lending Right Directive (Dir 92/100/EEC). Law 2121/1993 also protects the neighbouring rights of performing artists, producers of audio, visual or audio-visual recordings, broadcasters and publishers. Under Article 69 of Law 2121/1993 a new organisation will be set up known as the "Organisation of Intellectual Property"[63] and will be in charge of a number of copyright-related tasks presently falling under the competence of the Ministry of Culture.

Original intellectual creations of literature, art and science

Copyright protection is granted to any original intellectual creation of literature, art or science, expressed in any form. This general definition is followed by an indicative and extensive list of works that can be protected through copyright. Among categories of works of more topical interest, the

63 *Organismos Pneumatikis Idioktisias.*

law also mentions expressly: audio-visual works, databases (if the selection and arrangement of their contents is original), and computer programs and their preparatory design material. The conditions regarding interfaces and originality are practically identical to those of the Software Directive (Dir 91/250/EEC). Copyright protection is independent of the cumulative protection, if any, which a work may enjoy under other provisions and copyright protection is not subject to any formal conditions, such as fixation.

Authorship

The initial owner of copyright is its creator. There is a rebuttable presumption that the creator is the natural person whose name is mentioned on the material carrier of the copyright work and legal persons cannot qualify as creators. Law 2121/1993 distinguishes between co-operative, collective and composite works. Co-operative works are the products of co-operation on equal terms, and the relevant copyright is divided equally among their creators, unless otherwise agreed. Collective works are produced under the guidance of one person who is also the original owner of copyright on the whole work. Composite works are subject to joint co-authorship but separate exploitation rights, where this is possible. There is also a rebuttable presumption that the copyright of employees on works created in the framework of a work contract is transmitted to their employer, to the extent required for the purposes of the work contract.

Exploitation rights

The exploitation rights of the copyright holder consist of, *inter alia*, the right to permit or prohibit fixation, reproduction, translation, adaptation, putting into circulation, resale, rental, lending, public presentation, public performance and broadcasting of the work by any means. A rather confusing provision gives the author the exclusive right to import copies of a work produced abroad without his consent (essentially this provision enunciates the "exhaustion of rights" principle). The moral rights of the copyright holder consist of, *inter alia*, the right to decide on the conditions under which the work will be made accessible to the public, the acknowledgement of authorship of the work; the right to prohibit any amendment of the work, the right of access to the work (provided this causes the least inconvenience to the owner of the work where the owner is a person other than the author), and with regard to scientific and literary works (including computer programs) the right to rescind a contract involving the exploitation of the work, due to a change in the author's beliefs and subject to the payment of damages to the other party.

Term of copyright

Copyright runs for the life of the author and for 70 years after his death. After the termination of the protection, certain powers related to the moral right can be exercised by the Ministry of Culture. In the case of co-operative works, the 70-year period is calculated from the death of the last surviving author. In the case of anonymous or pseudonymous works, the term of protection runs for 70 years after the work is lawfully made available to the public. Law 2121/1993 contains detailed provisions on the transfer of pecuniary aspects of copyright in general, as well as specific categories of copyright-related agreements. The moral right cannot be transferred. The law distinguishes between exploitation contracts (in which the other party is obliged to exercise the powers transferred to it by the author) and exploitation licences (in which this exercise is optional). Both must be evidenced in writing, but only the author may challenge them as void if this formal condition is not fulfilled. In cases of doubt, exploitation contracts and licences are deemed to be non-exclusive, non-transferable and to have a duration of five years. In the absence of any contrary agreement, the transferee of the rights has legal standing to protect them, in his own name, against any infringement by a third party. Exploitation contracts and licences may not include all future works of the author, or methods of exploitation that were not known on the date on which they were concluded. As a general rule, subject to specified exceptions, exploitation contracts and licences must be concluded in consideration for a freely negotiable percentage of the proceeds from exploitation. Law 2121/1993 also includes special provisions for agreements on publishing and translation, audio-visual production, broadcasting, the publication of photographs, etc. Deviations from these provisions are only possible if they are more favourable to the author or authors involved.

The law of copyright of Iceland

In general

Although Iceland is not a Member State of the European Union, it does run a policy of self-determined harmonisation with the intellectual property law of the European Union and has been included in this work on that ground. The Icelandic Copyright Act 1972 governs the law of copyright in Iceland and was amended in 1984 and 1992. The purpose of the 1992 amendment was, among other things, to implement in principle the EC Software Directive (Dir 91/250/EEC). Under the Copyright Act 1972, the author of a literary or artistic work has full property rights in his work, including copyright, subject only to the limitations set out in the Act.

The nature of copyright

A copyright work is an original intellectual creation that bears some individual characteristics of the author. The idea that led to the work is not protected as such, but only in so far as it is integrated into the work. There are no requirements as to the quality or quantity of the work.[64] Adaptations and changes to a work can be protected as a new work, if they are the result of an independent intellectual creation. The person who adapts or changes the work will then be considered to be the author of the work in its changed version. Adaptations or changes do not prejudice the original author's rights to his work in any way. Contrary to most other intellectual property rights in Iceland, the protection of copyright is not conditional upon any sort of registration or other formal procedure on behalf of the author. A work is protected automatically once created within the meaning of the Copyright Act 1972 and the person who creates a literary or artistic work is its author. The copyright goes hand in hand with the creation of the work. Once the work has been created, a copyright is attached to it – normally exclusively to the author. Legal entities cannot qualify as authors and consequently the original copyright on works always rests with individuals; however, legal entities may acquire copyright to the extent that it is assignable.

In this context the Copyright Act 1972 does not contain any provisions regarding copyright in employer-employee relations. Provisions regarding the assignment of copyright may be included in a contract for employment. In some cases, such a provision can be regarded as being implicit in an employment contract, even if it is not mentioned expressly. Problems are most likely to arise when the employee's task is the creation of intellectual property and the employment contract is silent on copyright issues. In those situations, the employee's copyright is deemed to be assigned to the employer to the extent necessary to achieve the objective sought by the contract of employment. The 1992 amendment of the Copyright Act 1972 added a provision stating that employers become copyright owners or authors of computer programs created by their employees if, according to the contract of employment, the creation of computer programs is among the duties of the employee. As a rule, provisions on employees' copyright do not limit their moral rights. Employed authors, nevertheless, have to accept changes

64 Art 1(2) and (3) of the Act include a non-exclusive enumeration of examples of copyright works.

and adaptations necessary for the employer to make use of the work in his regular course of business. Technical advances can also lead to new possibilities which the employer could exploit in his regular course of business. An employer must, however, always be mindful of not encroaching upon the rights the author holds in respect of his creation.

Author's rights and term

The author has an exclusive right to make copies of his work for public distribution, be it in its original form or in an altered or adapted version. The author also holds an exclusive right to any kind of public presentation of his work. The duration of protection in the Copyright Act 1972 is in line with the rules of the Berne Convention, that is protection expires 50 years after the author's death, provided that the author was named. If the author was not named, this period starts running from the end of the year in which the work was first presented in any way. In cases of joint authorship, the 50-year period starts running from the death of the last survivor among the joint authors. All pecuniary rights in a copyright work are transferable. However, a waiver of moral rights is expressly prohibited under the Copyright Act 1992. The transfer of copyright is not subject to any formal requirements and an author may also transfer the rights of exploitation of a work through future, as yet unknown, means. Copying of copyright works for personal use is, as a rule, allowed. Nevertheless, there are exceptions to the rule. It does not apply to protected architectural, sculptural, industrial design or drawing works. Furthermore, it does not apply to musical or literary works if the assistance of professionals is sought for the copy making. Copying of protected computer programs is prohibited. The owner of a computer program can, nonetheless, make back-up and safety copies, as may be required for the use of the program. The right to use these copies is cancelled if the owner disposes of his original copy of the computer program.

The law of copyright of Ireland

In general

In Ireland copyright is a bundle of rights which automatically belongs to the author or creator of an original work. Copyright in relation to any work means the exclusive right to do and to authorise other persons to do certain acts in relation to the work. The law of copyright is governed by the Copyright Acts 1963 and 1987.

Based on UK legislation

The Copyright Act 1963 is based on the United Kingdom Copyright Act 1956. The Copyright (Amendment) Act 1987 was introduced to prevent designs of mundane objects from obtaining copyright protection as artistic works. A work will attract copyright protection if it is original in the sense that it is the author's own intellectual creation. Copyright will subsist in the expression of the idea rather than the idea itself. Copyright will subsist in every original unpublished literary, dramatic, musical and artistic work, if the author was a qualified person at the time when the work was created or, where the making of the work extended over a period, for a substantial part of that period. Copyright subsists in every published work if the work was first published in Ireland or the author of the work was a qualified person at the time of publication, or the author had died at that time but was a qualified person immediately before his death. A qualified person is an Irish citizen, or a person who is resident or domiciled in Ireland or, in the case of a body corporate, a company incorporated under Irish law. By two Government Orders of 1978, the definition of qualified person was extended on a reciprocal basis to citizens and residents of foreign countries which are parties to the Berne Convention, the Universal Copyright Convention, or the Rome Convention. Any original work can obtain copyright protection and there may be originality in the treatment of the subject, the form of expression or method of arrangement and selection. The author benefits from the presumption that the work is original. No protection will be given merely because labour and energy are expended creating the work if there is no originality. Under Irish copyright law the creator is protected against deliberate and accidental or inadvertent appropriation of his work.

Copyright protection was initially given to original literary, dramatic, artistic, and musical works. Artistic works include paintings, sculptures, drawings, engravings, and photographs irrespective of their artistic quality, and architectural works. Copyright also subsists in sound recordings, cinematograph films, broadcasts and Irish legal tender. The courts have included advertising slogans, examination papers, timetables, football pools coupons, letters, television listings codes and catalogues in the literary category.

Computer programs

The EC Software Directive (Dir 91/250/EEC) was implemented in Ireland in 1993 by Government Order. Regulation 3, subsection 1 of the implementing regulations states that "the Copyright Acts 1963 and 1987 shall apply to every original computer program as if it were a literary work and the legal protection so afforded shall apply to the expression in any form of a computer program".

Regulation 4 expressly provides that software created by the employee of a newspaper, magazine or similar periodical in the course of his employment will belong to the employer; and regulation 5 specifies the exclusive rights of the copyright owner or author within the meaning of Article 2 of the Directive. Under regulation 6 certain acts are not to be viewed as an infringement, in particular the making of a back-up copy by a person having the right to use the program and regulation 7 allows interoperability subject to the restrictions permitted by the Software Directive.

Ownership generally

No formalities such as registration are necessary. If the copyright work is made in the course of the author's employment under a contract of service or apprenticeship, his employer is entitled to the copyright in the work. However, if the work is created by the author in the course of his employment by the proprietor of a newspaper, magazine or similar periodical under a contract of service or apprenticeship and intended for publication in the newspaper, magazine or periodical, the employer owns the copyright in the work only in so far as it relates to such publication. If a photograph, painting, portrait, or engraving is commissioned and paid for in money or equivalent, the commissioner is the copyright owner. Copyright in a film vests in the "maker" who is defined as "the person by whom the arrangements necessary for the making of the film are undertaken".

Author's rights

Under Irish law, copyright is the exclusive right to reproduce the work in any form, publish the work, perform the work in public, broadcast the work, cause the work to be transmitted to subscribers to a diffusion service, make any adaptation of the work or to authorise others to do any of these acts. In Ireland, new legislation is required to introduce moral rights. Moral rights are protected under Article 6bis of the Berne Convention and while the Convention was implemented in Ireland under the Copyright Act 1963, moral rights were not created under the Act. The European Commission has stated that member states must at least implement Article 6bis. for it establishes a right of paternity which is the right of the author to have his name associated with the work and a right of integrity which means that the author may prevent an assignee from producing any derogatory treatment of his work. In Ireland the duration of copyright is for the life of the author plus 50 years. Under the Copyright Act 1963 copyright subsists perpetually in an unpublished work. In the case of photographs, sound recordings and films, the copyright subsists for a period of fifty years from first publication. The copyright owner may fully or partially assign his rights to someone else or he may grant licences. There is no register of copyright works, assignments or licences in Ireland and there is no legal requirement that an assignment or a licence be in writing; and there is no prohibition preventing a copyright owner from granting a licence to use his work through future, not yet known, methods of exploitation.

The law of copyright of Italy

In general

In Italy, copyright and neighbouring rights are regulated by Articles 2575–2583 of the Italian Civil Code of 1942 and by the Copyright Law No 633 of 22 April 1941, as amended. Copyright law protects all works, original or derivative, which belong to the categories of literary, musical, choreographic, artistic, architectural, cinematographic and photographic works (the latter provided they are not simple photographs protected by other provisions of the Copyright Law). It is not necessary for the work to take a material form, nor is it of any relevance whether the work is contrary to public order or accepted moral standards. As far as the requirement of creativity is concerned, according to an important school of thought, this is combined with the "subjective novelty" of the work, that is its capacity to express, in an original way, the personality and individuality of the author. However, another school of thought holds the view that works should not only be subjectively novel but also objectively novel, thereby differentiating themselves from all works that have appeared before. In any event, the degree of creativity required by law is small, and the Italian courts have given copyright protection to maps, legal maxims and to accounting tables. More recent decisions have recognised computer programs as being "creative" and therefore meriting copyright protection; however, it is submitted that the treatment of computer software under Italian law is still in its infancy and is by no means as advanced as in the United Kingdom. The protection provided by copyright in Italy is not conditional upon any formal requirement such as registration – it being sufficient that there has been an act of creativity. Decree No 244 of 3 January 1994 introduced a special public register for computer programs, managed by SIAE (the main Italian collecting society). Registrations of software in this register are optional, and creates a rebuttable presumption of authorship in favour of the person or persons claiming title in the register.

The "creation of a work from an intellectual effort"

Article 6 of the Copyright Law No. 633 tells us that "copyright shall be acquired by creation of a work from an intellectual effort". This definition excludes the possibility that a legal person may qualify as the copyright author of a work, the only exception being community or provincial state administrative bodies and private non-profit legal entities. Such bodies, according to Article 11(1)(a) of the Copyright Law No 633, may have copyright, including moral rights, for all works created and published under their name or on their account. Copyright works created under a contract of employment are not expressly regulated by the law. In any event, it seems that there is no doubt that, in the absence of a contrary agreement, if the creator is an employee, the employer takes ownership of all the economic rights of the work and the rights immediately become the property of the employer. Moral rights, however, always remain the property of the original author.

Legal commentators are not unanimous as to whether the same considerations can be applied by analogy in the case of freelance contracts. In such cases, it appears to be a question of case-by-case interpretation whether an express transfer of copyright ownership is required.

Collective works in Italy

It is submitted that a brief mention should be given to the cases of ownership of works created by a number of people (usually referred to as collective works, communal or combined works). Collective works consist of a number of distinct elements which have been co-ordinated. Rights in the collective work rest with the person in charge of co-ordination, without prejudice to the rights of the authors on the single component parts. Communal works are works in which the various elements merge together becoming indistinguishable. The rights are held by all the authors in equal parts and may be exercised in accordance with the rules set out in the civil code for rights held jointly. Combined works consist of a number of elements which are distinguishable but which integrate together to form an overall artistic effect. The law has not provided for a general category for this type of work but rather a series of particular cases, which from time to time indicate who is recognised as an author and who may benefit from the pecuniary rights. A typical and important example of a combined work, is a work of cinematographic art regulated by Article 44 of the Copyright Law No 633. The author of the subject, the author of the script, the composer of the music and the artistic director are considered co-authors of the cinematographic work while the pecuniary exploitation of the work is retained by the person who organised it. Furthermore, Article 47 of the Copyright Law No 633 gives the producer the right to make those modifications to cinematographic works which are necessary for cinematographic adaptation.

Author's rights

The author of a creative work becomes the owner of pecuniary as well as moral rights. The pecuniary rights of the author are independent of each other and can be transferred separately. The Copyright Law No 633 lists the most important of them, which are: the right to publish the work; the right to reproduce it; by whatever means (printing, photocopying, photographing, cinematography); the right to distribute and rent it; the right to transcribe the work (*e.g.* to transform an oral work into a written work or any other type of "fixed" format); the right to perform or recite the work in public (this does not include a performance or recitation within the normal family circle, school, college or institute of retreat or treatment which is not for profit), the right to diffuse the work over a distance through radio, television, telephony, broadcasting and other analogous means; and the right to translate the work into another language or dialect, and to modify or transform it in any other way.

The author's moral rights consist of the right of paternity, that is the right to claim authorship of the work; the right of integrity i.e. the right to object to any distortion, mutilation or any other modification of, and any other derogatory action in relation to the work, which would be prejudicial to the honour or reputation of the author; the right to prevent the work from being published; and the right to withdraw the work from commerce for serious moral reasons, subject to an obligation to indemnify anyone who has purchased the economic rights to the work which is withdrawn. The moral rights may not be renounced, they are not limited by statute, they may not be transferred and they are independent of the pecuniary exploitation rights. After an author's death, the rights of paternity, of integrity and the right not to have works published without his consent may also be asserted, without limitation in time, by the author's spouse, children and, in the absence thereof, a number of other relatives. The right to withdraw the work may only be asserted by the author personally and it extinguishes on his death.

Term of copyright

At the time of writing, the duration of the pecuniary rights is subject to parliamentary scrutiny in order to increase the protection from 50 to 70 years after the death of the author (or the death of the last of the co-authors) in accordance with the provisions of Directive 93/98/EEC. In some cases, protection starts to run from the first publication of the work (*e.g.* for films and computer software). Moral rights are not transferable. The rights of pecuniary exploitation of works and the neighbouring rights and are freely transferable, through assignments and licences, under all methods and in all forms permitted by the law, and are subject to the following rules: the transfer of rights of exploitation rights must be evidenced in writing[65], the transfer of one or more copies of the work does not entail a transfer of the related exploitation rights, unless the work is a mould, engraving plate or similar medium used to reproduce works of art; the rights of publication and exploitation of a published work, in so far as they belong personally to the author, may not be subject to pledge, seizure or sequestration; rights belonging to the author, with the exception of the right to publish a work during his lifetime, may be expropriated for reasons of state interest. The law only regulates publishing, printing and public performance contracts and it is undecided whether these rules may be applied to all other types of contracts, and the law is silent on this point.

The law of copyright of Luxembourg

In general

In Luxembourg copyright is protected under the Copyright Act of 29 March 1972, and under Article 1 of this Act, artistic creations in the broadest sense are protected. This Article also provides a non-exhaustive list of different types of artistic creations. Thus the Copyright Act 1972 protects, for example, speeches, musical creations, paintings, maps and translations of literary works and musical arrangements. The Court of Appeal decided in 1973 that a photograph is protected by copyright even if it does not have a distinct artistic character, and even if the author or artist did not accomplish an original intellectual creation. This decision was recently confirmed in 1990. It seems that the Court of Appeal made a literal interpretation of Article 1 of

65 There are two exceptions to this rule. The first exception applies where the mere transfer of a mould or analogous means of reproducing an artistic work implies the licensing of the right to reproduce the work. The second exception is related to photographs: the delivery of negatives implies a transfer of the right to reproduce them.

the Copyright Act 1972 and as this Article makes no reference to the concepts of "originality" or "artistic intellectual effort" the court protected simple photographs without considering the artistic value of the creation. If applied to other types of works, this interpretation makes it very easy for a work to qualify for copyright protection. There exists no specific copyright legislation concerning the protection of software programs (the Patent Law of 20 July 1992 expressly excludes software programs from patentability) but there seems little doubt that software programs can be protected by copyright. Even if the Copyright Act 1972 does not expressly mention software programs in its non-exhaustive list of artistic creations, some Luxembourg legal authors have made reference to French case law that has exercised considerable influence in Luxembourg and French law had accepted, fairly early, that computer programs could be protected by copyright.

General requirements

There are no formal requirements for copyright protection. However, the protection of certain neighbouring rights is conditional upon fixation. The person mentioned as the author on a work is presumed to be its author. If an artistic creation was accomplished by two or more persons, they can agree on the way copyright should be exercised by them. If no agreement has been reached, each author may exercise his rights separately. The publisher of an anonymous or a pseudonymous work is presumed to represent the author. However, if the author's identity is established, he or his legal representatives may freely use the rights and protection granted by copyright. In general terms, the author has an exclusive right of exploitation, consisting of the right to publish and reproduce the work.

Author's rights

More specifically, the authors of dramatic or musical creations have the exclusive right to authorise the public presentation or execution of these creations in front of an audience, as well as their public presentation or execution by any means; and the public transmission of the presentation or execution of the creation by any means.

The authors of literary creations have the exclusive right to authorise: the public reading or recitation of their creations, regardless of the means through which this takes place; the public transmission of these creations; the broadcasting of their creations or their public communication by any other means allowing the wireless transfer of signs, pictures or sounds; every public communication by or without wire of the broadcasted creation by a different organisation than the original broadcaster; and the public communication by loudspeaker or any other instrument transmitting signs, sounds or pictures. The author of a musical, dramatic or literary creation has the right to authorise translations, arrangements, adaptations or other transformations of these creations. The transfer of a work of art also implies transfer of copyright to the new owner. The author of a cinematographic creation has the exclusive right to authorise: the adaptation and the cinematographic reproduction of his works and the putting on the market of these adapted or reproduced creations; and the presentation and public execution, by any means, of the adapted or reproduced creations. The author may also protect his work against any action which might be considered detrimental to his honour or reputation. This right cannot be waived or transferred.

Term of copyright

The duration of protection of a copyright work lasts for 50 years after the death of the author. The protection of anonymous works or of those published under a pseudonym expires 50 years after the creation has been made available to the public. Protection by copyright of photographic creations or creations in the field of applied art lasts for 50 years following the creations of the photograph of the model. If the artistic creation results from a collaboration of two or more persons, copyright protection expires 50 years after the death of the last survivor among the joint authors.

Exceptions to protection

The Copyright Act 1972 provides many exceptions to copyright protection. Speeches held in assemblies, public court audiences, and political meetings may be freely published and broadcast. Speeches made in conferences may be published by newspapers and broadcast if such a use is justified for information purposes. Official declarations of any public authority are not protected by copyright. An example includes laws published in the Official Gazette. Any person has the right to make quotations or translations of artistic creations, to the extent that this may be in accordance with custom and justified under the circumstances. A quotation has to mention its origin as well as the name of the author, if his name appears in the source used by the person making the quotation. Case law has clarified that quotations may also be used freely for the purpose of criticism or discussion. Literary or artistic creations which have been presented or heard during a topical event may be reproduced or made available to the public during a report on this event by a photograph, a film or a broadcast. Topical articles relating to economical, political or religious discussions, published in newspapers, periodical journals or in broadcasts may be reproduced by the press, or broadcast originally or as a translation if the authors have given their permission. Nevertheless, the source of this article must be mentioned. An artistic creation in permanent exhibition in a public place may be reproduced and presented to the public by film or broadcasting.

The law of copyright of the Netherlands

In general

Dutch copyright law is set out in the Copyright Act 1912 (*Auteurswet*), which has been amended a number of times. In principle all "original" works enjoy copyright protection. The Copyright Act 1912 does not provide for a definition of originality, but the Dutch common law elaborated extensively on the concept of originality.

Originality

For a work to be considered original it should bear the "personal stamp of the maker" and Dutch case law has confirmed, for example, that a thesaurus could meet the originality criterion, as the selection of the words is based on a personal choice of selection criteria. It is not required that the work have any artistic or aesthetic value. The object of copyright is limited to the "expression" of ideas and concepts. The underlying ideas or methods are not eligible for copyright protection. However, a work can be expressed in both a material form (*i.e.* a book or painting) and an immaterial form (*i.e.* a lecture). The Copyright Act 1912 gives a non-exhaustive list of works which may enjoy copyright protection. Such works are *inter alia* books, music compositions, buildings, films, and photographs. A special feature of Dutch copyright law is the protection of all written material regardless of its originality. Written material which is lacking originality will enjoy limited copyright protection provided it is (or is intended to be) made public. Copyright in such cases will be limited to the possibility of forbidding straightforward copying. As a consequence, telephone directories, price lists and timetables will still be legally protected against straightforward copying, even if they lack any originality. Photographs are not considered to be "written material" within the 1912 Act and must therefore possess some originality to enjoy copyright protection. Computer programs were already protected by the old copyright regime if they were sufficiently original. As from 1 September 1994, computer programs and their preparatory design materials are explicitly mentioned in the Copyright Act as works eligible for copyright protection and a chapter implementing the EC Software Directive (Dir 91/250/EEC) and computer programs are now treated under Dutch copyright law as "written material".

Copyright is not subject to any formal requirements such as registration or payment of fees. The actual maker of a work will in principle be entitled to the copyright. If there are several makers of a work whose individual contributions cannot be distinguished, they all have a joint copyright on the totality of their contributions. If the contributions can be distinguished (e.g. in the case of music and images of a film, or the different audio-visual aspects of a computer games program), separate copyrights will be granted for each of the contributions. If the maker has used others to assist under his direction in the execution of the work, these assistants will not enjoy copyright on their contribution, except if their contributions relate to the conceptual part of the work. Employers are entitled to the copyright in works created by employees whose task includes the creation of such works. Works which are made public in the name of a corporation, public body or other legal entity are deemed to be made by such entity. This legal presumption can only be rebutted if the real author proves that he did not waive his rights to copyright. Special provisions exist for authors of audio-visual works. The contributors to an audio-visual work (*e.g.* a film, television programme, video-clip or, as indicated above, a games program featuring characterisations, music, animated action, and visual backgrounds which, in the computer games industry, are commonly produced by separate persons) such as the script-writer, costume designer etc are deemed to have assigned their exploitation rights to the producer unless they have reserved them in writing. The producer is defined as the person financially responsible for the production and distribution of the audio-visual work. This automatic transfer does not apply to composers and text writers of film music.

Author's rights

The Copyright Act 1912 states that the author has the exclusive right to publish or reproduce the work. Publication includes the exposure of a work to the public and covers, for example, the placing on the market of copies, the performance of a musical composition, or entry of an article into a database. Playing a record for family, friends or similar "closed" groups does not constitute a publication. However, playing a record for professional or commercial purposes to a limited audience (*e.g.* in the canteen of a company or during a funeral) is subject to the copyright owner's permission. A publication can be followed by a secondary publication. The Supreme Court has held that a public broadcast which is relayed by a cable-network operator is to be considered a further publication to the extent that this operator is not owned by the broadcasting company. The Supreme Court further held that the secondary use of a published work in a form other than the original publication, for example the sale of pictures of a published calendar as separate posters, constitutes a new publication. On the other hand, copyright is exhausted in regard to the renting or circulation of books, records and magazines, and the copyright owner cannot control their further use. Reproduction includes straightforward copying, but also translating, orchestration of a piano piece, adaptation of a book for theatre or film and – more generally – any imitation which does not amount to a new original work. The distinction between an imitation and a new work is unclear and will depend on a case-by-case assessment.

The author's moral rights also enjoy protection, even after the primary copyright is exhausted or after the copyright has been transferred to a third party. The author has the right to require to be mentioned as the author or creator; to oppose changes to the essence of the work; to oppose any deformation, mutilation or impairment of the work to the extent this could prejudice his reputation; to make certain corrections to the work – the author of a book can for example prevent an unchanged reprint of his work. The author can contractually waive the first and the second rights mentioned above, but it is not clear whether authors such as employers and legal entities can claim protection of moral rights.

Term of copyright

The duration of copyright in the Netherlands is 50 years after the year in which the author died. However, if the copyright is vested in a legal entity, the duration is 50 years after the year of first publication. A slightly different duration applies to cinematographic works, namely: 50 years after the year the work was "ready for showing". It is intended to extend the term of protection to 70 years in 1995. Copyright can be transferred by a simple deed. There are no particular formal requirements, except that the deed must expressly state the exploitation rights which are intended to be the subject of the transfer. Similar provisions apply to neighbouring rights. Licences which do not amount to a transfer of copyright are not subject to any formal requirements. Different provisions apply in the case of audio-visual works. The law includes a presumption that the authors have transferred their rights to the producer, exception being made for the composers of film music. The maker's moral rights cannot be transferred. The Copyright Act 1912 gives an important and exhaustive list of "fair dealings" which do not constitute a copyright infringement. It is submitted that the more important examples are: news can be copied without any restrictions; articles in the press (with exception of the photos and illustrations), radio or television emissions on topics of current interest can be copied if the source is mentioned and provided no reservation of copyright has been made; the short display in a television or radio program of a work is permitted to the extent necessary for the proper presentation of current events; copying of short pieces for educational or scientific purposes is allowed, provided the author is mentioned and a reasonable fee is paid; citation of a work is permitted, provided the source is mentioned and the extent of citation is reasonable; and importantly for computer programs as "written material", the copying for own use is permitted. The number of copies should not exceed two or three and short works can be copied in their totality, books and similar works only if they are no longer on sale.

The law of copyright of Norway

In general

The principal Act in the field of copyright law is the Act on Copyright in Literary, Scientific or Artistic Works, dated 12 May 1961. The preparation of this Act was conducted in close co-operation with the other Nordic countries and although Norway is not a Member State of the European Union, it has been included in this work on that ground. Therefore, the main rules of the Copyright in Literary, Scientific or Artistic Works Act 1961 correspond closely to those of the Copyright Acts of the other Nordic countries of Sweden, Finland, Iceland and Denmark. The Copyright in Literary, Scientific or Artistic Works Act 1961 has been amended several times during the years, especially in fields involving new technology (such as broadcasting, cable distribution and computer software). However, there have not been any major changes of the Act's basic principles. The essential substantive conditions which have to be fulfilled for the establishment of copyright protection are the following: the work created has to fall within the scope of the literary, scientific or artistic field; it has to be the result of an individual and creative "work of mind";[66] thus discoveries made by scientists are not regarded as creations and therefore fall outside the scope of copyright

66 This means that the work, at least to some extent, has to be the result of an original and individual creative process from the author. However, in the determination of whether the work qualifies as "work in mind", no subjective assessment of the work's literary or artistic standards may take place.

protection. As a further related condition, the work must have obtained its own existence and have been "disconnected" from its author; and it is required that the work be of a certain objective quality.

Requirements

There are no formal requirements, such as registration, to obtain copyright protection. Furthermore, it is not required that the work be fixed in any specific manner. However, as mentioned above, the work has to be the result of a "work of mind", and it should have its "own existence". As an example, a choreographic work is protected by copyright, even if it is not fixed on paper, tape or in other media. The legal requirements for copyright protection are that the choreographic work and any other type of work must be individualised and that it should be possible to make fixations of it, if necessary. The author is defined as the person who creates the work. The copyright always originates from an individual and if the work is created by two or more authors in co-operation, they enjoy joint authorship to the work. A legal entity may not be regarded as an original copyright owner. However, copyright may be transferred, either expressly or implicitly, from the author to a legal entity. As regards works created by employed authors, and where no specific agreement is concluded between employee and employer, the basic assumption is that the employer has the right to exploit the work to the extent reasonably necessary to fulfil the purpose of the employment contract. With regard to computer software, there is specific presumption in Article 39A of the Copyright in Literary, Scientific or Artistic Works Act 1961 concerning works created by employed authors. According to this presumption, the pecuniary rights to a computer program created by an employee within the framework of an employment contract, are, unless otherwise agreed, transferred to the employer.

Author's rights

The author of a copyright work enjoys an exclusive right to use, or to authorise the use of, his works. This includes the right to make copies of the work and to make the work available for the general public. If the work is recorded or otherwise transferred to technical devices which can reproduce the work, this is regarded as an act of copying the work. Furthermore, the work is made available to the general public when it is performed or exposed outside the private area, or when copies of the work are offered for sale, rental or lending or otherwise spread or exposed outside the private area. The right of distribution, including rental and lending rights, is exhausted when a work is published the first time. For computer programs the exhaustion of rights takes place when the work is sold, and for visual art works when the work is published or sold. There are certain limitations to this general rule. Copies of musical works, and computer programs are not subject to public rental without the consent of the author. As regards computer programs, the author's rights also include public lending. Provisions on rental and lending rights, in line with those of Council Directive 92/100/EEC are about to be introduced through the forthcoming revision of the Copyright in Literary, Scientific or Artistic Works Act 1961.

Moral rights

Article 3 of the Copyright in Literary, Scientific or Artistic Works Act 1961 protects the author's "moral rights". These include, *inter alia*, the right to be named as the author, both on copies of the work and when the work is made available to the public. Furthermore, if someone is authorised to change or adapt the work, or to make it available to the public, this may not be done in a way or in a context which is offensive to the author or to the work in question. The author may not waive the above-mentioned rights. The moral rights, however, do not include a right for the author to recall his work because of change of opinion. The copyright protection of works created by authors, as a general rule, lasts for 50 years after the death of the author. However, a special Act of 1955 extends the term of protection of works by authors deceased before the end of 1955 from 50 to 56 years after the death of the author, in order to compensate for losses sustained during World War II. All pecuniary rights arising under the Copyright in Literary, Scientific or Artistic Works Act 1961 may be transferred and licensed. No formalities apply to the transfer or licensing of these rights. The moral rights of the author cannot be transferred or licensed.

The law of copyright in Portugal

In general

It is only recently that intellectual property has achieved significant importance in the Portuguese legal system. The Copyright and Neighbouring Rights Code was adopted on 14 March 1985 (DL No 63/85), and it has been subject to subsequent revisions, the latest of which was on 3 September 1991 (DL No 11/91). The Industrial Property Code was adopted on 24 August 1940 (Dec No 30679) and the latest revision was on 27 January 1987 (DL No 40/87). These codes are at present in force in Portugal. However, a new

Industrial Property Code is in the process of being introduced at the time of writing, mainly aiming at bringing Portuguese law into compliance with the European Patent Convention, the Patent Co-operation Treaty and the First Trade Mark Directive (Dir 89/104/EEC). Copyright protects intellectual creations in the fields of literature, science and arts. Themes, thoughts and ideas are only protected when expressed in a material form. The work protected by copyright is the actual form in which an idea reflecting the author's thoughts has been expressed. The required originality refers to the form and not to the contents of the work. Novelty is not a requirement for copyright protection. Although the EC Software Directive (Dir 91/250/EEC) has not yet been implemented in Portugal, all recent decisions of Portuguese courts dealing with software have accepted copyright as the basis of protection. A work becomes eligible for copyright protection at the moment in which it is brought to the public's knowledge. Generally, there are no formal requirements. However, if the author so wishes he can register the work at the *Direcao-Geral de Espectaculas*. This facilitates proof of ownership in cases of dispute.

Author's rights

Portuguese law provides a non-exhaustive list of pecuniary rights, essentially allowing the owner of copyright to exploit a copyright work for economic purposes. In order to exercise these rights, authors can be represented by collecting societies, such as the *Sociedade Portuguesa de Autores*, which, at the moment, is the only collecting society in Portugal, and deals with all types of intellectual property rights. Portuguese copyright law also protects moral rights. The principal examples of such rights are the right to be named as the author and the right to protect the integrity of the copyrighted work. These rights are untransferable, imprescriptible and not renounceable. The author's name itself is protected by Portuguese law. The use of a similar name or sign, which could lead to confusion with that of another author, is prohibited. In such cases there is a special procedure enabling an author to obtain the immediate cancellation of the illegal use of his name (or of a similar name likely to engender confusion), and to claim compensation for any damages caused. Therefore, the protection of the author's name is guaranteed by exclusivity pertaining to the use of his name in works of literature, science and art. An author can register his name with the appropriate Register, although this is not a requirement in order for the name to be protected. The right not to publish a copyright work, and the right to withdraw works from circulation on moral grounds, as well as the right to modify works are other moral rights covered by Portuguese copyright law.

The author's moral rights are his personal property. They are not affected by an assignment or licence of the pecuniary right. Following the author's death, these rights are exercised by his successors for 50 years and thereafter they vest in the Portuguese state.

Term of copyright

Copyright and neighbouring rights last, generally, until 50 years have elapsed from the death of the author. Thereafter the work is deemed to be in the public domain and can be used freely, without any formalities. Only pecuniary rights can be assigned or licensed, wholly or partially. An assignment or licence of the whole of the pecuniary rights must be set in a notarised deed. A partial transfer need only be contained in a document bearing the duly certified signatures of the parties. The author can license the use of the work to a third party and, in the same manner as English law, this transaction does not involve a transfer of copyright; but such a licence must be in writing and must set out the conditions pertaining to the time, form, place, and price for which the licence is granted.

The law of copyright of Spain

In general

Spanish law traditionally recognises two different disciplines known as *Propiedad inteletual* (intellectual property) and *Propiedas industrial* (industrial property). The former concerns authors' rights over literary or artistic works and the latter aims to protect the rights of inventors in and users of trade marks and designs. This distinction is made because the protection required by an author – normally an individual – is seen in Spain as being different from the protection required, for instance, by a firm in protecting its distinguishing marks used to identify itself or its products. *Propiedad inteletual* are currently protected by the Intellectual Property Act 22/1987 of 11 November 1987, as modified by Act 20/1992 of 7 July 1992. This Act replaced legislation dating from 1879 and follows French laws to some extent. The main innovations of the new Act are its provisions on moral rights and the inclusion of collective works, "*droit de suite*", protection of computer programs and so-called neighbouring rights. Directive 91/250/EEC on the legal protection of computer programs was implemented by Act 16/93 of 23 December 1993.

Ownership

The Intellectual Property Act 1987 states that "the intellectual protection of a literary, artistic, or scientific work corresponds to the author merely by reason of its creation". An author might be required to prove actual authorship if this is disputed. The Act stipulates that the author is deemed to be the person who signs the work or who is named as such. According to Article 10 of the Intellectual Property Act 1987, the work must be original in some way to be considered as a creation, which is generally thought to mean that the work does not necessarily have to be innovative, but must be an individual expression of the personality and style of its author. Literary, artistic and scientific works are all protected and the Intellectual Property Act 1987 contains a non-exclusive and very detailed list of works covered by intellectual property protection. This list includes, for example, speeches and lectures, choreographs, films, applied or non-applied plastic artistic works and projects, plans and designs of architectural or engineering works, and computer programs. Importantly with respect to the copyright protection of computer programs, the Intellectual Property Act 1987 also provides for derivative rights over a work which, though based on another existing work, is modified by someone who leaves his own individual mark on the modified work. Derivative works are protected "without prejudice to the author's rights over the original work". Under this category of works, the Intellectual Property Act 1987 protects translations or adaptations, revisions, updates and musical arrangements.

Requirements

There are no formal requirements for the registration of copyright works in Spain and under Spanish law, intellectual property belongs as a matter of course to the author of the work. Therefore, the author can only be an individual, although the Intellectual Property Act 1987 does provide for some cases where legal persons can benefit from intellectual property protection. The work may, of course, be created by several authors in the case of collaboration. The Intellectual Property Act 1987 recognises common ownership rights for all authors involved. The rules of the Civil Code on joint ownership apply in such cases of collaboration, with certain variations. A slightly different case is that of compound works, defined under the Intellectual Property Act 1987 as new works incorporating other pre-existing works. Their exploitation requires prior consent from the author or authors of the pre-existing works, but not their collaboration. The author of a compound work takes elements or aspects from a previous work and creatively modifies it to produce another work. The author of the original work retains certain rights over the new work, depending on the agreement reached by both authors or what may be otherwise legally provided. Exceptionally, legal persons may acquire original copyright. This can be the case with collective works.[67] These are works created on the initiative of and coordinated by natural persons or companies which edit and publish them under their names, pooling the contributions of more than one author. The individual contributions form part of a unique and autonomous creation conceived by the promoter. Thus none of the co-authors are granted separate rights over the joint work. The Intellectual Property Act 1987 vests the rights to the collective work in the promoter of the work, but this rule is optional and the promoter and the co-authors may agree otherwise. When a work is created by an author during the normal course of his employment, the Intellectual Property Act 1987 provides for the automatic transfer of the rights to exploit the work to the employer. The parties may agree otherwise, but any such agreement must be made in writing. If not, the transfer is considered as exclusive, and its scope is defined by what is necessary for the performance of the company's normal business activity.

Author's rights

As in other civil law countries, Spanish legislation identifies within intellectual property a number of rights whereby the author can protect his personal interests in the work and the return which the work in question may bring him. Article 17 of the Intellectual Property Act 1987 invests the author with the exclusive right to exploit his work in whatever form. The Act further provides an indicative list of some of the more customary ways of exploiting intellectual property covered by the author's exclusive right. These include: reproduction, defined as setting the work in a medium which allows it to be communicated and copies to be obtained; distribution, which is an act by which the original or copies of the work are made available to the public on sale, for hire or through any other method; public communication, which covers any act whereby a number of people may have access to the work, provided that it does not take place in a purely domestic environment, that is theatrical performances, cinematographic and audio-visual projections, radio and television broadcasts, repeats of previous broadcasts by another media or their showings in public places, public exhibitions and public access to computer databases via telephone lines; alteration, a term which covers any translation, adaptation or modification of the work which may produce a

67 Art 8 of the Intellectual Property Act 1987.

new, derivative work. As mentioned already, the person altering the original work is considered the author of the new work, but this is without prejudice to the rights of the original author. Under Spanish law moral rights protect the personal and individual nature of the creative work of an author and they cannot be waived or transferred by the author.

Article 14 of the Intellectual Property Act 1987 enumerates, *inter alia*, the following moral rights: the right to decide if the work is to be published and in what form, and particularly if it is to be published under the author's name, pseudonym or anonymously; the right to claim recognition of authorship; the right to claim respect for the integrity of the work and to prevent any deformation, modification or alteration or other act that may prejudice the author's legitimate interests or impair his reputation; the right to modify the work, subject to respecting the rights acquired by any third party over the work (particularly when the work is being exploited); the right to recall the work from the market-place because of a change of intellectual or moral convictions. For this right to be exercised, the Intellectual Property Act 1987 expressly sets out that the holders of the rights to exploit the work should receive prior compensation for damages. Furthermore, if the author decides, at a later date, to exploit the work again, he must offer this right first to those persons originally exploiting the work. This right does not allow the author to demand the work to be moved from one place to another.

Term of copyright

The duration of the pecuniary rights is limited, generally lasting for the lifetime of the author and another 60 years after his death. Moral rights generally lapse upon the death of the author; however, the Intellectual Property Act 1987 entitles certain persons to exercise some of the author's moral rights in order to defend the value of the work and the reputation of the author, and to ensure the conservation of the work. These persons are those named by the author in his will, or, if there is no will, his heirs. If there are no heirs, then the rights in question can be exercised by the government/administration. The moral entitlement to exercise the right not to publish a work lasts for 60 years following the death of the author. There is no time limit set for the above-mentioned persons to exercise other moral rights. The personal nature of moral rights makes them non-transferable. Pecuniary rights, on the other hand, may be transferred by the author, although his prior consent is required before a third party can exploit any of his works in any way. The rights to exploit the work may be transferred by any of the cases of transfer on death recognised by law. The Intellectual Property Act 1987 also allows transfers *inter vivos*, but these must specify the rights transferred, the types of exploitation, and the period and the territory for which the transfer is made. If no period is set, the assignment is deemed to be for five years; if no territory is specified, it is deemed to be the country where the agreement takes place; and if the type of exploitation is not stated, it is deemed to be defined through strict interpretation of the contract. The Intellectual Property Act 1987 requires such transfers to be made in writing; but prohibits the transfer of all of the author's future works; any warranty by the author not to undertake any further works; and the extension of the contract to methods of using or disseminating works which are not yet known.

The law of copyright of Sweden

In general

Swedish intellectual property ("IP") rights are dealt with in a substantial number of separate Acts, but the controlling Act for the purposes of this work is the Act on Copyright in Literary and Artistic Works (1960:729). This Act affords protection to works of a literary and artistic character.[68] Anything expressed in a literary or artistic form is protected immediately upon termination of a creative act by a human being resulting in something which possesses an independently achieved original character.

Originality

The necessary degree of originality is present when the work has risen to a modicum of creativity in relation to what already exists and what might possibly come into existence independently.[69] There are no quality requirements, nor any quantitative requirements. However, the Act on Copyright in Literary and Artistic Works (1960:729) only protects the form of what has been expressed, not the intellectual essence of the expression. This means that ideas, facts, plots, news items etc, fall outside the scope of the Act. Literary works include any kind of work of a descriptive nature. Such descriptive works may be addresses, dictionaries, newsletters, as well as drawings, maps and the like, apart from fictional and non-fictional literature, poems and dramatic works.

---

68 Act on Copyright in Literary and Artistic Works (1960:729), s 1.

69 Supreme Court of Sweden, NJA [1965] 523, *Svensk bokkatalog*, NJA [1990] 440, *Gotlandsmotiv*, NJA [1994] 74, *Smultron*.

Computer programs

Computer programs are, generally considered to be of a descriptive nature, are potentially protected by the Act on Copyright in Literary and Artistic Works (1960:729) as literary works, if they are original. This was also the case before the 1988 amendment to the CA Act on Copyright in Literary and Artistic Works (1960:729) in which computer programs were expressly mentioned among the categories of works protected by copyright. Since then, the EC Software Directive (Dir 91/250/EEC) has been implemented in Sweden. The required level of originality of computer programs has not yet been tested by the Supreme Court, but there are several Appeal Court judgments. However, in cases dealing with the originality requirement after the implementation of the Software Directive it is clearly assumed that a modest but distinctive degree of individuality is necessary. Artistic works are non-literary works in a form created with the purpose of generating an artistic (non-descriptive) effect. Among them one may find all kinds of pictorial arts as well as sculptures, models and works of architecture and applied art, such as furniture and ornaments. Musical works in any medium also belong to this group, as do film works and dramatic works as performed, including ballets, pantomimes and marionette shows. Further, original photographic pictures are also protected as artistic works.

Optional registration

The copyright in a work according to the Act on Copyright in Literary and Artistic Works (1960:729) requires no formalities, such as fixation or registration, or any act other than an author's effort resulting in the creation of an original work. However, there is one optional registration procedure available. Under section 7(1) of the Act on Copyright in Literary and Artistic Works (1960:729), it is possible, without paying any fees or other charges, to register voluntarily a notification with the Ministry of Justice that makes known the name of the author of a work published anonymously or under a pseudonym. The creator of a literary or artistic work, irrespective of what kind, is always the original owner of the copyright in that work. Without exception, Swedish copyright law initially confers copyright solely to one or, as the case may be, several individual persons. All creative contributors to, for instance, an audio-visual work are therefore considered as the authors of that work, provided of course that their contributions are original. However, in accordance with the EC Software Directive (91/250/EEC), rights in a computer program created by an employee in the execution of his duties or following the instructions given by his employer, may be exclusively exercised by the employer, unless otherwise provided by contract[70], notwithstanding that an individual person (or several) is still the original author of the computer program.

Author's rights

Economic or pecuniary rights are dealt with in section 2 of the Act on Copyright in Literary and Artistic Works (1960:729). They include the right to exploit the work by producing copies of it and by making it available to the public, be it in original or in a changed form, in translation or adaptation, in other literary or artistic forms or by other technical means. The reproduction right covers any production of a copy of the work, including the very first one and any item in which a work is fixed as a copy, irrespective of the technique used. The expression "making a work available to the public" includes, *inter alia*: "distributing copies of the work to the public; displaying or exhibiting a work to the public;[71] or performing the work in public, be it in front of a live audience or via radio, television, cable, films, video, recordings, computer program or any other medium." Moral rights are dealt with in section 3 of the Act on Copyright in Literary and Artistic Works (1960:729). They constitute an important part of copyright protection, and are available not only to authors but also to performing artists, within the scope of protection afforded to them by neighbouring rights. The author's moral rights include the author's rights to be mentioned, when copies of a work are produced or when the work is made available to the public, to the extent and in the manner required by proper usage.[72] Section 3(2) of the Act protects the integrity of a work. Under this provision, a work may not be changed in a manner which is prejudicial either to the author's literary or artistic reputation or to his individuality, nor may it be made available to the public in such a form or context as to prejudice the author.

Term of copyright

Pursuant to section 43 of the Act on Copyright in Literary and Artistic Works (1960:729), an author's copyright subsists from the moment of creation until the end of the fiftieth year after the year in which the author died or, in the

70 Act on Copyright in Literary and Artistic Works (1960:729), s 40a.

71 Displaying also includes the appearance or expositions of an art object or a copy, but without any performance. The projection of a film qualifies as a performance, but showing a work of art in a broadcast television programme is also a display in the terms of the Act on Copyright in Literary and Artistic Works (1960:729).

72 Act on Copyright in Literary and Artistic Works (1960:729), s 3(1).

event of works of joint authorship, after the year in which the last surviving author died. A protection period of 70 years after the death of the author is being considered along the lines of EC Directive (Dir 93/98/EC). Under section 27 of the Act, the exclusive pecuniary rights of the author may be transferred to others, be it individuals or legal entities, entirely or in part, without any restrictions as to the required form of the transfer. Under section 28 of the Act, a person to whom copyright has been transferred may not transfer those rights to others without the original author's permission. The Act on Copyright in Literary and Artistic Works (1960:729) also contains a set of rules on publishing contracts, and contracts on public performances and audio-visual works. All statutory rules on contracts and transfers are optional apart from the presumption in favour of employers regarding computer programs created by their employees.[73] Moral rights as such cannot be transferred, only waived, and only in respect of clearly specified uses of the work.[74] This mandatory rule applies to all types of literary and artistic works, as well as to the performances of artists, protected by the Act on Copyright in Literary and Artistic Works (1960:729). However, the application of this rule to moral rights on employees' software appears to be unclear. According to section 40a of the Act on Copyright in Literary and Artistic Works (1960:729), the rights of an employee in a computer program are automatically transferred to his employer. Unlike the EC Software Directive (91/250/EEC), the Swedish Act on Copyright in Literary and Artistic Works (1960:729) does not include any express restriction of this transfer solely to economic rights, but seems to have a bearing on all the rights of the author.

The law of copyright of Switzerland

In general

Although Switzerland is not a Member State of the European Union, it does run a policy of self-determined harmonisation with the intellectual property law of the European Union and has been included in this work on that ground. Switzerland enacted a new Code on Copyright and Neighbouring Rights and its implementing Ordinance on 1 July 1993. As under the previous Act, Swiss copyright law aims at the protection of intellectual creations which have an individual character in the fields of literature and art, irrespective of their purpose or value. A non-exclusive list identifies the categories of works which are normally encompassed by this rather broad

73 Act on Copyright in Literary and Artistic Works (1960:729), s 40a.
74 Act on Copyright in Literary and Artistic Works (1960:729), s 3(3)(c).

definition and they include literary and musical works, artistic works such as drawings, paintings and sculptures, works with scientific or technical content, works of architecture, works of applied art, photographic and cinematographic works, choreographic works and pantomimes. Furthermore, the Code now also explicitly treats computer software as copyright-protected works. Swiss courts are traditionally prepared to extend copyright protection to minor creations, as long as they have been created by human beings (as opposed to animals, computers or other types of machines) and show a certain level of individuality. The level of individuality required to trigger copyright protection depends on the category to which a work belongs. The creator of works of applied arts or a computer program may enjoy less freedom of individual expression, owing to aspects of functionality which influence their creation. That does not mean that such works are deprived of copyright protection under Swiss law. Copyright originates upon creation of a work and is initially vested in the author. Only the individual who has created the work is considered to be the author and therefore the first owner of the copyright. This is also the case where the work was made by an employee in the course of his employment or was created by one or more freelance commissionees performing their contractual duties. There is an exception, however, regarding the copyright in computer software which was created by employees in the course of their employment. Under the Code the employer is exclusively entitled to the exploitation of such software. The question of first ownership in the copyright and the subsistence of moral rights relating to computer software created by employees are not covered by the Code; but it is generally taken to be the case that the creator of the computer program is its author and the initial owner of the copyright. The employer is granted a licence for commercial exploitation including first publication. The moral rights subsisting in the computer program, however, remain with the employee.

Author's rights

The copyright owner has the exclusive right to exploit the copyright work, that is to reproduce the work and to issue copies of it to the public, to alter or adapt the work, to perform the work in public, to record or broadcast it, to retransmit the broadcast work and to communicate broadcasts and retransmissions to the public. Additionally, copyright in computer software includes an exclusive rental right but currently, Switzerland has no plans to introduce lending and rental rights for musical and audio-visual works. Swiss law traditionally protects moral rights, that is the right to be identified as author, the right to decide on the date and manner of the first publication of the work and the right to object to derogatory treatment of the work. The right to recall a work because of a change of opinion, as known to other jurisdictions, is not protected in Switzerland. Instead, the Code on Copyright and Neighbouring Rights 1993 added three new powers which, it is submitted are similar to moral rights. Under these the owner of a copyright work is obliged to give the author access to the work at any time in so far as execution of the copyright requires him to see the work; the author is entitled to claim the work for the purpose of an exhibition in Switzerland, if he can demonstrate an adequate interest; and prior to destroying an original work of art of which no other original editions exist, its owner is obliged to offer it to the author for an amount not exceeding the value of the material incorporated therein. The Code on Copyright and Neighbouring Rights 1993 extended the term of copyright protection from 50 to 70 years from the end of the calendar year in which the author dies. However, in the case of computer software, protection expires 50 years from the end of the calendar year in which the author dies.

Copyright can be assigned or licensed in part or in its entirety. There are no formal requirements for copyright assignments or licences. It should be noted that moral rights are regarded as being part of the author's personal rights which are unassignable; however, the author may waive moral rights within reasonable limits. According to the prevailing doctrine and practice in Switzerland, an exclusive licensee is only entitled to take defensive actions against copyright infringers if he is contractually bound to defend the copyright. A number of acts which may be carried out in relation to copyright works are not considered copyright infringements, either because of the existence of a prevailing public interest or because of the mere impossibility of control and enforcement. The most important of such "fair dealings" are the private and domestic use of a copyright work and its use for educational purposes.

The Code on Copyright and Neighbouring Rights 1993 entitles the copyright owner to share in the benefits of such mass exploitation by means of a statutory royalty levied on copiers used in companies and within the administration; a fee levied on blank video and audio tapes; and a statutory royalty imposed on the rental to the public of copyright works, with the exception of works of architecture and works of artistic craftsmanship (applied arts), in cases in which a business engages in such rental for money or money's worth. Under the Code on Copyright and Neighbouring Rights 1993, "fair dealings" also includes: the right of the licensee of computer software to decompile its interface information in order to develop an independent but compatible program if the interface information is not readily available.

Chapter 11

Aspects of International Copyright

Introduction

The computer software industry as a community is global and is constituted not only of software houses that operate in one legal jurisdiction only: the majority of software houses will operate across the borders of sovereign states in some fashion or other. A British software house might, for instance, be a true multinational organisation and own subsidiaries in other parts of the world; on the other hand the British software house might not own subsidiaries abroad, but have foreign independent distributors that licence the use of its software overseas. In any event, it is highly likely that the indigenous computer software house will source component parts for integration into its own computer software products from abroad by licensing, outright purchase or, in the case of a multinational, from development teams producing copyright works operating within its own subsidiaries but outside the United Kingdom. This chapter will accordingly consider the nature of international copyright and the application of the Copyright, Designs and Patents Act 1988 to copyright works produced outside of the United Kingdom. A brief explanation will also be made of the operation of the principal international conventions on the law of copyright. Unfortunately, a detailed examination of international copyright law is beyond the scope of this work. Instead, this chapter will seek to focus in brief on the manner in which English law treats the copyright works that arise outside of the United Kingdom so as to give some insight into their status when viewed alongside works which have arisen under the aegis of the Copyright, Designs and Patents Act 1988.

INTERNATIONAL CONVENTIONS

Generally

International conventions are agreements entered into by and between sovereign states, in the context of the law of copyright, so that their local laws do not discriminate against each other's authors and publishers. Under British constitutional law private citizens derive no rights from such conventions, which is why it is necessary to enact statutes and to make Orders in Council so as to give effect to the UK's international obligations. The conventions are important, it is submitted, for two principal reasons: firstly, the international copyright conventions assist in the interpretation of UK legislation on copyright since there is a presumption that Parliament will frame legislation in accordance with the United Kingdom's international obligations;[1] and secondly, conventions form a means of recognising and dealing with foreign copyrights under the aegis of the English law of copyright.

The United Kingdom is party to two principal international conventions: the Berne Copyright Union which began in 1886 and the Universal Copyright Convention which originated in 1952. They are broadly similar in effect in that the parties to them undertake to provide a degree of copyright protection under their own domestic laws which conforms at least to the minimum standards laid down by the conventions. Generally speaking, the signatories to the conventions must give protection to the copyright works of citizens of the other signatories, which have been first published therein, on the same terms as native authors. Under the Berne Copyright Union system no formalities are required, the minimum term of protection is longer, and the scope of protection is laid down in greater detail and is more extensive than the system arising under the Universal Copyright Convention. Under the Universal Copyright Convention system, the only formality that can be required as a condition of protection is the use of the universal copyright symbol "©" on all published copies of the work, accompanied by the name of the copyright owner and the year of first publication, placed in such a manner and such a location as to give reasonable notice of the author's or copyright owner's claim to protection.

---

1 **Hogg v Toye & Co Ltd** [1935] Ch 497 at 520; **Warwick Film Productions Ltd v Eisinger** at 521; **The Jade** [1976] 1 All ER 920 at 924.

The Berne Convention

The system generally

The Berne Convention was amended by the Paris Act on 1 March 1989 and as a result many countries, including the major members of the Berne Union[2] have adhered to the Paris Revision of the Berne Convention. The United States acceded to the Paris Act with effect from 1 March 1989 and the United Kingdom ratified the Paris Act on 29 September 1989 with effect from 2 January 1990. There are theoretically two systems which are possible to effect in international copyright agreements. Perhaps the most satisfactory system would be a complete copyright code which applied to every signatory to the agreement and their nationals directly. Perhaps a less satisfactory system, merely from this international standpoint, would be one which requires each signatory state to give the nationals of other signatory states the same protection as it would apply to its own nationals; but this would result in varying degrees and modes of protection when considering each signatory state. The Berne Convention adopted a compromise between these two types of system and the Paris Act has tended to extend the principle of a copyright code which is common to all signatory states. Of course, the Berne Convention originally never anticipated the emergence of computer programming technologies; but the manner in which it has approached the concept of intellectual property in literary and artistic works has generally been well drafted, well anticipated and accepted throughout the world. For instance, the solution of expressly adopting computer programs as a form of copyright work has gradually emerged as the preferred and most appropriate (or least controversial) form for the protection of computer programs in the European Union. The European Union took the view that as copyright protection does not require any formalities that could stifle the rapid development of new software and benefitted from an existing and long-established system for international protection based on multilateral agreements[3] which have been ratified by a very large number of countries throughout the world, it opted for copyright as the appropriate vehicle for the harmonisation of the legal protection of computer programs.

Protection of computer programs

This led to the adoption of the Council Directive of 14 May 1991 on the

2 Including the UK.
3 The Berne Convention on Copyright and the Universal Convention on Copyright.

legal protection of computer programs.[4] This Council Directive on the legal protection of computer programs[5] seeks to protect computer programs by copyright, as literary works within the meaning of the Berne Convention on copyright. Article 2(1) of the Berne Copyright Convention (Paris Revision, 1971) defines "literary and artistic works" as including:

> "every production in the literary, scientific and artistic domain, whatever may be the mode or form of its expression, such as books, pamphlets and other writings; lectures, addresses, sermons and other works of the same nature; dramatic or dramatico-musical works, choreographic works and entertainments in dumb show; musical compositions with or without words; cinematographic works to which are assimilated works expressed by a process analogous to cinematography; works of drawing, painting, architecture, sculpture, engraving and lithography; photographic works to which are assimilated works expressed by a process analogous to photography; works of applied art; illustrations, maps, plans, sketches and three-dimensional works relative to geography, topography, architecture or science."

Accordingly this protection applies to the expression, in any form, of a computer program, including preparatory design material.[6]

Article 3 of the Paris Act contains the general criteria for eligibility for copyright protection and provides as follows:

> "(1) The protection of this Convention shall apply to:
> (a) Authors who are nationals of one of the countries of the Union, for their works, whether published or not;
> (b) Authors who are not nationals of one of the countries of the Union, for their works first published in one of those countries, or simultaneously in a country outside the Union and in a country of the Union.
> (2) Authors who are not nationals of one of the countries of the Union but who have their habitual residence in one of them shall, for the purposes of this Convention, be assimilated to nationals of that country."

Publication and protection

The concept of publication in the Paris Act is similar to that adopted by the Copyright, Designs and Patents Act 1988[7], and all that is required to constitute publication in a particular country is that copies should be made available for sale in that country, with the consent of the copyright owner, and sufficient to satisfy the reasonable requirements of the public there, having regard to the nature of the work. The protection afforded to copyright

4 Council Dir 91/250 of 14 May 1991 on the legal protection of computer programs – 91/250/EEC; OJ 1991 L122/42.

5 *Ibid.*

6 See Chap 3 above for an explanation of the nature of preparatory design material.

7 Copyright, Designs and Patents Act 1988, s 175.

works under the Paris Act of the Berne Convention is provided for in Article 5 of the Paris Act as follows:

> "(1) Authors shall enjoy, in respect of works for which they are protected under this Convention, in countries of the Union other than the country of origin, the rights which their respective laws do now or may hereafter grant to their nationals, as well as the rights specially granted by this Convention ......
>
> (3) Protection in the country of origin is governed by domestic law. However, when the author is not a national of the country of origin of the work for which he is protected under this Convention, he shall enjoy in that country the same rights as national authors."

One can see that a distinction is made between the extent of protection in the country of origin and in other countries of the Union, since protection in the country of origin is governed by the domestic law but, in countries other than the country of origin, the author is given not only the rights which are given under their domestic law, but also the rights granted by the Convention. Thus it can be seen that under Article 5 of the Paris Act, authors are protected in countries other than the country of origin, and that a distinction is drawn as to the type of protection afforded in the country of origin and other countries. Article 5(4) defines the expression "country of origin"as follows:

> "The country of origin shall be considered to be:
>
> (a) in the case of works first published in a country in the Union, that country; in the case of works published simultaneously in several countries of the Union which grant different terms of protection, the country whose legislation grants the shortest term of protection;
>
> (b) in the case of works published simultaneously in a country outside the Union and in a country of the Union, the latter country;
>
> (c) in the case of unpublished works or of works first published in a country outside the Union, without simultaneous publication in a country of the Union, the country of the Union of which the author is a national provided that:
>
> (i) when these are cinematographic works the maker of which has his headquarters or his habitual residence in a country of the Union, the country of origin shall be that country, and
>
> (ii) when these are works of architecture erected in a country of the Union or other artistic works incorporated in a building or other structure located in a country of the Union, the country of the Union shall be that country."

The Berne Convention provides that there are not to be any formalities precedent to obtaining copyright, for instance, registration or some reservation of copyright, nor any formalities precedent to the bringing of an action for infringement, such as registration prior to the commencement of proceedings. Consequently, apart from the express stipulations of the Convention, the extent of protection, as well as the means of redress to be secured by the copyright owner, are governed exclusively by the laws of the country where protection is claimed.

Participating countries

At the time of writing this work, the following countries form the Copyright Union under the Berne Convention:

Argentina	Australia	Austria	Bahamas
Barbados	Belgium	Benin	Brazil
Bulgaria	Burkino Faso	Cameroon	Canada
Central African Republic	Chad	Chile	Columbia
Costa Rica	Cyprus	Czechoslovakia	Denmark
Egypt	Fiji	Finland	France
Gabon	Germany	Great Britain	Greece
Guinea	Holy See	Honduras	Hungary
Iceland	India	Irish Republic	Israel
Italy	Ivory Coast	Japan	Lebanon
Lesotho	Liberia	Libya	Liechtenstein
Luxembourg	Malagasy Republic	Malaysia	Mali
Malta	Mauritania	Mauritius	Mexico
Monaco	Morocco	Netherlands	New Zealand
Niger	Norway	Pakistan	Peru
Philippines	Poland	Portugal	Rumania
Rwanda	Senegal	Spain	Sri Lanka
Surinam	Sweden	Switzerland	Thailand
Togo	Trinidad	Tobago	Tunisia
Turkey	Union of South Africa	United States of America	Uruguay
Venezuela	Yugoslavia	Zaire	Zimbabwe

The Universal Copyright Convention

Generally, the effect of the Universal Copyright Convention as revised in 1971 is that each contracting sovereign state undertakes to give to the unpublished works of the nationals of all other contracting states the same protection as it gives to the unpublished works of its own nationals in addition to the protection specifically granted by the Convention. Computer programs are covered by the ambit of the obligations set out in Article I of the Universal Copyright Convention[8] where it states:

> "Each Contracting State undertakes to provide for the adequate and effective protection of the rights of authors and other copyright proprietors in literary, scientific and artistic works, including writings, musical, dramatic and cinematographic works, and paintings, engravings and sculpture."

8 Paris Revision, 1971 Cmnd 4905.

The contracting states further undertake to give to the published works of the nationals of the other contracting states wherever first published, and to published works of the nationals of any country if first published in one of the other contracting states, the same rights as it gives to works first published in its own territory as well as the protection specifically provided for by the Convention. In addition to this, such published works, if first published outside of the territory of the contracting state in question and not being the work of a national author, are to enjoy the protection without any formalities provided that from the time of first publication all copies bear the universal copyright symbol "©" accompanied by the name of the copyright owner and the year of first publication, and placed in such a manner and location as to give reasonable notice of the copyright owner's claim to the copyright subsisting within it.

Ambit of protection

With respect to the ambit of the protection sought to be given by the Universal Copyright Convention, the Convention provides that each contracting state should give adequate and effective protection to the rights of authors and other copyright proprietors in literary, scientific and artistic works, including writings, musical, dramatic and cinematographic works, and paintings, engravings and sculpture. It is further provided that these rights are to include the basic rights ensuring the author's economic interests; including the exclusive right to authorise reproduction by any means, public performance and broadcasting, and are to extend to the work either in its original form or in any other form recognisably derived from the original. Any contracting state to the Convention may make exceptions to these rights that do not conflict with the spirit and provisions of the Convention, but ought nevertheless to accord a reasonable degree of effective protection to each of the rights to which exception has been made. It is also provided in the Convention that such rights include the exclusive rights to make, publish and authorise the making and publication of translations of works; but the contracting state may make provision for compulsory licence to translate if, after the expiration of a period of seven years from the date of first publication, a translation has not been published in a language in general use in that state. This last provision also seems to encompass computer program and would, it is argued, cause the computer program menus and other visual textual manifestations to be translated into the language in general use in that state. It is contended that this provision is not directed to the concept of computer programming languages.

Participating countries

At the time of writing the following countries are parties to the Universal Copyright Convention:

Algeria	Andorra	Argentina	Australia
Austria	Bahamas	Bangladesh	Barbados
Belgium	Belize	Brazil	Bulgaria
Cambodia	Cameroon	Canada	Chile
Columbia	Costa Rica	Cuba	Czechoslovakia
Denmark	Dominican Republic	Ecuador	El Salvador
Fiji	Finland	France	Germany
Ghana	Great Britain	Greece	Guatemala
Guinea	Haiti	Holy See	Hungary
Iceland	India	Irish Republic	Israel
Italy	Japan	Kenya	Korean Republic
Laos	Lebanon	Liberia	Liechtenstein
Luxembourg	Malawi	Malta	Mauritius
Mexico	Monaco	Morocco	Netherlands
New Zealand	Nicaragua	Niger	Nigeria
Norway	Pakistan	Panama	Paraguay
Peru	Philippines	Poland	Portugal
Rwanda	Saint Vincent	Senegal	Spain
Sri Lanka	Sweden	Switzerland	Trinidad
Tobago	Tunisia	United States of America	Venezuela
Yugoslavia	Zambia		

Protection of foreign works by the Copyright, Designs and Patents Act 1988

By section 159 of the Copyright, Designs and Patents Act 1988, Her Majesty is authorised, by order in Council, to make provision for applying any of the provisions of Part I of the Act dealing with copyright to a country[9] to which Part I does not extend, so as to secure that the provisions of Part I:

(i) apply in relation to persons who are citizens of that country or are domiciled or resident there, as they apply to persons who are British citizens or are domiciled or resident in the United Kingdom, or

(ii) apply in relation to bodies incorporated under the law of that country as they apply in relation to bodies incorporated under the law of a part of the United Kingdom, or

9 The expression "country" includes any territory by virtue of s 178 of the Copyright, Designs and Patents Act 1988.

(iii) apply in relation to works first published in that country as they apply in relation to works first published in the United Kingdom, or

(iv) apply in relation to broadcasts made from or cable programmes sent from that country as they apply in relation to broadcasts made from or cable programmes sent from the United Kingdom.

Thus by an Order in Council made under section 159 of the Copyright, Designs and Patents Act 1988 which came into force on 1 August 1989[10], various provisions of the Copyright, Designs and Patents Act 1988 were applied in various degrees to works originating in a number of foreign countries which are enumerated below.[11] The Copyright (Application to Other Countries) Order is not, it is suggested, particularly straightforward and the explanation of its action that follows should be viewed purely as a guide, since a comprehensive and in-depth construction and exposition of it is considered to be beyond the scope of this work. Having said this, it is submitted that when considering the Copyright (Application to Other Countries) Order, two matters need to be borne in mind. Firstly, Article 6 of the Copyright (Application to Other Countries) Order provides that nothing in the Order is to be taken as derogating from the effect of paragraph 35, Schedule 1 of the Copyright, Designs and Patents Act 1988. This paragraph provides that every work in which copyright subsisted under the Copyright Act 1989 is to be deemed to satisfy the requirements of Part I of the Copyright, Designs and Patents Act 1988 as to qualification for copyright protection. It is submitted that this matter is still germane to computer programs since a significant number of modern commercial computer software products continue to contain computer programs, logic, sub-routines and code which pre-date the commencement of the Copyright, Designs and Patents Act 1988. It will be recalled that Part I of the Copyright, Designs and Patents Act 1988 includes sections 153–156 which deal with the qualification for copyright protection.

The second matter to be borne in mind is that the articles of the Copyright (Application to Other Countries) Order which grant protection[12] are made subject to Article 7 of the Order. Article 7 contains a provision, applicable

10 The Copyright (Application to Other Countries) (No 2) Order 1989 (SI 1989 No 1293), as amended by the Copyright (Application to Other Countries) (No 2) (Amendment) Order 1989 (SI 1989 No 2415) and the Copyright (Application to Other Countries) (No 2) (Amendment) Order 1990 (SI 1990 No 2153) which, collectively and for the purposes of this chapter, will be referred to as "the Copyright (Application to Other Countries) Order".

11 See p 272.

12 The Copyright (Application to Other Countries) Order, Arts 2, 3 and 4.

where copyright subsists in a work by virtue of the Copyright (Application to Other Countries) Order, but did not subsist prior thereto, which deems certain acts not to be infringements which are not or were not infringements at the relevant time; unless the owner of the copyright or his exclusive licensee (if any) pays such compensation as, failing agreement, may be determined by arbitration. Now section 1 of the Copyright, Designs and Patents Act 1988 protects as copyright works literary, dramatic, musical and artistic works, sound recordings, films, broadcasts, cable programmes, the typographical arrangement of published editions and film sound-tracks. The Copyright (Application to Other Countries) Order gives protection to all such works in the designated countries, other than cable programmes with the exception of Singapore. In consequence Article 2(1) of the Copyright (Application to Other Countries) Order provides that sections 153–155 inclusive of the Copyright, Designs and Patents Act 1988 are to apply in relation to:

(i) persons who are citizens or subjects of a country specified in Schedule 1 to the Order or are domiciled or resident there as they apply to persons who are British citizens or are domiciled or resident in the United Kingdom;

(ii) bodies incorporated under the law of such a country as they apply in relation to bodies incorporated under the law of a part of the United Kingdom; and

(iii) works first published in such a country as they apply in relation to works first published in the United Kingdom.

The expression "first published" includes simultaneous publication under section 155(3) of the Copyright, Designs and Patents Act 1988. This overall prima facie entitlement to copyright is then withdrawn in specialised cases by Article 2(2) in respect of certain works because of circumstances relating to their first publication. Where copyright does subsist in a work by virtue of Article 2(1), then Article 2(3) provides that the whole of Part I of the Copyright, Designs and Patents Act 1988 including Schedule 1 thereto applies in relation to the work, except in the case of designs of typefaces, as to which there are limitations.[13] Schedule 1 to the Copyright (Application to Other Countries) Order includes Singapore and Taiwan, but not Indonesia. There are special modifications to Article 2 in Schedule 4 to the Copyright (Application to Other Countries) Order in respect of Singapore and Taiwan.

13 Although it could be argued that this exception with respect to typefaces is not germane to this computer program orientated work, it has been included so that the statement could not be construed as misleading.

The Copyright (Application to Other Countries) Order applies to the following countries in respect of all species of copyright works except broadcasts and cable programmes:[14]

Algeria	Andorra	Argentina	Australia
Austria	Bahamas	Bangladesh	Barbados
Belgium	Belize	Benin	Brazil
Bulgaria	Burkina	Cameroon	Canada
Central African Republic	Chad	Chile	Columbia
Congo	Côte d'Ivoire	Cuba	Cyprus
Czechoslovakia	Denmark	Dominican Republic	Ecuador
Egypt	El Salvador	Fiji	Finland
France	Gabon	Germany	Ghana
Greece	Guatemala	Guinea	Haiti
Holy See	Hungary	Iceland	India
Ireland	Israel	Italy	Japan
Kampuchea	Kenya	Korea (Republic)	Laos
Lebanon	Liberia	Libya	Liechtenstein
Luxembourg	Madagascar	Malawi	Malaysia
Mali	Malta	Mauritania	Mauritius
Mexico	Monaco	Morocco	Netherlands
New Zealand	Nicaragua	Niger	Nigeria
Norway	Pakistan	Panama	Paraguay
Peru	Philippines	Poland	Portugal
Romania	Rwanda	Saint Vincent	Senegal
Singapore	South Africa	Spain	Sri Lanka
Suriname	Sweden	Switzerland	Taiwan
Thailand	Togo	Trinidad	Tobago
Tunisia	Turkey	United States of America	Uruguay
Venezuela	Yugoslavia	Zaire	Zambia
Zimbabwe			

The United States of America

The United States of America is both a highly important producer of and market-place for computer software products; and many UK software houses either distribute computer software products of US origin, purchase the copyright in computer software products developed in the United States of America, or are licensed by American software house to integrate copyright works originating in the United States into UK software products. Accordingly, this short section with respect to the treatment of works from

14 Sch 1 to the Copyright (Application to Other Countries) Order describes the countries as being "either ... parties to the Berne Copyright Convention and/or the Universal Copyright Convention or otherwise give adequate protection under the law."

the United States under the Copyright Act 1956 and the Copyright, Designs and Patents Act 1988 has been added and is submitted, for the sake of clarity, to be germane.

Copyright under the Copyright Act 1956 was originally conferred in respect of copyright works originating in the United States by reason of the United States's adherence to the Universal Copyright Convention; but the provision of the Orders conferring this right were not retrospective in relation to published works.[15] However, this position changed after the United States acceded to the Paris Act of the Berne Convention with effect from 1 March 1989. This was because, it is submitted, the most recent Order concerned with conferring copyright under the Copyright Act 1956 on copyright works of the US origin was amended, as from 8 March 1989, in such a way as to remove US copyright works from the qualification on protection in such Order of works first published in the United States before 27 September 1957.[16] As this amendment appeared to grant copyright to works not previously entitled to copyright protection, the amending Order contained a general provision preserving the existing rights of persons who, before the commencement of the Order, had incurred expenditure or liability in connection with the reproduction or performance of any work or other subject-matter. It is argued that in any event many existing works would have obtained UK copyright protection under the Copyright Act 1956, by having been simultaneously published in the United Kingdom or a Berne Convention country, without the necessity of reliance upon these Orders in Council. However, the Copyright (Application to Other Countries) (No 2) Order 1989 (SI 1989 No 1293), as amended by the Copyright (Application to Other Countries) (No 2) (Amendment) Order 1989 (SI 1989 No 2415) and the Copyright (Application to Other Countries) (No 2) (Amendment) Order 1990 (SI 1990 No 2153) made under section 159 of the Copyright, Designs and Patents Act 1988 now applies the copyright provisions of the Copyright, Designs and Patents Act 1988 directly to works originating in the United States.

15 Except in so far as such works had already acquired copyright under the Orders made during World War II.

16 The Copyright (International Conventions) Order 1979 (SI 1979 No 1715) as amended by the Copyright (International Conventions) (Amendment) Order 1989 (SI 1989 No 157).

Appendix

PRECEDENTS

INTRODUCTION

The purpose of these precedents is to give simplified and worked examples of component parts of real-life contracts which key-in to the legal analysis earlier in this text. Only those contractual areas which are concerned with issues of copyright or computer programming technology are given with attendant comment given in footnotes. All other aspects of the agreement such as clauses concerned with delivery, services, payment, warranties and their exclusion, limitation and exclusion of damages, *force majeure*, waiver, entire agreement provisions etc have been excluded. The practising draughtsman will have his or her preferred solutions and will, no doubt, refer to practitioner's textbooks which concentrate on these specialist areas. The following precedents are therefore offered as a guide as to how, in the framework of the modern law of copyright and current computer programming technologies, the premise of identifying and considering the technology first and allowing the legal analysis to follow is applied as an adjunct to drafting technique.

Precedent (A) *Extract from a Licence and Maintenance Agreement for the use of a Computer Software Product*

The definitions clause has been included in this precedent to show how useful a tool this can be in assisting the description of the ambit of the licence grant. The licence grant and its restrictions follow the most prevalent current practice amongst the suppliers of commercial computer software products in restricting use to nominated machines at nominated places and further restricting the number of concurrent users permitted. It is through these tools that the commercial software industry exploit their intellectual property rights.

1. Definitions

For the purposes of this Agreement the following words shall have the meaning set forth against them:

"Commencement Date" shall mean the date of execution hereof by <*Software House*>.

"Software Product" shall mean the computer software products set forth in Schedule I, including all and/or any modifications and/or error correction made thereto.[1]

1 This definition of the product to be licensed includes the upgrades, bug-fixes and enhancements which are supplied in the maintenance service. These upgrades etc may very well be copyright works in themselves and will need to be the subject of a licence grant.

"Customisation"	shall mean the use of certain facilities of the Software Product which modify and/or augment the functionality of the Software Product so as to more closely match the Licensee's operational requirements.[2]
"Software Customisation Toolset"	shall mean the computer software products supplied by <*Software House*> and used to effect Customisation.
"Software System"	shall mean the Software Product and the Software Customisation Toolset collectively.
"Authorised Hardware"	shall mean the computer hardware system, being the property of or under the control of the Licensee, as more particularly set forth in Schedule II.[3]
"Location"	shall mean the postal address at which the Authorised Hardware is situate, as more particularly set forth in Schedule II.[4]
"Users"	shall mean the maximum number of concurrent users of the Software Product permitted hereunder as specified in Schedule I.[5]
"Source Code"	shall mean any computer program, whether stored on or in any magnetic or optical medium, in any computer memory of whatsoever kind or in eye-readable form, from which it is possible to discern the logic, algorithms, internal structure, operating features and any other design characteristic of such computer program.[6]
"Object Code"	shall mean the computer executable binary code derived from compiled Source Code for execution on a computer hardware system.
"User Manual"	shall mean any instruction manual, designed to and intended to teach, aid and assist in the operation and use of the Software System.[7]

1 *(cont.)*
Thus, if the maintenance service is optional, the grant of the licence for upgrades and the like will need to be addressed elsewhere in the agreement; otherwise the licensee will have an automatic right to them by virtue of the breadth of the initial licence grant.

2 Due to the large number of mainstream software application products that include some method for altering the computer programs operation by the end-user (often a type of 4GL (Fourth Generation Language), this definition has been included to give an example of how this form of technology may be addressed contractually.

3 This form of licence restricts the licensee to use the software on a specific computer.

4 This form of licence restricts the licensee to use the software on a specific computer at a specific location; a very common mechanism in the software industry.

5 With the advent of multi-user, networked and, more recently, client-server systems, many software houses have elected to price their software not only with respect to the hardware upon which it is run, but also with respect to the number of users who will be using the system concurrently.

6 Due to the capacity of computer software experts to disagree on the nature of source and object code and so as to increase constructional certainty, definitions of technical computer terminology should be included, especially when licence restrictions may be attached to them.

7 It should be borne in mind that user manuals and technical documentation are copyright works in themselves. Thus a licence will be needed with respect to them should the user be given the right to copy them or substantial parts thereof.

"Licence"	shall mean the rights granted to the Licensee with respect to the Software System in Clause 2 hereinbelow.[8]

2. The Licence

2.1 The grant

2.1.1 <*Software House*> hereby grants to the Licensee a personal, non-transferable, non-exclusive and revocable licence to use the Software System on the Authorised Hardware at the Location.[9]

2.1.2 The Licensee shall use the Software System only for the Licensee's benefit in the course of its normal business activities. The Software System may be executed only at the Location and on the Authorised Hardware by employees of the Licensee or by staff under contract to the Licensee and under the Licensee's direct supervision who require such access in order to permit and enable the use by the Licensee of the Software System in the manner contemplated by this Agreement.

2.2 The restrictions

2.2.1 The Licensee shall not permit:

(i) any other person or entity to use the Software System; nor

(ii) a greater number of Users than that specified in Schedule I to use the Software Product at the same time.

2.2.2 The Licensee acknowledges that the continued integrity of the Software System, provision of maintenance and the performance of other obligations by <*Software House*> hereunder are dependent upon the proper use and maintenance of the Software System by the Licensee. Concomitant upon such acknowledgement the Licensee undertakes to properly use and maintain the Software Product. Proper use and maintenance means that the Licensee will:

(i) preserve the Software System code intact;

(ii) use the Software System in accordance with the User Manual and all other documentation supplied by <*Software House*>;

(iii) follow the Authorised Hardware manufacturer's instructions for maintaining and updating the system software used upon it;

(iv) follow <*Software House*>'s instructions for installing new releases[10] and for correcting and circumventing errors in the Software System.

2.3 <*Software House*> makes available at reasonable charges a range of information which could assist the Licensee in the creation of independent computer programs to operate with the Software System. In view of this ready availability, the Licensee undertakes to respect the confidentiality of the Software System and the trade secrets therein and not to use any disassembly, decompilation or

---

8 It is submitted that it can often be useful, as a constructional device, to gather the licence grant into one clause and then to define it. In this way easy reference may be made when certain proscribed acts or termination provisions are directed to non-observance of the licence provisions.

9 The species and the ambit of the licence grant needs to be set out as comprehensively as possible. This licence is specifically expressed to be a "non-exclusive licence" rather than an "exclusive licence" See Chap 7.

10 If the software house's upgrade methodologies are particularly complex, it is often advisable to define such items as "upgrades" or "releases" to increase the constructional certainty of the agreement.

reverse compilation techniques or any other similar or like method to gain access to the Source Code to the Software System and/or to determine any design, structure, concepts and/or methodology employed in the Software System; whether to incorporate within any product or computer program of its own creation or for any other purpose whatsoever.[11]

2.4 The parties hereto specifically represent, each to the other, their acknowledgment of the importance of each and every part of this Clause 2. Concomitant on such acknowledgement, the parties agree that each and every term of and obligation arising from this Clause 2 shall be in the nature of a condition and fundamental to the operation of this Agreement as a whole.

Precedent (B) *Extract from an Evaluation Licence Agreement with respect to a Computer Software Product*

Many software houses allow their prospective clients to "trial" or "evaluate" their computer software products before the decision is made to purchase a licence. The following extract is directed to the licence component of such an agreement.

2. The Licence

2.1 The grant

2.1.1 <*Software House*> hereby grants to the Licensee a bare, personal, non-transferable, non-exclusive and revocable licence to use the Licensed Program on the Authorised Hardware at the Location solely for the purposes of evaluating the Licensed Program.[12]

2.1.2 The Licensee shall use the Licensed Program only for the Licensee's benefit of evaluating the Licensed Program in the course of its normal business activities and shall not use the Licensed Program so as to rely on the performance of the Licensed Programs and/or the results that it may produce in any circumstances other than those of a test.

2.1.3 The Licensed Program may be used only at the Location and on the Authorised Hardware by employees of the Licensee or by staff under contract to the Licensee and under the Licensee's direct supervision who require such access in order to permit and enable the use by the Licensee of the Licensed Program in the manner contemplated by this Agreement.

11 This clause avoids s 50B Copyright, Designs and Patents Act 1988 giving the end-user the right to reverse engineer. See Chap 7.

12 It will be noticed that this licence closely follows the general "shape" of the licence in Precedent A.

Precedent (C) *Extract from a Source Code Licence Agreement with respect to a Computer Software Product*

In this agreement, the software house is permitting its licensee access to the source code of one or more of its computer software products. In such a situation, greater attention will be needed to be paid to the confidentiality provisions of the agreement and those contractual mechanisms which control the security to be applied to the safe-keeping of the source code and the control of access to it.

1. Definitions

For the purposes of this Agreement the following words shall have the meaning set forth against them:

"Commencement Date"	shall mean the date of execution hereof by <*Software House*>.
"Licensed Program"	shall mean the computer software products (in whatsoever form or format) set forth in Schedule I.[13]
"Authorised Hardware"	shall mean the computer hardware system, being the property of or under the control of the Licensee, as more particularly set forth in Schedule II.
"Location"	shall mean the postal address at which the Authorised Hardware is situate, as more particularly set forth in Schedule II.
"Source Code"	shall mean any computer program, whether stored on or in any magnetic or optical medium, in any computer memory of whatsoever kind or in eye-readable form, from which it is possible to discern the logic, algorithms, internal structure, operating features and any other design characteristic of such computer program.
"Licensed Program Source Code"	shall mean the Licensed Program in Source Code form.
"Object Code"	shall mean the computer executable binary code derived from compiled Source Code for execution on a computer hardware system.
"User Manual"	shall mean any instruction manual, designed to and intended to teach, aid and assist in the operation and use of the Licensed Program.
"Licence"	shall mean the rights granted to the Licensee with respect to the Licensed Program Source Code in Clause 2. hereinbelow.
"Modifications"	means all and any additions, alterations, adaptations, modifications, enhancements and/or changes made to the Licensed Program Source Code by the Licensee including, but not limited to, all accompanying,

13 As has been suggested elsewhere in this work, a thorough examination of the technology to hand should be made before any legal analysis, and therefore, drafting, is proceeded with. Thus, in these circumstances, the draughtsman ought to be concerned whether any preparatory design materials are to be supplied along with the source code itself. In such a circumstance, these species of copyright work will also need to be covered and controlled by the licence grant.

supporting and related documentation and technical literature written by the Licensee in connection with and/or related to such additions, alterations, adaptations, modifications, enhancements and/or changes made to the Licensed Program Source Code by the Licensee.[14]

"Schedule" shall mean the provisions set out in any schedule attached hereto and made part hereof.

All references to Clauses, Sub-clauses, Schedules and Appendices are to Clauses, Sub-clauses, Schedules and Appendices of this Agreement.

Words importing the singular number only shall include the plural number and vice versa; words importing the masculine gender only shall include the feminine gender; and words importing persons shall include corporations.

References to accounts, records and/or information shall include any means or modes of storage or retrieval of the same including (but without limiting the generality of the foregoing) computer disk, tape, cassette, microfiche and the like.

2. The licence

2.1 The grant

2.1.1 The <*Software House*> hereby grants to the Licensee a personal, non-transferable, non- exclusive and revocable licence to make Modifications to the Licensed Program Source Code on the Authorised Hardware at the Location solely for the purpose of *correcting errors intrinsic in the Licensed Program so as to secure and safeguard the benefits of use derived by the Licensee from the provisions of the Licence Agreement.*[15]

2.1.2 The Licensee shall make Modifications to the Licensed Program Source Code only for the Licensee's benefit in the course of its normal business activities. Modifications to the Licensed Program Source Code may be made only at the Location and on the Authorised Hardware by employees of the Licensee who require such access in order to permit and enable the use by the Licensee of the Licensed Program Source Code in the manner contemplated by this Agreement.

2.1.3 The <*Software House*> hereby grants to the Licensee a personal, non-transferable, non- exclusive and revocable licence to use the Licensed Program and the Modifications on the Authorised Hardware at the Location.

2.1.4 The Licensee shall use the Licensed Program and the Modifications only for the Licensee's benefit in the course of its normal business activities. The Licensed Program and Modifications may be used only at the Location and on the Authorised Hardware by employees of the Licensee

14 It is here that the draughtsman must capture all of the species of copyright works that arise or may arise when the licensee modifies the source code. The software house may take the view that modifications to its product ought to belong to it and therefore such works will need to be the subject of a copyright assignment.

15 It is suggested that in these circumstances, where the licensee may be dealing with very sensitive and secret material, that the licence is confined not only to an activity but the purpose of the activity so as to confine the licensee's activities in every respect. The italicised portion of this text contains the "purpose".

or by staff under contract to the Licensee and under the Licensee's direct supervision who require such access in order to permit and enable the use by the Licensee of the Licensed Program and the Modifications in the manner contemplated by this Agreement.

2.1.5 Upon the production of any Modifications, the Licensee shall forward such Modifications to the <*Software House*> by pre-paid, first-class, registered mail within seven (7) days of the production thereof in machine-readable and eye-readable Source Code form.

2.2 The restrictions

2.2.1 The Licensee shall not permit any other person or entity access to the Licensed Program and/or Modifications or permit such access of the Licensed Program and/or the Modifications by at, or by means of any telephonic or other means of electronic access from computers and/or locations other than the Authorised Hardware at the Location.

2.2.2 The Licensee specifically undertakes not to use the Licensed Program and/or the Modifications as part of a Computer Bureau operation or business.

2.2.3 The Licensee undertakes to respect the confidentiality of the Licensed Program Source Code and the trade secrets therein and not to use any design, structure, concepts and/or methodology employed in the Licensed Program Source Code other than for the purposes of this Agreement.

2.3 The critical nature of the licensed program source code

The Licensee specifically acknowledges that the Licensed Program Source Code contains design concepts, structures, algorithms and methodologies of a highly sensitive and secret nature which are the trade secrets of the <*Software House*> and critical to the <*Software House*>'s business. Concomitant upon such acknowledgement, the Licensee hereby undertakes and agrees:

(i) to keep the Licensed Program Source Code in a safe and secure place where only such employees of the Licensee with a bona fide need to have access to the Licensed Program Source Code will have such access thereto; and

(ii) that money damages would not be a sufficient remedy for any breach of this Agreement by the Licensee and that the <*Software House*> shall be entitled to specific performance and injunctive relief and all other remedies for such breach. Such remedies shall not be deemed to be the exclusive remedies in respect of the Licensee's breach of this Agreement but will be in addition to all other remedies available at law to the <*Software House*>.

2.4 The parties hereto specifically represent, each to the other, their acknowledgment of the importance of each and every part of this Clause 2. Concomitant on such acknowledgement, the parties agree that each and every term of and obligation arising from this Clause 2. shall be in the nature of a condition and fundamental to the operation of this Agreement as a whole.

Precedent (D) *Extract from a Translation Agreement with respect to a Computer Software Product*

There are occasions when a software house operating in, for example, the United Kingdom would wish a firm of technical authors or another software house in another country, to translate the screen displays of their computer software product into another language. Once again, it is suggested that the draughtsman must take care to examine the technology to hand. For example, but rarely in a modern programming environment, the screen displays may be "hard coded" into the main body of the program and therefore a great deal of computer programming may need to be done. However, it is more likely that the text for screen displays is held in separate and discrete files and only this text will need translating. Movement from a roman type script to a Cyrillic or, more importantly, a pictogram form of script may call for extensive programming activity despite language text being held in separate files. The precedent below assumes that there might be sufficient programming carried out to give rise to new copyright works. The precedent does not contain the usual warranties and indemnities which go to the content and quality of the translation, nor that the translation should not include anything which might be lewd or defamatory, for example.

1. Definitions

For the purposes of this Agreement the following words shall have the meaning set forth against them:

"Commencement Date"	shall mean the .... day of .... 199....
"Licensed Program"	shall mean the computer software products set forth in Schedule A, including all and/or any enhancements, additions, modifications and/or upgrades thereto; but, for the avoidance of doubt, not including new computer software products whether based on the Licensed Program or not.
"User Manual"	shall mean any instruction manual, designed to and intended to teach, aid and assist the operation and use of the Licensed Program.
"Local Language Adaptation"	shall mean an adaptation of the Licensed Program whereby all manifestations of the Licensed Program in eye-readable form have been modified to appear in a tongue other than English and as specified in Schedule B and where, for the avoidance of doubt, such adaptation does not include the meaning assigned thereto by Section 21(4) of the Copyright, Designs and Patents Act 1988.[16]
"User Manual Translation"	shall mean an adaptation or translation of the User Manual into a tongue other than English as specified in Schedule B.

16 Note here that for constructional purposes, the use of the word translation is made clear so that it may not be confused with the type of translation where a computer program is being translated from one computer language to another; *e.g.* Visual Basic to C++.

“Translation Service” shall mean the process of modifying, changing and developing the Licensed Program into a Local Language Adaptation and translating the User Manual into a User Manual Translation.

“Source Code” shall mean any computer program, whether stored on or in any magnetic or optical medium, in any computer memory of whatsoever kind or in eye-readable form, from which it is possible to discern the logic, algorithms, internal structure, operating features and any other design characteristic of such computer program.

“Object Code” shall mean the computer executable binary code derived from compiled Source Code for execution on a computer hardware system.

“Software Tool” shall mean any computer program or computer software product provided on loan by the *<Software House>* to the Translator to aid the Translation Service.[17]

“Milestone” shall mean the dates by which certain stages of the Translation Service are to be completed by the Translator as set forth in the timetable of events (hereinafter referred to as the “Translation Service Timetable”) as set forth in Schedule C.

“Deliverable” shall mean the Local Language Adaptation and the User Manual Translation or any part thereof to be delivered to *<Software House>* by the Translator in accordance with the Timetable and Milestones.

“Schedule” shall mean the provisions set out in any schedule attached hereto and made part hereof.

All references to Clauses, Sub-clauses, Schedules and Appendices are to Clauses, Sub-clauses, Schedules and Appendices of this Agreement.

Words importing the singular number only shall include the plural number and vice versa; words importing the masculine gender only shall include the feminine gender; and words importing persons shall include corporations.

References to accounts, records and/or information shall include any means or modes of storage or retrieval of the same including (but without limiting the generality of the foregoing) computer disk, tape, cassette, microfiche and the like.

2. Licence grants

2.1 The *<Software House>* grants to the Translator a personal, non-exclusive, non-transferable, revocable, royalty-free licence to use, modify, copy, change and/or alter the Source Code to the Licensed Program so as to develop the Local

17 It is often the case that software houses either use proprietary or develop their own software tools to manipulate or build their product’s displays. In such a circumstance, the software house might want to loan these tools to the translator. Care needs to be taken, where the software tool is a preparatory one owned by a third pay, that the software house has the copyright capacity to effect the “loan” which will amount to the grant of a licence. The draughtsman will also need to take a view as to the ambit and complexity of the licence that needs to be drawn with respect to the use of the software authoring tool.

Language Adaptations in the tongues set forth in Schedule B (hereinafter referred to as the "Tongues").

2.2 <*Software House*> grants to the Translator a personal, non-exclusive, non-transferable, revocable, royalty free licence to translate the User Manual into the Tongues.

2.3 In so far as any new copyright arises in the Local Language Adaptations and/or User-Manual Translations, the Translator as beneficial owner of such changes, modifications, developments, additions, enhancements to and translations of the Licensed Programs, User Manual including, but not limited to, the Licensed Program Adaptations and User Manual Translation (hereinafter collectively referred to as the "Translator Works") hereby assigns to <*Software House*> all the copyright, including but not limited to all future copyrights and all audiovisual aspects to the Translator Works as defined, mentioned and made reference to in the Copyright, Designs and Patents Act 1988, throughout the territory to which that or any other Act may at any time hereinafter extend, together with the copyright and all other rights of a like nature as are conferred by the laws in force in all other territories and lands throughout the world, and such other rights as may hereafter be conferred or created by law or international agreement or convention in any part of the world, whether by way of new or additional rights not now comprised in copyright or by way of extension of the period of then or now existing rights of and in the Translator Works.

3. The translation service

3.1 The <*Software House*> shall deliver the Licensed Program in Source Code and Object Code forms and the User Manual to the Translator in machine readable form together with the Software Tool (where and as appropriate). The Translator agrees to provide thereafter the Translation Service as set forth herein and to deliver the Deliverables in strict accordance with the Milestones and the Timetable recognising that time is of the essence.

3.2 The Translator agrees to provide reasonable assistance and information to such employees of the <*Software House*> as the <*Software House*> may, from time to time, nominate with respect to the performance of the Translation Service and the production of the Licensed Program Adaptation and User Manual Translation. Such assistance and information shall be provided at no additional charge to the <*Software House*>.

3.3 In the event that the Translator anticipates or ought reasonably to anticipate at any time that the Translator will not satisfy any Milestone then the Translator shall give the <*Software House*> immediate written notice thereof and the <*Software House*> may, at its sole discretion:

(i) amend the Timetable; or

(ii) treat such failure as a breach of this Agreement and require such breach to be cured within the provisions of Clause 10.[18] hereinbelow.

18 Cross-referencing to the termination provisions in the agreement.

3.4 The Translator agree to include the <*Software House*>'s copyright notice on all copies of the Licensed Programs and Local Language Adaptations in the following form:

©[19] 1989, 1990, 1991, 1992, 1993, 1994, 1995 <*Software House*> Limited
All Rights Reserved

Precedent (E) *Extract from a Technology Transfer Agreement*

In this precedent, Software House ABC is selling a computer software product to another software house, Software House XYZ. Usually, in such situations, a service needs to be applied from the seller to the purchaser to transfer their knowledge and understanding of the software product. Thus these agreements are often referred to as "Technology Transfer" agreements. Although this precedent is only comprised of the definitions clause and assignment clauses, it thereby illustrates how the agreement needs to be structured so as to identify the incoming copyright works and the copyright works that will arise when ABC employee's produce documentation for XYZ employees in the technology transfer process.

1. Definitions

For the purposes of this Agreement the following words shall have the meaning set forth against them:

"Commencement Date"	shall mean the .... day of .... 1993.
"ABC Software"	shall mean the computer software products including, but without derogation of the generality of the foregoing, computer programs, flow-charts, technical specifications and descriptions, algorithms, routines and computer program code described in Schedule A, including all and/or any enhancements, developments, additions, changes, adaptations, modifications and/or upgrades made by ABC thereto.
"Trade Mark"	shall mean the names, devices and logos set forth in Schedule B.
"User Manual"	shall mean any instruction manual, designed to and intended to teach, aid and assist any user of the ABC Software in its operation and use.
"Source Code"	shall mean any computer program, whether stored on or in any magnetic or optical medium, in any computer memory of whatsoever kind or in eye-readable form, from which it is possible to discern the logic, algorithms, internal structure, operating features and any other design characteristic of such computer program.
"Object Code"	shall mean the computer executable binary code derived from compiled Source Code for execution on a computer hardware system.

19 Ensure the inclusion of the universal copyright symbol and not a letter "C" in brackets – (C).

"Program Specification"	shall mean such documentation, technical literature, specifications and stipulations set forth in Schedule C or made reference to in Schedule C describing, *inter alia*, the functionality, operation and technical aspects of the ABC Software.[20]
"Technology Transfer Service"	shall mean the consultancy service provided by ABC to XYZ as more particularly described in Schedule E hereof.
"Technology Transfer Works"	shall mean the literary and artistic works[21] (including, but without derogation of the generality of the foregoing, computer programs, flow-charts, technical specifications and descriptions, manuals, algorithms, routines and computer program code) produced by ABC as a result of or in connection with the provision by ABC of the Technology Transfer Service.
"Schedule"	shall mean the provisions set out in any schedule attached hereto and made part hereof.

All references to Clauses, Sub-clauses, Schedules and Appendices are to Clauses, Sub-clauses, Schedules and Appendices of this Agreement.

Words importing the singular number only shall include the plural number and vice versa; words importing the masculine gender only shall include the feminine gender; and words importing persons shall include corporations.

References to accounts, records and/or information shall include any means or modes of storage or retrieval of the same including (but without limiting the generality of the foregoing) computer disk, tape, cassette, microfiche and the like.

2. Copyright and trade mark assignments

2.1 Copyright assignment

ABC, as beneficial owner of the ABC Software, User Manual and Technology Transfer Works (hereinafter collectively referred to as the "ABC Works") hereby assigns to XYZ all the copyright, including but not limited to all future copyrights[22] and all audiovisual aspects to the ABC Works as defined, mentioned and made reference to in the Copyright, Designs and Patents Act 1988, throughout the territory to which that or any other Act may at any time hereinafter extend, together with the copyright and all other rights of a like nature as are conferred by the laws in force in all other territories and lands throughout the world, and such other rights as may hereafter be conferred or created by law or international agreement or convention in any part of the world, whether by way of new or additional rights not now comprised in

20 This specification can be used later in the agreement as a yard-stick for measuring or producing performance warranties for the software being purchased.

21 Care will need to be taken here in framing this definition. In a business application environment it is suggested that this definition will be sufficient, but in an entertainment program environment, the definition may need to be drawn more broadly to include films, sound recording and the like. Alternatively, as a matter of drafting prudence, the definition may be cast very broadly to include all species of copyright works.

22 Notice that the assignment captures the future copyright in the works which will be produced during the technology transfer.

copyright or by way of extension of the period of then or now existing rights of and in the ABC Works.

2.2 Trademark assignment

ABC, as beneficial owner of the Trademark and all of the good will subsisting therein hereby assigns to XYZ all the copyright, including but not limited to all future copyrights, and all trade mark rights and good will (whether subsisting by virtue of the common law or statute) in the Trademark as defined, mentioned and made reference to in the Copyright, Designs and Patents Act 1988 and the Trade Marks Act 1938, throughout the territory to which that or any other Acts may at any time hereinafter extend, together with the copyright, trade mark rights and all other rights of a like nature as are conferred by the laws in force in all other territories and lands throughout the world, and such other rights as may hereafter be conferred or created by law or international agreement or convention in any part of the world, whether by way of new or additional rights not now comprised in copyright or in trade mark law or by way of extension of the period of then or now existing rights of and in the Trademark.

Precedent (F) *Extract from an International Distributor Agreement*

The following extract sets out the "front-end" of a standard international distributor agreement whereby the software house appoints a distributor in a certain territory. For the purposes of this precedent, any competition law dimensions have not been addressed.

1. Definitions

For the purposes of this Agreement the following words shall have the meaning set forth against them:

"Commencement Date"	shall mean the .... day of .... 199....
"Licensed Program"	shall mean the computer software products set forth in Schedule A, including all and/or any enhancements, additions, modifications and/or upgrades thereto; but, for the avoidance of doubt, not including new computer software products whether based on the Licensed Program or not.
"Source Code"	shall mean any computer program, whether stored on or in any magnetic or optical medium, in any computer memory of whatsoever kind or in eye-readable form, from which it is possible to discern the logic, algorithms, internal structure, operating features and any other design characteristic of such computer program.
"Object Code"	shall mean the computer executable binary code derived from compiled Source Code for execution on a computer hardware system.

"Software Licence & Maintenance Agreement"	shall mean the form of agreement set forth in Schedule C.[23]
"End-User"	shall mean any person, partnership, firm, company or any other entity or organisation being a client or customer of the Distributor and who enters into a Software Licence & Maintenance Agreement with the Distributor for the use of the Licensed Program.
"User Manual"	shall mean any instruction manual, designed to and intended to teach, aid and assist any End-User in the operation and use of the Licensed Program.
"Territory"	shall mean those countries, states, republics, territories, principalities and geographic areas set forth in Schedule B.
"Trade Mark"	shall mean the name of the Licensed Program as set forth in Schedule A.
"Marketing"	shall mean the general promotion of the Licensed Program to prospective End-Users and the market-place of the Licensed Program in general which shall include, but not be limited to, market research, market definition, the construction of and implementation of promotional campaigns, the placing of advertisements, the preparation and distribution of sales literature and all other types of communication material.
"Sales"	shall mean the general activity of granting sub-licences for the use of the Licensed Program to End-Users, such activity including, but not limited to, customer identification, customer proposal preparation and presentation, contract negotiations, continued client relation activities and all other activities usually carried on by a competent sales function.
"Product Support"	shall mean the general activity of supporting the End-User in its use of the Licensed Program, such activity including, but not limited to, liaison with End-Users on errors in the Licensed Program, advice on User Manual interpretation and the update of End-Users with releases of enhancements and updates to the Licensed Program.
"Software Key"	shall mean any number, sequence of numbers, computer program or code provided by *<Software House>* to the Distributor to be entered into the Licensed Program during its execution so as to enable the full and continuing use of the Licensed Program by any End-User.[24]
"Schedule"	shall mean the provisions set out in any schedule attached hereto and made part hereof.

23 The software house's own "Software Licence and Maintenance Agreement" is exhibited. This will be useful in setting out the minimum number and types of obligations with respect to the software house's copyright that needs to be applied to the end-user.

24 This definition anticipates the use of some authorisation device produced by the software house which activates the software so that a bona fide end-user can use it. Such mechanisms are becoming very common in the software industry.

All references to Clauses, Sub-clauses, Schedules and Appendices are to Clauses, Sub-clauses, Schedules and Appendices of this Agreement.
Words importing the singular number only shall include the plural number and vice versa; words importing the masculine gender only shall include the feminine gender; and words importing persons shall include corporations.
References to accounts, records and/or information shall include any means or modes of storage or retrieval of the same including (but without limiting the generality of the foregoing) computer disk, tape, cassette, microfiche and the like.

2. Appointment and licence grant

2.1 <*Software House*> hereby appoints the Distributor as its exclusive distributor for the Marketing, Sales and Product Support of the Licensed Program in the Territory. Such exclusivity shall be subject to any constraints set forth in Schedule B, and <*Software House*> undertakes, subject to the performance by the Distributor of all of its obligations arising herein, not to appoint another distributor during the term of this Agreement.

OR

2.1 <*Software House*> hereby appoints the Distributor as its non-exclusive distributor for the Marketing, Sales and Product Support of the Licensed Program in the Territory.[25]

2.2 <*Software House*> hereby grants to the Distributor a personal, revocable, non-exclusive and non-transferable licence to Market, Distribute, supply Product Support and deal in the Licensed Program and to use the Licensed Programs for sales demonstrations and promotions in the Territory only. For the avoidance of doubt, this licence includes the right of the Distributor to grant sublicences to third parties to use the Licensed Program but does not include the right for the Distributor to appoint sub-distributors and/or dealers.[26]

3. Acceptance of appointment

The Distributor accepts such appointment and agrees to the following:

(i) to develop, organise and maintain business facilities and business intelligence to fully and properly exploit the market potential of the Licensed Program in the Territory;

(ii) to establish, develop and maintain a competent Sales and Marketing office network throughout the Territory structured in such a way that the market for the Licensed Program subsisting within the Territory can be efficiently and effectively penetrated and serviced;

(iii) to staff such Sales and Marketing offices with personnel who are well trained in the demonstration, installation, operation and use of the Licensed Program;

(iv) to establish, develop and maintain a competent Product Support office network throughout the Territory structured in such a way that the End-Users throughout the Territory may be properly and efficiently supported

25 An alternative provision for a non-exclusive distributor.

26 It is suggested that in such circumstances, the licence grant is always kept separate from the appointment even though it might appear to be a duplication. In this way the chance of inadvertently granting an exclusive licence into an exclusive territory is avoided.

with respect to those services set forth in the Software Licence & Maintenance Agreement;

(v) to staff such Product Support offices with personnel who are well trained in the technical aspects of the demonstration, installation, operation and use of the Licensed Program;

(vi) to make available services for training in the use of the Licensed Program which End-Users may, at their option, take up;

(vii) prior to the transfer of any Licensed Program from the Distributor to any prospective End-User, the Distributor shall enter into an agreement with the prospective End-User substantially and materially in the form of the Software Licence & Maintenance Agreement;

(viii) to ensure that all Software Licence & Maintenance Agreements include an effective provision whereby, upon the termination of this Agreement, such Software Licence & Maintenance Agreements shall automatically and effectively be assigned to <*Software House*>;[27]

(ix) that in the event of an End-User wishing to take only a licence to use, or only maintenance services, with respect to the Licensed Program; then the Distributor may only enter into such an agreement with the prior written permission of <*Software House*>;

(x) to forward a copy of all such Software Licence & Maintenance Agreements to <*Software House*> promptly following the execution thereof;

(xi) to maintain a complete record of all such Software Licence & Maintenance Agreements and permit <*Software House*>, upon reasonable notice and during normal the Distributor business hours to inspect and make copies of such agreements upon the request of <*Software House*>;

(xii) to maintain a complete record of all prospective End-Users for the Licensed Programs and to forward a copy of such record to <*Software House*> upon the request of the same by <*Software House*> and in any event at least once in every three (3) months;

(xiii) to provide <*Software House*>, on a three (3) monthly basis with a sales and promotional plan which, *inter alia*, identifies and describes the number of licences granted, current prospective End-Users, details promotional activities undertaken by the Distributor and generally describes the state of the market within the Territory. Such sales and promotional plan shall include such other information as <*Software House*> may reasonably, from time to time, request;

(xiv) to support the Licensed Program licensed to End-Users substantially and materially in accordance with the terms of the Standard Software and Licence Agreement;

(xv) to promptly inform <*Software House*> of all enquiries from End-Users and prospective End-Users outside the Territory.

27 This provision avoids the common situation where software house and distributor have a "falling out" occasioning the termination of the distributor agreement whilst leaving a large number of end-users in the territory who cannot be directly accessed by the software house. Such a provision may need to be supplemented by mechanisms which go to the distributor's obligations to ensure the efficacy of such a provision in their own legal jurisdiction.

Index

Rs. 750.00